This Was a Poet

THIS WAS
A POET

A CRITICAL BIOGRAPHY

OF

Emily Dickinson

By

GEORGE FRISBIE WHICHER

ANN ARBOR PAPERBACKS

THE UNIVERSITY OF MICHIGAN PRESS

TO
MY OTHER SELF
AND TO
"OUR BEST THIRD"

Preface

EMILY DICKINSON's poems, the final and artistically the most perfect product of the New England renaissance, have quietly attained the rank of an American classic. The fame that she would not pursue in life has overtaken her now that she has "passed out of record into renown." From the time, nearly fifty years ago, when the first selection from her work appeared, she has won an increasing number of readers who have realized the high integrity of her poetic craftsmanship and who would no more think of leaving her out of American letters than they would think of ignoring Poe, or Emerson, or Whitman. But the long-delayed and piecemeal publication of the whole body of her work has encouraged a tendency to forget the ground from which it sprang and the organic relation of one poem with others. Now, however, that nearly a thousand of her intense and poignant lyrics are contained within a single volume, it is possible to discern the larger scope of her achievement and to define her position in relation to the forces current in her time. This I have attempted to do in the latter half of the present book.

Before considering Emily Dickinson's poems as the consummate expression of a region and a period, it has been necessary to consider the poet herself in relation to her background. I have, therefore, devoted the first half of this book to a study of the village where she lived, her education, her important friendships with the several men whom she regarded as her tutors, and her years of seclusion when the greater part of her poetry was written, though not published. Since 1930, when two attempts were made, with doubtful success, to clarify Emily Dickinson's biography, a considerable body of fresh evidence has come to light. I hope I may have used it with effect to terminate the persistent search for Emily's unknown lover. I have tried to show conclusively that her love poems are nothing more than the reverberations in an uncommonly sensitive nature of a devotion whispered in the heart's chambers, but never outwardly expressed, save in poetry. Had it been otherwise we should not have had the poems. The quintessence of the New England spirit was embodied in Emily Dickinson. She cannot be rightly understood except in terms of her heritage.

With few exceptions the poems quoted or referred to in the following pages may be found in the inclusive collection entitled *The Poems of Emily Dickinson,* edited by Martha Dickinson Bianchi and Alfred Leete Hampson, and published by Little, Brown and Company, 1937. This is an indispensable book. No finer body of lyric poetry by an American author of the nineteenth century can be found, and if lovers of unforgettable verse are not moved to open their copies of Emily Dickinson by what I have written, then my book will have failed of its intention. To facilitate reference I have frequently given in parentheses page numbers in Arabic numerals joined with poem numbers in small Roman numerals. The same numbers will serve for *Poems: Centenary Edition* (1930), except that this edition does not contain the final section called "Additional Poems."

Emily Dickinson's prose writing is often as exciting as her verse. The best single-volume collection is *Letters of Emily Dickinson,* edited by Mabel Loomis Todd, new and enlarged edition, published by Harper and Brothers, 1931. I have quoted

PREFACE

enough from its pages, I hope, to cause any who do not know it to add it to their list of imperative reading.

In conclusion, I wish to thank Mr. Charles R. Green of the Jones Library, Amherst; Miss Margaret R. Hitchcock, curator of the Edward Hitchcock Memorial Room, Amherst College; and the officials of the Mount Holyoke College Library, the Harvard College Library, the Yale Library, and the American Antiquarian Society of Worcester for valuable assistance afforded me during the writing of this book. I am grateful also to many friends, and to strangers on the way to becoming friends, who have generously given me information and help of various kinds. It would be a pleasure to name them here, but since many, for understandable reasons, have asked not to be named, I can only express my appreciation to them all, collectively and anonymously.

GEORGE F. WHICHER

Amherst College

Contents

CONTENTS

PART THREE
THE SOURCES OF A STYLE

PART FOUR
POETRY AS PLAYMATE

PART ONE

THE LITTLE TIPPLER

The Village

NEAR midnight on December 10, 1830, Emily Dickinson was born in the brick house on Main Street built by her grandfather and occupied by her father. Her birthplace, one of the few houses in Amherst that might be called a mansion, was the substantial dwelling of a prosperous country lawyer. The carved marble fireplaces in the best parlor bespoke unusual elegance, and the white-painted woodwork set off gleaming mahogany, her mother's dower, brought from Monson by ox-cart. A canvasser for Andrew Jackson, who had been elected President two years earlier, would not have thought it worth his while to call at the Dickinsons'. The stately house had an air of Whig gentility. Nevertheless it lacked conveniences that we now take for granted. Through the long New England winters it was only partially heated by air-tight stoves, running water was unknown except for a pump in the kitchen, and interior bathrooms were an unheard-of luxury. Astral lamps burning whale-oil, or tallow dips, supplied illumination. Housekeeping during Emily's girlhood was an incessant burden upon the women of the family, even when the heavier tasks were performed by a stout Irish maid.

The brick house had its barn and carriage shed and a notable woodpile like other comfortable Amherst houses. There were flowering shrubs in the yard, lilacs and syringas, a flower garden and a patch for vegetables, and many fruit trees, for the Dickinsons like all their neighbors took pride in apples and pears of fragrant name—Early Harvest, Bell Flower, and Seek-no-further among the Baldwins and Russets, and for pears Winter Neilis, Sugar, Flemish Beauty, and the ever-popular Seckle. Cherries, grapes, plums, and peaches came to the table in season, and any October day after the first frosts had visited the lawns with marl a pocketful of chestnuts, black walnuts, or hickory nuts could be gathered in the course of a short stroll.

Below the hemlock hedge and picket fence that guarded the dooryard ran the dusty road, traversed by the four-horse yellow stagecoach from the shire town of Northampton to Belchertown, Palmer, and far-away Boston. Across the road, dipping gently to a ravine where a small brook flowed eastward, lay the Dickinson meadow, a sunny spot of greenery in summer, where grasshoppers leaped and butterflies floated and cicadas shrilled. On winter nights the moonlight gleamed on its untrodden snow.

The Amherst of Emily Dickinson's childhood was a tiny cluster of houses and farms, hardly distinguishable among the woods of western Massachusetts. Just outside her window was a tall pine, whispering like the ocean. On the knoll behind the house stood a heavy growth of oaks. Whichever way she looked from her hilltop were trees and yet more trees. They filled with a sea of branches the western interval between the village and the Connecticut River, they sent their green waves to the south around the base and up the sides of the Holyoke Range, to the east they overspread the Pelham slope, and they fairly inundated vast tracts northward to the hills of Sunderland and Deerfield. All about the village stretched a lovely and unspoiled countryside, greatly admired by tourists. Reverend Timothy Dwight, viewing the great bowl of the Connecticut Valley from the tower of the first Amherst meeting-house in 1803, broke into superlative raptures over what he chose to call its "fine collection of scenery." He considered it one of the most impressive and delightful spectacles that the United States afforded. "A handsomer piece of ground," he declared, "is rarely seen; more elegant slopes, never. The lines by which they are limited, are formed by an exquisite hand, and with an ease and grace, which art cannot surpass."

Every week-day morning Squire Edward Dickinson took his high hat and cane and made a stately progress along Main Street to his office at the town center, where Main Street and Pleasant Street crossed. On the diagonal corner stood Elijah Boltwood's tavern, a renowned hostelry, where travellers from the Hartford-Brattleboro and Albany-Boston stages gratefully sought refreshment. To the south stretched the town common, some few acres in extent, surrounded by a one-rail fence to which buggies and farm-wagons were hitched. The Amherst of the 1830's was not the trim village of today. Helen Hunt Jackson, who played in childhood under the syringa bushes of the Dickinson yard, has preserved an unflattering recollection of it in *Mercy Philbrick's Choice*. To the critical eye of her heroine, accustomed to the neat cottages of Cape Cod, the inland town appeared "untidy and huddled." The common was overrun with weeds and in part marshy.

On the left-hand side of the hotel, down the eastern slope of the hill ran an irregular block of brick buildings, no two of a height or size. The block had burned down in spots several times, and each owner had rebuilt as much or as little as he chose, which had resulted in as incoherent a bit of architecture as is often seen. The general effect, however, was of a tendency to a certain parallelism with the ground line: so that the block itself seemed to be sliding down hill; the roof of the building farthest east being not much above the level of the first story windows in the building farthest west. To add to the queerness of this "Brick Row," as it was called, the ingenuity of all the sign-painters of the region had been called into requisition. . . . There was a painted yellow horse with a fiery red mane, which was the pride of the heart of Seth Nims, the livery stable keeper; and a big black dog's head with a gay collar of scarlet and white morocco, which was supposed to draw the custom of all owners of dogs to "John Locker, harness-maker." There was a barber's pole, and an apothecary's shop with the conventional globes of mysterious crimson and blue liquids in the window; and, to complete the list of the decorations of this fantastic front, there had been painted many years ago, high up on the wall, in large and irregular letters, the sign stretching out over two-thirds of the row, "Miss Orra White's Seminary for Young Ladies." . . .

On the other side of the common, opposite the hotel, was a row of dwelling-houses, which owing to the steep descent had a sunken look, as if they were slipping into their own cellars. The grass was too green in their yards, and the thick, matted plantain-leaves grew on both edges of the sodden sidewalk. . . . To the south, there was again a slight depression; and the houses, although of a better order than those on the eastern side of the common, had somewhat of the same sunken air.

Amherst landmarks and actual names may be easily recognized in this description, though Mercy Philbrick unaccountably failed to see the tower of the College Chapel, conspicuous on its elevation south of the common, or to remark on a street running west the whitewashed brick building of Amherst Academy. During Emily Dickinson's lifetime, while the village increased in numbers from 2631 to 4199, the unsightly common was drained and planted with elms, largely through the efforts of her brother, William Austin Dickinson. The hotel was twice burned and replaced each time by a more pretentious structure; and the line of brick shops, still the least attractive feature of the town, gradually extended itself along the north and west sides of the common.

On Sundays the Dickinsons walked to church, morning and afternoon, the Squire in his invariable broadcloth and tall white stock, Mrs. Dickinson on his arm in her best black silk, and the children, Austin, Emily, and Lavinia, in decorous rank behind, dressed as they may still be seen in the group portrait painted not improbably by O. A. Bullard about 1840. The meeting-house of the First Parish (now College Hall), a large oblong building of yellow-painted brick, rigidly rectangular in all its lines save for a cupola belfry and a portico supported by four enormous white columns, stood on the west side of the common near its southern extremity. The grounds about it were still rough and ungraded. Inside, the pulpit and pews and galleries were as square and orthodox as the preaching. Two tiers of uncurtained windows on each side let in a flood of daylight; there was nothing dim and religious about Congregational worship. The pews all had doors so that their occupants were "buttoned in tight" during service, and the high pulpit, like a pine coffin on end, was so narrow that the minister had to mind his elbows if he attempted a gesture. Stoves, the first of a series of innovations dubiously accepted, had been installed in the vestibule in 1833; the stovepipes, radiating little heat downward, ran the whole length of the two aisles to chimneys in the west end and were equipped with tin troughs to catch the drip of creosote. Pews for the growing colony of free Negroes were provided in the far corners.

The precentor's pitch-pipe was no longer heard. In the gallery sat a choir of ten or fifteen singers, with an instrumental accompaniment consisting of a violin, a flute, and a bass-viol. The last instrument, a recent accession, was "managed," in Austin Dickinson's recollection, by Deacon Josiah Ayres, "and the tones he drew from its lower chords in his accompaniment to the singing of some of Watts' Favorite Hymns haunt me even now. Such lines as 'That awful day will surely come,' 'That last great day of woe and doom,' and 'Broad is the road that leads to death,' etc., seemed to me sufficiently depressing in plain print; sung with the accompaniment, they were appalling— to a boy." Emily Dickinson was reminded of the nursery rhyme of Jack and Jill, with the bass-viol in the rôle of Jill literally tumbling after, while the choir as Jack "galloped insanely on."

The parson in 1840 was a young man fresh from Andover Seminary, the Reverend Aaron M. Colton, who had won Edward Dickinson's unqualified approval by his tireless energy during his period of trial. "That Colton," exclaimed the Squire, "is a marvel of a man—to visit two hundred families in one week, and tire out seven committee-men, and pat every woman's baby." His doctrines, of course, were flawlessly orthodox. It was during Mr. Colton's earnest ministry, in the great revival of 1850, that Edward Dickinson at last gave in and joined the church. Susan Gilbert, soon to become his daughter-in-law, was another of the sixty-eight who made profession of faith on this occasion.

The Congregational ministry numbered in its ranks men of deep spirituality and fiery zeal. Their sermons not infrequently struck home to the hearts of their hearers. Going to meeting in Emily Dickinson's youth was no perfunctory formality, as two passages from her letters will serve to show. Both happen to be concerned with the preaching of visiting clergymen, but she also noted occasions when Mr. Colton, or later Mr. Dwight, the regular incumbent, "preached wonderfully" so that she wished her brother had been there to share the privilege of listening to him. In December, 1851, she wrote:

Oh Austin, you don't know how we all wished for you yesterday. We had such a splendid sermon from that Professor Park—I never heard anything like it, and don't expect to again, till we stand at the great white throne, and "he reads from the Book, the Lamb's Book." The students and chapel people all came to our church, and it was very full, and still, so still the buzzing of a fly would have boomed like a cannon. And when it was all over, and that wonderful man sat down, people stared at each other, and looked as wan and wild as if they had seen a spirit, and wondered they had not died.

A year or two later, after hearing a sermon of a different type, she hastened to communicate her feelings to Doctor and Mrs. Holland, with just a hint of the ironical peeping out from behind her seriousness.

The minister today, not our own minister, preached about death and judgment, and what would become of those, meaning Austin and me, who behaved improperly—and somehow the sermon scared me, and father and Vinnie looked very solemn as if the whole was true, and I would not for worlds have them know that it troubled me, but I longed to come to you, and tell you all about it, and learn how to be better. He preached such an awful sermon though, that I didn't much think I should ever see you again until the Judgment Day, and then you would not speak to me, according to his story. The subject of perdition seemed to please him, somehow. It seems very solemn to me. I'll tell you all about it, when I see you again.

Emily, alone of her family, never became a church member, but she was a regular attendant at services until at least her twenty-fifth year. Throughout her life "Mr. and Mrs. Clergyman," whoever they happened to be, were always numbered among her friends. She shared her father's admiration for Mr. Colton, but she was better acquainted, if we may judge from her letters, with some of his successors, notably Reverend Edward S. Dwight, pastor from 1853 to 1860; Reverend Jonathan L. Jenkins (1867–77), a man of great social gifts and her brother's intimate friend, who once interviewed Miss Emily on the subject of her soul and reported to her father that she was on the whole "sound"; and Reverend Forrest F. Emerson (1879–83), whose words brought her comfort in time of deep affliction.

The ministers who successively filled the Amherst pulpit were no more remarkable than the people who sat under them. Among the two thousand or more small communities scattered through New England, western New York, and northeastern Ohio, Amherst came as near as any to realizing the ideal possibilities of the type. The village was economically independent, a complete microcosm, little beholden to the outside world for the satisfaction of its needs. The necessaries of life were mostly supplied at home. Nearly every family owned a house and a few acres of land, raised potatoes, corn, green vegetables, and fruit, and kept hens, pigs, and a cow or two. An unusual number of the inhabitants were college graduates. For the literary society of the town the bookstore run by the kindly, intellectual John S. Adams served as a rallying point. The local printer published books in a modest way and also issued one of the best country newspapers in New England, *The Hampshire and Franklin Express*. Native wits of a somewhat lower grade were apt to gather in the carpenter shop of David Parsons, son of the first minister of the parish, who had inherited a faculty for shrewd and pithy speech. One of his father's sayings, "Grace never cured squint eyes," was long repeated as an adage. Inspiration of a still cruder kind was supplied by a distillery, where cider was converted into a potent apple brandy, until about 1850 the conscience of the village was roused to drive the demon alcohol from its borders. Gradations of rank were recognized, but the distinction between rich and poor was not strongly marked. One of Emily Dickinson's earliest memories was of riding with her father when the Squire drove with his grain to the mill. The President of Amherst College hoed his own potatoes.

Six generations of Calvinistic teaching had borne fruit in a high sense of personal responsibility. Upon each individual rested the supreme duty of self-improvement in mind and character. Only by earnest effort could the elevation of mankind be attained. Most New Englanders responded eagerly to the stimulus of self-discipline, though there were occasional recalcitrants and backsliders. A surplus of moral energy became the most characteristic product of the region. The leading men of Amherst, all of them zealous Congregationalists, were a group whose character and abilities raised them far above the status of small-town merchants and professional men. Many of them had held public office and were known and respected throughout the state. A representative figure was that of Deacon David Mack, the founder of a prosperous straw-hat factory, who bought the Dickinson house in 1840 and occupied it until his death in 1854, the Dickinsons meanwhile living in his former house on Pleasant Street. Austin Dickinson has left a vivid portrait of him.

General Mack was a man to command attention anywhere, tall, erect, of powerful build, with a fine head finely set, clear, exact, just, a believer in law and penalty for its breach; strong as a lion, pure as a saint, simple as a child, a Puritan of the Puritans: I remember my first sight of him—I was four years old—I thought I had seen God. He was moral and spiritual tonic to any community he entered.

Closely associated with him in the conduct of church affairs were two other business men: Deacon John Leland, Edward Dickinson's predecessor as treasurer of the College, an intelligent, liberal, public-spirited citizen who served some years in both branches of the Massachusetts Legislature; and at a slightly later period, Deacon Luke Sweetser, the proprietor of the general store, a genial, active, generous, conscientious man, whose name stood for honor, integrity, and high Christian character.

Among the lawyers, Lucius Boltwood was notable as a man of considerable property, whose beautiful home was a center of hospitality. For many years he served the College as secretary of the Board of Trustees and as a commissioner of its Charitable Fund. The Liberty Party, which as an early abolitionist he helped to organize, chose him as its first candidate for Governor. He is said to have been "overflowing with good humor, remembering everything he ever heard, and with slight prompting from Mrs. Boltwood everything that ever occurred; of sincere convictions and the courage of them." His wife, famous for a flow of conversation as spell-binding as the Ancient Mariner's, was a first cousin of Ralph Waldo Emerson. Osmyn Baker and Charles Delano, both potential congressmen, were also practising law in Amherst in the early forties.

The village physician, or the most noteworthy of several, was Doctor Timothy J. Gridley, a graduate of Yale and a mine of curious information: "that strange, queer, eccentric, fascinating man; doctor, politician; hated, admired, distrusted, believed to carry life in his hand; apparently not knowing day from night, that Sunday came the same day every time, his own house from another's; who wouldn't go straight if he could go across; regular only in being irregular; a most picturesque character." So Austin Dickinson described him. To Austin's classmates of

1850 the doctor was better known as the father of two vivacious daughters.

The list of striking and original personalities might be indefinitely extended, for the people of Amherst came of a refractory, stiff-necked, and rebellious stock. The marvel is that so many independent integers were somehow welded into a body politic capable of recognizing common interests and of taking common action. But welded they were, less by any power of leadership than by an ingrained habit of giving to town and church their exact due. The level of plain living and high thinking attained in the small New England towns before country talent was drawn to the cities has seldom been equalled. In the opinion of a modern historian, "The standards which they maintained represented one of the highest community achievements in history."

The temper of the village in the three decades before the Civil War was strongly conservative, yet the influences of an expansive age were not altogether to be denied. One by one the old ways were modified. Innovations proposed by progressive citizens were nearly always vehemently resisted, but in the end nearly always prevailed. A church organ smacked of Episcopacy and Rome, but an organ was installed; chandeliers made the sacred edifice resemble that devil's instrument the theatre, but chandeliers were put in. The opponents of a change, once they were "dealt with" and made to see its desirability, not infrequently became the most effective agents in bringing it to pass. Some deep-seated religious prejudices were abandoned more quickly in Amherst than in other places. A student who came to college in 1846 was astonished to find that godly people saw nothing wrong in taking a quiet stroll on Sabbath afternoons; after reflection he decided that the practice, in a small town, did not "tend to countenance dissipation" as it was thought to do in his home town of Newport, Rhode Island. By the 1860's sectarian rancors had largely disappeared. The orthodox majority welcomed the establishment of an Episcopal Church in 1864, and within a decade the Episcopal fashion of celebrating Christmas and Easter was in general vogue. The Congregationalists of this period were in fact more tolerant than the Episcopal rector, who once appeared plunged in gloom at an evening party, and when asked the reason replied that it saddened him to think that he could not enjoy the society of such pleasant friends in the world to come. This was long a village joke. When *The Springfield Republican* ventured to appear on Sunday, there were bitter protests from Amherst, but several families managed to reconcile the tradition of Sabbath observance with the gospel according to Samuel Bowles by the expedient of accepting Sunday delivery while refraining from reading the paper or paying for it until Monday. In the early 1870's a Maypole dance was held in College Hall, late the meeting-house. Merry Mount had at long last come into its own.

The Puritanism of the village, though staunch, was never of a virulent type. Yet if life in Amherst failed of completeness in any respect, it was probably on the side of relaxation. It was undeniably tense, with few outlets for emotional release. The young gentlemen of the College sometimes blew off steam in an informal game of wickets, but for adults there was no form of play. Card games and dancing, though tolerated in worldly Northampton, were frowned upon in Amherst. The reading of novels was considered a symptom of dissipation. Concerts were rare and the theatre non-existent. Besides religious objections to amusements, there were two reasons why New Englanders of the period remained indifferent to the lighter side of life. One was that creative enterprises—the founding of schools and colleges, the building of railroads, the establishment of banks and factories and public utilities—were springing up on every hand. Men engaged in the business of keeping their community abreast of the age were completely and almost thrillingly busy. It was fun, like the adventures of the Swiss Family Robinson. They felt no need of artificial entertainments. The other reason was that the women of the community had little leisure from the heavy routine of housekeeping.

Yet there was some visiting about in the evening, when the elders gravely discussed affairs of village and church or listened to the reading of the sententious poetry then in vogue, while the youngsters perhaps organized a gayer party of their own in the kitchen. Formal dinners were seldom given before the sixties, but entertaining at informal suppers or "handed teas" was common. On state occasions the dignitaries of the town and College held "levees" or evening parties, ending invariably at ten o'clock. When students were invited the festivities were apt to be more protracted, though hardly less stiff. A contemporary record of an evening party in 1846 gives us a brief glimpse of some of Emily Dickinson's schoolmates, though not of Emily herself.

[November 10.] Evening. French, one of our class who lives here in Amherst, invited the whole class to his house this evening. The faculty and their ladies were there, also both the tutors, the class, *en masse*, and young ladies to match. Was astonished to find how well our class could appear in emergencies. Was introduced to a great many young ladies I never saw before and never wish to see again: also to some that I do. Miss French is not pretty but very lively: Miss Jones, her cousin, is ditto. Miss Sarah Gridley was present. Was introduced to Miss Emily Fowler, one of the reigning belles, with rather a pretty face, but a figure like a jar of sweetmeats: also to Miss Livia Coleman, another belle and the prettiest girl I have seen in A. except perhaps Jennie G.: also Miss Adams, a rather pretty, pleasant girl. . . . Also to Mrs. Prof. Warner. The evening passed quickly, in talking, promenading, music, and *feeding*. Was surprised to find it nearly 11 P.M. when I got home.

The household engaged in giving a party was deeply involved in the anxiety of preparation for it, and there were not infrequent flurries behind the scenes as ladies made quick transitions from the part of cook to that of hostess. When a reception was impending at President Hitchcock's, about 1850, the daughter of the house begged her brother to be present in order that the "ice-creams" might not be experimentally treated by their scientific father. "I really wish you could be here," she wrote, "for I expect Pa will insist on so many chemical principles down in the cellar that he will spoil them. The fact is, Chemistry is a great deal better in theory than it is in practice—especially in the kitchen."

The simple social life in which Emily Dickinson freely participated as a girl became somewhat more elaborate about the time that she was withdrawing from the world. Improved means of communication were making less possible the survival of parochial angularities, and the general increase of wealth and comforts permitted the women of the better families to take the lead in social affairs. With the coming to Amherst of men of broad worldly experience like William A. Stearns, the first President of the College drawn from outside the immediate locality, Professor Edward Tuckerman, and Professor Richard H. Mather, the era of Amherst hostesses commenced. John W. Burgess, who saw the village from the perspective of a Southern upbringing, characterized the Amherst society of the 1860's as "really charming in its simplicity, geniality, and intellectuality," though limited to half a dozen houses. "It was, of course, a somewhat provincial society, but it was sound to the core, educated, refined, and at times approached brilliancy. When I went to New York later to reside, I found nothing better." The elegance of dress, the lights and flowers and good talk of this gayer era, were unknown to Emily Dickinson, save as her sister-in-law reported them. She had closed the valves of her attention to all society but that of her own choosing. The one concession to the world that she made for some years after her retirement was to greet her father's guests on the occasion of the Dickinson tea, always given on the Wednesday of Commencement week. "At a moment when conversation lagged a little," says Professor

Burgess, "she would sweep in, clad in immaculate white, pass through the rooms, silently courtesying and saluting right and left, and sweep out again. She seemed more like a spirit than a human body."

The College Commencement, which fell on a Thursday early in August, and Cattle Show, held about the middle of October, were the two red-letter days in the village calendar. Commencement, the culmination of four days of celebration, was attended by all the neighboring clergy, returned missionaries, graduates of the College, and dignitaries from far and near, including often the Governor and his staff. Since each and every senior was entitled to "exhibit" at the conclusion of his course, the oratorical outpouring in the village church commonly lasted from nine until three. The guests of the College then sat down to an abundant but cold collation. An English visitor in 1834 noted the spectacle presented by the thronged common.

The green which opened before us on quitting the dinner-table, offered a lively and busy sight. There were innumerable carriages of all descriptions, which had brought the present visitors to the spot; and numbers of persons, who had come rather in search of amusement than profit. Yet there was no sport, no show, no merrymaking of any kind. But there was, as remarkably characteristic, in the midst of this bustle, a Yankee auctioneer resolved to improve the occasion. He was mounted in a cart and selling, or trying to sell, books, prints, harness, and carriages—the very carriage he came in.

Cattle Show, or more properly the exhibition of the Hampshire Agricultural Society, occupied one or two days and included prize competitions for every variety of livestock, agricultural produce, and article of domestic manufacture known to New England. The Dickinsons, father and son, were always prominently concerned in the management of the fair, and sometimes exhibited their carriage horses. The ladies of the family sent flowers and choice cookery. It was a season of high excitement. Village and countryside packed the hall, many like the writer of the following description (1847) fully aware that

> The show is not the show,
> But they that go.

A great cattle show and fair in the village to-day. A rich display of human as well as animal nature. Never in all my life before did I see such specimens of humanity. . . . Spent an hour in the fair after dinner, enjoying with Jenks the refreshing verdure of the scene. The evening however was *the* occasion. All the big turnips etc. were cleared away, and nothing left but the tables of the ladies society. Went up into the parlor after tea, and escorted Sabra H. to the hall. It was crowded: the beauty and fashion of Amherst were there in full array, going about seeking whom they might sell something to: many of the students there and every other inch of room filled with a dense mass of rowdies and nobodies. It was full to suffocation. Everybody was present, even the Faculty, *en masse*. One could neither walk, stand, or sit in peace nor hardly preserve his *individuality*. Crowded about, made an unsuccessful speculation in the ring-cake, and walked home with Mrs. Warner. . . . Back to the fair: crowded about and talked to various ladies. Went to the P.O. and wrote some letters, by special invitation of Cate Hitchcock. Got two: awful flat. . . . Went home with Sabra, of course, and stayed a little while. Then to the fair again: had my fortune told with great success: saw the end of all things and finally went home with Miss Shepard. Thus endeth the cattle show, brute and human.

After Cattle Show peace settled upon the village until the next Commencement. Through the long winters lyceum lectures provided a mild diversion, and occasional orators, John B. Gough, Wendell Phillips, Daniel Webster, Charles Sumner, enthralled large audiences by their rolling eloquence. Most of the lectures, however, were of a semi-religious type. Emily Dickinson mentioned in 1846 a series of talks by a converted Jew and another by a returned missionary. In 1849 an Ojibway Indian and his wife, both in full costume, startled the College by appearing in chapel for morning prayers; the same evening he spoke before a crowded house on the subject of Temperance.

At rare intervals a travelling circus passed the Dickinson house, and Emily, who cared nothing for the performance, would sit at her window all night if necessary to see the "Algerian procession" go by. It seemed to her that she "tasted life" at such moments, though all she could report next day was that "they said, 'Hoy, hoy' to the horses."

An outsider might easily have concluded that existence in Amherst was dull. In the early seventies the Episcopal rector's wife, who was a daughter of Harriet Beecher Stowe, missed the larger stir of Hartford and hopefully sought to remedy the situation by introducing game suppers in place of the traditional and stereotyped "teas." But the village was not to be seduced. Inhabitants to the manner born preferred a life whose sources were interior and which showed few outward manifestations. The external sameness of their days was protective; it gave them room to experience the satisfactions of religion, of practical affairs, and of good neighborliness, and these sufficed them. A clever woman succinctly stated the village attitude in saying, "We wish to remain elegantly plain."

In one respect the village was fortunate in possessing a means of enlarging the scope of its interests. Amherst College, the tangible expression of its evangelistic tendencies, was from the first the object of its constant solicitude and pride. The infant institution, founded in 1821 for the classical education of "indigent and pious young men," was tacitly designed to become a stronghold of orthodoxy against the Unitarian heresies of Harvard. Its founders hoped, as Noah Webster in a private letter candidly stated, that it would grow up "to check the progress of errors which are propagated from Cambridge." This was a cause of common concern to the Congregational churches of western Massachusetts and Connecticut, and they rallied to support it. Amherst College was not imposed upon the region by an outside benefactor; it was created by the region, in spite of poverty, to be an instrument for perpetuating and extending

begat Nathan, Nathan begat Nathan, Jr., and Nathan, Jr., begat Samuel Fowler Dickinson, who was Emily's grandfather. It was the first Nathan, with his wife Thankful Warner, who in 1742 established the family in the "Third Precinct" of Hadley, which later became the town of Amherst. Neither of the Nathans can be set up as a leading citizen, though Dickinsons not in Emily's direct line played a spirited part in the local disputes attending the outbreak of the Revolution.

The Dickinson dynasty, which was to rule Amherst for three generations, began with Samuel Fowler Dickinson, born October 9, 1775, the son of Nathan Jr., and Esther Fowler Dickinson. He graduated in 1795 from Dartmouth College, where he was so imperfectly educated that he remained all his life a fanatical believer in the virtue of education. Though trained to the law and considered by many the best lawyer in Hampshire County, he spent himself and his substance recklessly in the promotion of public-spirited enterprises. For nearly forty years he was a deacon of the First Church, for fourteen years town clerk, for twelve years a representative in the General Court, and for one term a member of the Massachusetts Senate. But not content with official services, he became a kind of secular evangelist, yearning and laboring to promote the world's enlightenment with all the means at his disposal. He was the soul of the movement that led in 1814 to the founding of Amherst Academy, his name heading the first subscription list. No sooner was the Academy a going concern than he pressed for the addition to its program of certain collegiate courses, and when this scheme failed to find support, he leaped with sublime audacity to the conception of establishing a full-fledged college. For a short period it was hoped that Williams College might be moved from the Berkshires to a more available location either in Amherst or in Northampton, but the legislature blocked the proposal. Squire Dickinson then with a small group of enthusiasts rallied the support of the region and proceeded to build on little more than faith the Collegiate Institution which later become Amherst College. He not only gave liberally of his time and money, but again and again pledged his entire resources to help the struggling college through financial crises. Meanwhile his private practice suffered from neglect, and in his early fifties the Squire found himself an impoverished man. In 1833 he went to Ohio to serve as fiscal agent for Lane Seminary, and later to occupy a similar position at Western Reserve College. He died at the latter post, on April 22, 1838, still faithful to his vision of Protestant education, a hopeful and sanguine projector to the end.

His wife, married on March 31, 1802, was Lucretia Gunn of Montague, a March bride with much of March in her disposition. She lived until 1840, and legends of her peppery temper lived after her. Her grandchildren, when they needed an alibi for some impulsive act, used to claim that it survived in them. Emily Dickinson, however, probably had few distinct memories of her paternal grandparents. The grandmother mentioned in one of her letters to her brother was her mother's stepmother.

Edward Dickinson, the eldest of the nine children of Samuel Fowler Dickinson, was born in Amherst on January 1, 1803. The Academy, his father's darling project, was founded just in time for him to attend it, but he was ready to go on before the local college had come into being, and for two years he continued his education at Yale. When the Collegiate Institution at Amherst opened its doors in September, 1821, Edward matriculated as a member of the junior class. He returned to Yale, however, to graduate in 1823. The infant college at home had failed to receive a charter, and it was not in his nature to risk his academic standing. Armed with a bachelor's degree of unimpeachable soundness, he proceeded to study law in his father's office and for a third year at the Northampton Law School. He was admitted to the bar in 1826 and established his office squarely in the center of Amherst, on the corner of Main Street opposite the hotel. Squarely in the center of Amherst he remained for the rest of his life, seldom leaving the town except to serve its interests. He was elected to the Massachusetts Legislature in 1839 and 1840, and to the Senate in 1842 and 1843. When Governor George N. Briggs was in office —the "Governor B." immortalized in the *Biglow Papers*— Edward Dickinson served with distinction as a member of the Governor's Council. In 1852 he was a delegate to the Whig Convention in Baltimore, one of the defeated minority that sought to nominate Daniel Webster for the presidency of the United States. He was a member of Congress from 1853 to 1855, and in the autumn of 1860 he was nominated for the post of Lieutenant Governor by the "Bell and Everett party," but declined the nomination. Thereafter his only appearance as a candidate for public office was in 1873–74, when he sought and obtained election to the General Court in order to promote the construction of the Massachusetts Central Railroad. The projected line was to pass through Amherst. While speaking before the house on a bill connected with the Hoosac tunnel, he suffered a stroke and died in Boston on June 16, 1874.

The bringing of railroads to Amherst—he had helped to establish the Amherst and Belchertown Railway in 1853—was only one of the many public measures that Edward Dickinson fostered. Did the church building need repair, his subscription was ready and his name was sure to be included on the building committee. He was equally ready to encourage the founding of Episcopal and Catholic churches. For nearly forty years he was a trustee of Amherst Academy, and from 1835 to 1873 treasurer of Amherst College, not only managing its funds but taking general charge of its buildings and grounds. During his term of office the institution passed through the most difficult period in its history, when for a time it seemed that the declining college could not long survive. But the portion of the sky that rested on Edward Dickinson's shoulders was never allowed to fall. In the crisis he was a rock of faithfulness and integrity. Not a dollar was ever lost or wasted. Men knew that what he said he meant and what he promised he would perform. His unbending firmness of purpose and his great freedom and boldness of speech under excitement gained him enemies, both personal and political, but he had no opponent who did not respect the force of his character, the purity of his motives, and the intensity of his public spirit.

In Edward Dickinson's generation the substantial aristocracy of New England flowered less ostentatiously but not less perfectly than the plantation aristocracy of the South. He was a typical Whig gentleman of the old school, every inch a leading citizen, solid and deliberate in judgment, generous in intention, vigorous in action. His professional occupations, public service in which he met on equal terms the leaders of other sections of the state, a well-ordered home, and innumerable private charities brought him complete fulfillment. It was characteristic of him to propose to the woman who was shortly to become his bride that they prepare themselves for "a life of rational happiness" rather than "a life of *pleasure!*" Trivial joys were no part of his regimen; he hardly felt the need of them in his constant preoccupation with the affairs of the village, the College, and the church. He had the fine skill in living to find his pleasures within the scope of his duties. Thomas Wentworth Higginson, meeting him casually in 1870, thought him "thin, dry, and speechless," but Edward Dickinson had no small talk for the Higginsons of this world. Words to him were the equivalent of deeds, and he respected them accordingly. Praise from his lips was an accolade that the recipient never forgot. His meticulous bearing and the black broadcloth and glossy beaver that he invariably wore as a sort of professional uniform gave an impression of stately formality. An outsider might have been misled further by a certain gyroscopic instinct in him which caused him to lean away from his emotions, so that, as his daughter keenly observed, he was capable of becoming "really sober from excessive satisfaction." But the flash of his deep-set brown eyes was ready to betray him. No one who knew him intimately could fail to perceive that beneath his dignified reserve lay an unusual sensitiveness, tenderness, and power of enjoyment.

"Father steps like Cromwell when he gets the kindlings," wrote Emily, but none knew better than she how much there was to offset the stiffness of his bearing. Two or three slight incidents may be mentioned. It was young Edward Dickinson among other students at Amherst who roused the concern of good President Moore by attending a late oyster supper given by the wilder blades at the Academy; "the following facts appeared," according to the President's letter:

that after supper they had cherry-rum and gin—that they drank to excess—that about 12 o'clock they all of them came to the Institution—that they there behaved in a very indecent and riotous manner, and made great disturbance in and about the Institution, to the extreme annoyance of those residing in it, till one o'clock or later.

It was Edward Dickinson, the leading lawyer of Amherst, who drove the fastest horse in town, and it was he also who rang the bell of the Baptist Church one afternoon in late September, 1851, to call the attention of his startled fellow townsmen to an extraordinarily brilliant sunset. And it was Edward Dickinson, an old man of seventy-one, who noticed the birds sitting disconsolate in an April snow and "went to the barn in his slippers and came back with a breakfast of grain for each, and hid himself while he scattered it, lest it embarrass them." If these were the acts of a strait-laced Puritan, we shall need to revise our ordinary conception of the Puritan character.

To Emily Dickinson her father was a cardinal fact. Only when he is taken for granted, beside her and in her, can her personality be correctly interpreted. His gods were her gods;

his granite integrity was hers also. As a child she stood in no little awe of him, and there were moments in her later girlhood when flesh and blood threatened to mutiny. But defiance of her father was defiance of what was deepest in herself, an instinct of rightness that could not be denied. She could not fail him. So sure and unquestioning was her response that she could dally with playful indirections, teasing him, or more often teasing herself, by suggesting possibilities of waywardness that she might carry out if she chose—only she did not choose. It was in high fun that she delighted to picture herself as a rebel incarnate. Precisely because her character was as firmly rooted as his, she could permit her fancy to frisk with squirrel-like irresponsibility, secure of its refuge. If her father's life seemed stark and rigorous in its sacrificial effort to sustain for a little time the precarious order of humane living, it was her part to contribute grace and wit, lightness and diversion. There were desserts to make and the piano to be played after supper. With the passing of years her allegiance to him deepened to a profound, unspoken tenderness. She came to understand and respect him as her own soul. She had known other brilliant and prominent men, Governor Briggs among them, but none to match her father. "His heart was pure and terrible," she wrote after his death, "and I think no other like it exists."

Edward Dickinson married on May 7 (or May 6), 1828, Emily Norcross, the third of the nine children of Joel Norcross of Monson and his first wife, Betsey Fay Norcross. It was a local saying in Monson that the Norcrosses could not manage to raise their girls, but Emily's mother escaped the family doom and lived to be seventy-eight. She was a year and a half younger than her husband, whom she met presumably while he was a student at Yale and she a pupil in a young ladies' finishing school in New Haven. His courtship, as already indicated, may have lacked impetuosity, but it was not in her nature to be exacting. She was the type of gentle, submissive woman that stirs the possessive and protective instincts of intensely masculine men, a type that to the regret of later readers appealed strongly to Scott and Fenimore Cooper. Nothing in Milton's specifications for Eve would have shocked her, except perhaps the fact that his heroine was unclothed. She reverenced her husband and devoted her life to making his home a silken nest. Both were content that he should be the integer and she the cipher that "swelled the man's amount." Emily, whose element was lifeblood, found it difficult to be aware of her unassertive mother; Higginson, a little stunned, recalled that she had said to him in her summary way, "I never had a mother. I suppose a mother is one to whom you hurry when you are troubled." Mrs. Dickinson was hardly qualified to be a tower of strength, but ten years after Higginson's visit Emily would not have been able to dismiss their relationship so cavalierly. Just twelve months after her husband's death Mrs. Dickinson became paralyzed and lingered for seven years an invalid. Since Emily left contacts with the outside world entirely to her sister Lavinia, a large part of the care of her mother must have fallen to her share. Their positions were reversed—her mother had become her child. Helplessness served in lieu of more positive traits to make the sufferer precious. Before Mrs. Dickinson died, on November 14, 1882, Emily had learned that she had a mother.

Though there were frequent visits between Amherst and Monson, no record has survived of Emily's impressions of her mother's father, who died when she was fifteen. His second wife made her portentous appearance at the Dickinsons several times in the early 1850's; "you certainly don't think I'd allude to a Hippodrome in the presence of that lady!" wrote Emily to Austin on one such occasion. "I'd as soon think of popping fire-crackers in the presence of Peter the Great."

On both sides of the family were uncles and aunts—twelve, not counting relations-in-law, were living when Emily was born

—besides unnumbered cousins of all degrees. A favorite aunt was her mother's sister Lavinia, who married a cousin named Loring Norcross and died in 1860, leaving her two daughters to be doubly orphaned by their father's death three years later. With Louisa and Fanny Norcross, the "little cousins" of her published letters, Emily maintained a tender intimacy until the end of her life. Hardly less close to her for a time were two other orphaned cousins, Clara and Anna Newman, the younger daughters of her father's sister Mary, who married the New York publisher and bookseller Mark Newman. After the death of their parents the two girls became Edward Dickinson's wards and lived in the Austin Dickinson house next door to their guardian. Emily took an affectionate interest in their education and welcomed their confidences, sometimes in secret reading her poems to Clara.

From Worcester, where Edward Dickinson's brother William had established himself as a banker and manufacturer, came William Hawley Dickinson, the "Cousin Willie" of Lavinia's diary, two years younger than Emily and a congenial escort of the Dickinson girls in their early twenties. It was with him that Emily dashed away from a funeral on a roundabout and indecorous buggy-ride home.

Of the Dickinson aunts, Aunt Lucretia (Mrs. Asa Bullard), wife of the general agent of the Massachusetts Sabbath School Society, was a stately occasional visitant. Aunt Katie (Mrs. Joseph A. Sweetser) was sweetly cherished for her gracious and lovely ways, while Aunt Elizabeth (Mrs. Augustus N. Currier) was known in the family as "the only male relative on the female side." She was distinctly not a favorite, though Emily's second name, Elizabeth, was apparently given in her honor.

Edward Dickinson's younger brothers, Samuel Fowler, Jr., Timothy, and Frederick, of whom the first two had settled in the South, seem to have maintained little connection with the

Amherst Dickinsons, but Mrs. Dickinson's youngest brother, Joel Warren Norcross, was a lively visitor in the early 1850's and his failure to write on one occasion prompted one of the gayest letters in Emily's published correspondence.

No complete picture of the intercourse between the Dickinsons and their large circle of relations can be reconstructed from the fragmentary evidence available, but it is clear that the Amherst home was a center of hospitality. Kinsmen, friends, and former neighbors were constantly dropping in, and in those days of leisurely movement dropping in might mean staying for several days or even weeks. In the swirl of comings and goings that beset Emily from her earliest years a few moments to herself might easily come to seem the best part of the day. Decidedly human intercourse was a thing that one could have too much of.

For forty-eight years the glossy gray beaver and gold-headed cane of Edward Dickinson passed up and down Main Street, saluted by fellow-townsmen as the outward emblems of royalty. When at last they were seen no more, the planter's sombrero of Austin Dickinson succeeded them. Father and son together ruled the little kingdom of Amherst for a span of seventy years.

William Austin Dickinson, born on April 16, 1829, and educated at Amherst College and the Harvard Law School, possessed in full measure the Dickinson integrity, force of character, and sagacity in practical affairs. His career, though closely patterned after the paternal model, never brought him into the thick of life or called out all his capacities. Its lines were those of a familiar classic, now reprinted and abridged. Edward Dickinson had moved in the counsels of state and nation, Austin confined his energies to his own community. There he filled many offices, organizing a Village Improvement Association, succeeding his father as treasurer of the College and trustee of the now inactive Academy, founding and directing banks and public utilities, supervising the building of a new church, laying out a new cemetery, and serving for twenty years as moderator of town meeting. His local attachments grew to be the consuming interests of his life. He became intensely parochial, hating to leave town even for a pleasure trip. When he died, on August 16, 1895, town, College, and church paid fitting honor to the memory of a beloved and faithful citizen. The power that was in him to be more than that was never used.

It was not altogether Austin's fault that he remained a large frog in a small puddle. As a young man he had wished to establish himself in a flourishing Western city to grow up with the country, but he was overpersuaded by his father to remain at home. At that time Amherst was one of many self-sufficient and independent communities whose leading men were responsible for shaping the policies of the country. New England by sheer force of incisive conviction then occupied a position of influence out of all proportion to its numbers. In 1856, when Austin made his decision, few could have foreseen that the Civil War was to bring all this to an end. The era of business expansion which followed subordinated the small towns to the rapidly growing cities. The country gentleman was thrust aside by the entrepreneur, the statesman by the politician. New England, strongly committed to its traditions, could not immediately adjust itself to the new state of affairs. The fate of the Adams family, whose marked capacity for intelligent public service was no longer in demand, was repeated on a smaller scale in the generations of the Dickinsons. The times were out of joint for Austin. There was nothing for him but an intensity of devotion to small affairs.

Temperamentally he was very different from his father. In reaction from the monumental solidity and gravity of the elder Dickinson, he was quick, sensitive, outspoken, humorous. It was easy to strike sparks from Austin, and he himself enjoyed seeing them fly in the give and take of conversation with a worthy opponent such as Samuel Bowles. Even with his father, whom he idolized, he was often, as Emily said, "at fisticuffs." He loved music, painting, and poetry, and his instinctive good taste found an outlet in transforming the unkempt village common and college grounds into well-planted parks. He could be firm and even vehement, but not aggressive. "His nature," said *The Springfield Republican,* editorially, "was all gentleness and refinement, and there was a shyness and reserve in his composition, coupled with an intensity of feeling. . . . He was best liked by those who knew him best." But even those who knew him slightly perceived the whole-souled kindliness that made Austin Dickinson the ready friend of any man who needed his aid or sympathy.

His marriage, which took place on July 1, 1856, brought into the closely knit Dickinson family an alien and dazzling personality. Susan Huntington Gilbert, a former schoolmate of Emily's at Amherst Academy, possessed a quick mind and a superficially opulent nature. As the daughter of a village tavern-keeper, she had been early touched by worldly influences. As an orphan from her eleventh year, living now with an aunt and now with a married sister, she had not known the security of a well-established home. She craved the excitements of society and was always at her best when surrounded by a lively and distinguished company. On such occasions her wit was ruthless, and neither bonds of friendship nor regard for truth were allowed to spoil a good story. Those who knew her only as a vivacious hostess have left abundant testimonies to her charm. Between public appearances her charm was less notable. Some of her guests, at least, were able to penetrate beneath the glittering surface. Professor John W. Burgess, who graduated from Amherst College in 1867 and returned to teach there from 1873 to 1876, was a courtly Tennessean but an accurate historian, and his sketch touches gently some of the complexities that mingled in Sue's disposition like the variegated strands in shot silk.

The social leader of the town was Mrs. Austin Dickinson, a really brilliant and highly cultivated woman of great taste and refinement, perhaps a little too aggressive, a little too sharp in wit and repartee, and a little too ambitious for social prestige, but, withal, a woman of the world in the best sense, having a very keen and correct appreciation of what was fine and admirable. Her imagination was exceedingly vivid, sometimes so vivid that it got away with her and she confounded its pictures with objective things. If she had had sufficient application, she would have rivaled Cervantes as a writer of romance and adventure. . . . Mrs. Dickinson was, I suppose, by descent a Puritan, but she was not much of a Puritan in her mentality.

The available evidence, which may not be complete, does not warrant the belief that Susan Gilbert was among Emily's most intimate friends at the Academy, but from the time, about 1852, when Austin became attached to her, Emily accepted her future sister-in-law with overflowing enthusiasm. To "dear Susie" she gave her confidence and love without reserve. For some years after Sue became mistress of the house next door the relationship continued unshaken. Emily was much in her brother's house and Sue in hers. Messages flew between them. Emily showed the poems she had written, and Sue suggested improvements. But it is impossible to accept without serious qualifications the statement that Emily never changed in her attitude of adoration for "Sister Sue."

Austin, like Emily, was at first fascinated by his lady's gaiety and freedom, but in the end he reverted to a strong preference for a more Puritan mentality than she possessed. We need not elaborate the unhappy story of the man who discovers too late that cake is an unsatisfactory substitute for daily bread. The profound alienation that separated Austin from his wife and his two eldest children is important only in its bearing on the life of Emily Dickinson. Both Emily and Lavinia were unquestioningly loyal to their brother. He was with them so often each day, as Emily wrote in 1883, "we almost forget that he ever passed to a wedded home." Indeed Austin himself was in danger of forgetting it. There was no open break, but for weeks at a time intercourse between the sisters-in-law was suspended. Sue was no doubt busy with scintillation, and Emily had her poems to attend to. Insensibly they drifted further and further apart. Then a few notes would pass, sometimes extravagant in protests of affection, and there would be a momentary resumption of a relationship which rang more and more hollow. The one link between the two divided households was Austin's second son Gilbert, a true Dickinson and the darling of his father and his aunts alike, but when the entrancing child died in 1883 the link was broken. The unfaltering yes that Emily once gave to Sue was tacitly revoked.

This is not a matter of doubtful inference. The signs of strain are only too evident. They come to the surface in 1866 when Sue betrayed Emily's confidence in allowing one of her poems to be printed in *The Springfield Republican*. On this occasion Emily was thoroughly outraged and used a downright and unsisterly word: "it was robbed of me." We may guess that thereafter Sue saw fewer poems. Again in 1879 Emily wrote to Higginson that her brother and "pseudo-sister" lived next door. The word speaks volumes, for Emily was not capable of sacrificing a friend for the sake of a casual pun. One of her last notes sent across the lawn declares that Sue has given her more knowledge than any one except Shakespeare, and adds that this is "strange praise." The knowledge referred to can only be knowledge of the human heart, and if one reflects that Shakespeare had revealed to her the dark secrets of an Iago, a Lady Macbeth, a Goneril, and a Regan, then this is strange praise indeed. Could Emily, who knew her Shakespeare thoroughly, write as she did without hearing the echo of Cordelia's scorn: "Shall we not see these daughters and these sisters?"

Between the worldly woman and the "passenger of infinity" that Emily increasingly became there could be little in common. "I showed her heights she never saw," wrote Emily in a poem that pleads for sympathetic companionship on the part of a woman, of course unnamed, whose friendship she considered of desperate moment to her. "She could not find her yes." Even when the speaker sacrifices what is holiest to her on the altar of friendship, the result remains inconclusive.

From the heights of her withdrawal Emily could on occasion look back on the world she had left with devastating vision. She did so in another poem which is of interest in this connection, for if she had needed a model to sit for this portrait, she had not far to search. The overwhelming impression of Sue's glancing talk, already intimated by Professor Burgess and repeatedly confirmed by those who met her socially, was that "she loved to get her little poniard in."

> She dealt her pretty words like blades,
> As glittering they shone,
> And every one unbared a nerve
> Or wantoned with a bone. . . .

Was this, we wonder, one of the poems sent across the lawn? And why did Emily once entreat her sister-in-law to write the one assurance, "Emily has not grieved me"?

Besides little Gib, who died in childhood, an elder nephew and a niece were growing up in the house next door. Toward them Emily was always a model of the affectionate aunt, helping to solve their dilemmas with sympathetic comprehension, delighting in their sayings, and watching their games with amused interest. For Ned, a sufferer from serious illness, she wrote extravagantly irreverent poems. But her confidences were more freely given to the Newman sisters, who lived in the same household and took care of the younger children, than to either her nephew or her niece.

Emily Dickinson's younger sister Lavinia, born on February 28, 1833, was her lifelong companion and trusted confidante. To a friend of her later years Emily wrote: "Your bond to your brother reminds me of mine to my sister—early, earnest, indissoluble. Without her life were fear, and Paradise a cowardice, except for her inciting voice." It was to her sister only, and to one other person outside her family, that Emily spoke of the man who was closest to her heart. She could smile at Vinnie's bustling ways and at her monstrous regiment of cats, but the love that united the two was absolute and never faltered.

Like all the Dickinsons Lavinia was something of a "character," with an extraordinary power of vivid and incisive speech. "To me," wrote Professor Joseph K. Chickering, who knew her from about the time of her father's death, "she was unique, rather than peculiar. She never said things as other people said them. I think she abhorred the commonplace in speech almost more than the vulgar. I never made ready to call upon her without feeling that I must purge my vocabulary of triteness. Her views of life were those of an onlooker, not a participator in the affairs of men, and they were at once shrewd and amusing to a remarkable degree." Though Vinnie was a church member, she detested religious cant almost as much as Emily, and was quick to detect it.

In Amherst "Miss Lavinia" is still recalled as a little old lady who lived alone in the huge brick house on Main Street, guarded by her faithful Irish servant Maggie Maher. Gossip said that mistress and maid ate in the same room for company, but with their backs turned to each other so that a proper decorum might be observed. Many knew of her touching devotion to the memory of her sister. Lavinia had been a pretty girl, full of flashing vitality. She too wrote verses, though her little poems about fireflies and stars were undistinguished. If love ever beckoned to her, she was unwilling to heed it. Apparently without any such psychic crisis as Emily underwent she remained at home and quietly accepted her destiny as high priestess of the Dickinson household. Whatever her father, brother, or sister did or said or thought was right in her eyes. No other view was possible. She indulged Emily in her desire for polar privacy, sparing her the slightest inconvenience. Both sisters to the end of their lives wore a style of dress vaguely reminiscent of that in vogue in their youth, and since they were of the same size, Emily's gowns of invariable white were always fitted to Lavinia. Thus Lavinia held the world at bay, while Emily confronted eternity. When all who were dearest to her were gone, Lavinia clung to her accustomed life with quiet courage. While she was there her father's house should not lack honor nor her sister's flowers fail for want of cherishing; and woe to the marauding boy who dared to intrude on the Dickinson orchard. Ultimately it was owing to Lavinia's child-like faith in the supreme importance of anything her adored sister had written that Emily's "letter to the world" was not irrecoverably lost. Before she died, on August 31, 1899, Lavinia knew that Emily's triumph was secure.

Seven generations of Dickinsons uncompromisingly going their own way and thinking their own thoughts had built up the rich soil of Emily's inheritance. Now a new sap was running in the Puritanism of her race and region. New England's flowering time had come. She had grown up in an atmosphere of controlled energies that might at any moment break loose. It was only necessary that her imagination be stirred and she would respond. Let her will be crossed and the response would become electric. Under pressure no Dickinson had ever failed to take an independent line and follow it to the edge of doom.

3

Amherst Academy

I WENT to school," Emily Dickinson wrote to Higginson, "but in your manner of the phrase had no education." Though she was anxious to claim as little as possible for herself, there was no reason why she should have felt called upon to speak humbly in the presence of a Harvard graduate. She had, as a matter of fact, received a better formal education than commonly fell to the lot of a New England gentlewoman at that period. But looking back on her schooldays some fifteen years later, she may well have felt that her studies had taught her little compared to what life had taught her since. Decidedly she was no academic product. Like any other first-hand thinker, she had absorbed from education what she needed without ever being dominated by the process. Yet her debt to school and seminary, though not of the letter, was still considerable. All her young life she had lived in an atmosphere of eager learning which was a tonic to her mind. Amherst Academy and Mount Holyoke formalized not too rigidly the seeking after knowledge which was going on anyhow. Emily Dickinson was too much a child of the region that produced these institutions to be as clearly aware of their influence as an outsider would have been, but we cannot fully understand her without considering how school and seminary confirmed and tested certain ingrained elements of her character.

Her niece is authority for the statement that Emily with her brother and sister learned her rudiments at the district school.

How long this phase of her education lasted we have no means of knowing, but it can hardly have occupied more than three or four years at most. Before her eleventh birthday she had begun to attend Amherst Academy. No memory of her earliest schooldays has survived in her published writings, and only the child portrait, already mentioned, remains to tell us what she was like as a schoolgirl.

Before 1860 the public schools of Amherst were ungraded, and their inadequacies were one of the reasons why the citizens of the town, including Emily's grandfather, organized an academy. One of Noah Webster's daughters, who must have attended the school of the "West Middle" district about 1812, has left a description of what the schools of that period were like:

> I remember well the forlorn, unpainted, and unshaded building on one side of the village green. There was an entry way where hats and cloaks were kept and then one large room with an open fire place at each end and in winter full of green logs with the sap oozing out of them. Two or three rows of hard benches with desks before them were on each side and a tall desk in the centre of the room was for the teacher. There were no maps or pictures of any kind—no maps or equipments for the teacher, but I remember that the children were happy and anxious to learn.

A generation later the school at the village center was greatly improved. A two-story building of whitewashed brick was erected in 1826 on a plot of land, purchased from Samuel F. Dickinson, on the west side of Pleasant Street, almost opposite the house in which Edward Dickinson and his family lived from 1840 to 1855. Beside the bare, barnlike structure stood the woodshed and school pump. The interior was probably not markedly different from that of the old school on the village green. One would have found the same vestibule for wraps, the same large desk-lined rooms on upper and lower floors, and the same rows of benches before the teacher's desk where classes came to recite. This was the "Primary School"—so called to distinguish it from the Academy—which the little Dickinsons and their neighbors in the village attended. It is hardly surprising that Emily should have ignored in later life an experience that contributed nothing to her mental stores except the power to read, write, and cipher. Her mastery of arithmetic at this time was very doubtful, for according to local tradition she was accustomed to write compositions for certain of her schoolmates who in return did her sums for her.

If there was no lifeblood in the district school, there was enough and to spare in Amherst Academy and Mount Holyoke Seminary. The later phases of Emily Dickinson's education brought her into stimulating contact with the current of evangelistic, humanitarian piety which was one of the most vital forces of her generation. Amherst Academy, Amherst College, and Mount Holyoke Seminary were alike conceived in the faith that the spread of Christian doctrines as interpreted by orthodox Congregationalism would free the world of its miseries and corruptions. The explosive force of this conviction, thundered from a thousand pulpits, was incalculable. It led thrifty farmers and shrewd lawyers, as well as devoted teachers and clergymen, to give more than they could afford to promote educational institutions and missionary enterprises. Women and children hoarded their mites to foster the cause. Families scrimped and saved to send their sons—less frequently their daughters—to college, where an intensified piety was fortunately ballasted by a sound classical training and some knowledge of science and philosophy. Graduates of Amherst and Mount Holyoke went forth to teach and preach, to plant schools and churches in the West, to enlighten and evangelize the Sandwich Islands, Turkey, Persia, India, China. No one brought up in such an atmosphere could be unaffected by it; either one became a soldier of the faith or one found sufficient reasons for not enlisting. Making the momentous choice called for long searching of the heart.

In its effect on character, therefore, the education of those days was not superficial.

Amherst Academy, when Emily Dickinson entered it, was a flourishing New England school. It was conducted by a principal with one or more male assistants, and a preceptress who was specially charged with the education of the girls. The connection between the College and the Academy, though informal, was very close. Of the seven principals who served while Emily Dickinson was a pupil, five were recent graduates of Amherst, and many of the assistant teachers were Amherst seniors. Youth was leading youth, but with a high sense of dedication. They were serious-minded young men, these principals. Two of them subsequently entered the ministry, two became missionaries, and one died before completing his theological training.

Over two hundred pupils, most of them drawn from the immediate vicinity, attended the Academy in the course of the year, but barely half that many were in attendance at any one time. The academic year was divided into four terms of eleven weeks each, commencing normally on the first Monday in June, September, December, and March, and ending with a public exhibition or examination. Two weeks of vacation intervened between one term and the next. Pupils attended school term by term as their circumstances permitted. Emily Dickinson, during the two and a half years when we can follow her through her letters, was never in school for four consecutive terms. Besides taking part in daily worship and in the weekly rhetorical exercises on Wednesday afternoons, pupils usually carried four studies in a given term.

The formal record preserved in the printed catalogues of Amherst Academy shows that Emily and Lavinia Dickinson were enrolled in the "English course" at some time during the year 1840–41. The next year both girls were listed in the "Classical course," where Emily remained in 1842–43. A star opposite her name indicated that she was studying French, an "extra." No catalogues were published for 1844, 1845, or 1846. In the 1847 catalogue Emily and Lavinia appear again as students in the English course. There is no further mention of Emily in later catalogues, though her niece states that after her year at Mount Holyoke she continued to study at the Academy. She may have attended certain classes without becoming formally enrolled.

Several letters that have only recently come to light give a charming picture of Emily as a little scholar. They were written to her friend Jane Humphrey, the daughter of Doctor Levi W. Humphrey of Southwick. Apparently Jane made long visits to the Dickinsons while she attended the Academy and on these occasions shared Emily's bedroom. The earliest letter, dated May 12, 1842, covers with exemplary neatness the first page of a folded sheet of foolscap, but at the top of page two the writer ran out of material and abruptly concluded. Even so this is a precocious performance for a child of eleven. (The passages omitted are concerned chiefly with family news):

My dear Jane
I have been looking for a letter from you this long time but not receiving any I plucked up all the remaining courage that I had left and determined to make one more effort to write you a few lines. I want to see you very much for I have got a great deal to tell you about school matters—and besides you are one of my dear friends. . . . I miss you more and more every day, in my study in play at home indeed every where I miss my beloved Jane. I wish you would write to me. I shall think more of it than of a mine of gold. when you write me I wish you would write me a great long letter and tell me all the news that you know of. . . . this afternoon is Wednesday and so of course there was Speaking and Composition. there was one young man who read a Composition the Subject was think twice before you speak. . . . he is the sillyest creature that ever lived I think. I told him that I thought he had better think twice before he spoke. what good times we used to have jumping into bed when you slept with me. I do wish you would come to Amherst and make me a great long visit. how do you get along

in Latin. I am in the class that you used to be in in latin. besides Latin I study History and Botany. I like the school very much indeed. . . . My Plants grow beutifully. you know that Eldest [?] old Rooster that Austin thought so much of—the others fight and killed him. answer this letter as soon as you can. I can think of nothing more to say now yours   affectionately

EMILY

Another vignette of Emily and her little friend occurs as a bit of reminiscence in a later letter (April, 1852):

I think I love you *more* when spring comes—you know we used to sit in the front door, afternoons after school, and the shy little birds would say chirrup, chirrup, in the tall cherry trees, and if our dresses rustled, hop frightened away; and there used to be some farmer cutting down a tree in the woods, and you and I, sitting there, could hear his sharp ax ring. You won't forget it, Jennie, Oh no, I'm sure you won't, for when you are old and gray, it will be a sweet thing to think of, through the long winter's day! And I *know I'll* remember it, for it's so precious to me that I doubt if I *could* forget it, ever, if I should try.

Unconsciously Emily Dickinson was building up in childhood the store of little, nameless, but vividly remembered experiences that constitute the poet's stock in trade.

From early in 1845, when she had just passed her fourteenth birthday, Emily's published letters to a second friend and former schoolmate, Abiah Root (later Mrs. Samuel W. Strong), give us a much livelier impression of her life at the Academy than can be gleaned from official records. As the correspondence opens, Emily had apparently just completed the winter term, and was looking forward to the spring and summer terms, which she also attended. "We have a very fine school," she wrote on May 7, and added that she was studying Mental Philosophy, Geology, Latin, and Botany. "How large they sound, don't they? I don't believe you have such big studies." She also spoke of having written one composition, "exceedingly edifying to

myself as well as everybody else." Besides her studies at the
Academy, she was going to singing-school on Sundays, and
expected shortly to begin piano lessons with "Aunt S——."
She was interested in gardening and offered to supply local
wild flowers for her friend's herbarium,—"'most all the girls
are making one." The letters of the ensuing months bubble over
with minor ecstasies. "I never enjoyed myself more than I have
this summer; for we have had such a delightful school and
such pleasant teachers, and besides I have had a piano of my
own."

The principal in charge of the Academy at this time was the
Reverend Lyman Coleman, an experienced educator and a ripe
scholar, who had recently returned from a period of study in
Berlin. He combined his duties at the Academy with teaching
Greek and German at the College, where he was the first to
give instruction in the German language. During the winter of
1845–46 Emily Dickinson was one of a large class that recited
to Mr. Coleman in this then little known tongue: "father
thought I might never have another opportunity to study it."
Mr. Coleman was assisted by a young man from Union College
named Jesse Andrews, who subsequently became principal for
two terms. There was no preceptress at this time, and Emily
asked her friend Abiah repeatedly for news of a former preceptress, Miss Elizabeth C. Adams, "our dear teacher." Perhaps
the learned Mr. Coleman, though he was said to be a genial
man, was a bit overpowering. To a fourteen-year-old schoolgirl
the road ahead looked long. "We'll finish an education some-
time, won't we?" she wrote. "You may then be Plato, and I will
be Socrates, provided you won't be wiser than I am." The note
of wistfulness, if this is wistful, was never to occur again in her
references to her school, except when she found herself unable
to attend it.

Four studies and two hours a day at the piano were apparently too much for Emily's frail physique. She was not allowed

to continue at the Academy during the fall and winter of 1845: "Mother . . . had rather I would exercise." Housekeeping—she was learning to make bread and was doing the family sewing—gardening, music and German lessons, must suffice. But such exercise did not prevent coughs and colds from becoming too neighborly. She was ill in January, but was able to enter the Academy at the beginning of the spring term. Then followed a struggle with poor health, and eventually defeat. She was obliged to drop out of school at the end of eleven weeks, though "dear Miss Adams" was again at her post, and Emily now knew that she was to be sent to Mount Holyoke. The summit of her ambition was to be one of Miss Mary Lyon's pupils. "It has been in my thought by day, and my dreams by night, ever since I heard of South Hadley Seminary." How could one be sick when such opportunities beckoned?

To save his eager daughter from overtaxing her strength Edward Dickinson seems to have practised a paternal stratagem. Late in August he sent her to stay with a favorite aunt in Boston, where in visiting such sights as the Chinese Museum, Mount Auburn, the Bunker Hill Monument, and the Horticultural Exhibition, four weeks glided insensibly by. When Emily returned to Amherst the fall term at the Academy was already well under way and her parents were able to persuade her to remain out of school. If she commenced the winter term of 1846–47, as she expected to do, her attendance must have been irregular, since she contracted influenza in late February and was ill for three or four weeks. But the spring term saw her back in school at last, studying Ecclesiastical History, Algebra, and Euclid, and reviewing Arithmetic (one notes the concentration on long-neglected mathematics), and she remained at the Academy through the summer. She was then prepared to enter the middle class at Mount Holyoke.

What was the effect of Emily's seven years at Amherst Academy on her unfolding mind? Her formal accomplishments were probably not exceptional. She had studied three languages, Latin, French, and German, and in the first of these she was a proficient scholar. The French that she learned from Charles Temple, Jr., an Amherst senior, and the German acquired from the Reverend Lyman Coleman, can hardly have amounted to more than a smattering. So far as is known, she never read any masterpiece of either literature in the original. Mathematics, it is only too evident, was merely a hurdle to be surmounted in order to qualify for the Seminary. The "Mental Philosophy" recited by a girl of fifteen from Upham's manual cannot be taken seriously, nor can her acquaintance with Ecclesiastical History be supposed to have been more than perfunctory. The sciences, however, enlisted her interest, and her work in English composition called out her best powers.

In the natural sciences the pupils of the Academy were admitted to "the very valuable Lectures of the Professors in Amherst College." Among these was the powerful personality of Edward Hitchcock, an eccentric and dyspeptic Yankee, but a nationally known scientist and a born teacher who communicated his enthusiasm to a host of young disciples. In 1845 he became president of the College at a time of financial crisis when it seemed as though the institution must collapse. He was able to extricate it, however, after some years of Spartan self-denial on the part of his faculty. One of his first moves when things had begun to look brighter was to call to his aid, as professor of Zoology, his former pupil Charles Baker Adams, whose zeal as a collector and teacher was so extreme that he could hardly bear to snatch the necessary hours for food and sleep. A third impassioned collector, this time of minerals, had joined the Amherst faculty a year or two earlier in the person of Charles Upham Shepard, a first cousin of Ralph Waldo Emerson. In 1848 the College celebrated its relief from financial stringency by building a cabinet for the combined collections of these three scientists, and an observatory in the faith that

Providence would shortly provide an appropriate telescope. (Providence did.) A religious impulse had originally brought the College into being, but it owed its permanence to the scientific renaissance under President Hitchcock.

No one could be in touch with Amherst College during these years of struggle, almost of martyrdom, and of faith triumphant, without feeling the pulse of its devotion to scientific study. Whether Emily Dickinson sat in Hitchcock's classroom or learned Geology under the enthusiastic tutelage of one of his students, she could not have found it a dull subject. From an early age she could name the stars, and though in one mood she protested against the collecting and classifying mania of the day, she was herself an ardent botanist and knew the haunts of the rarest wild flowers of the region. The scientific information that she acquired was, of course, very limited. It was communicated by deeply religious men whose avowed object was to exhibit the glorious handiwork of the Creator as manifested in the world of nature and who were themselves untouched by the materialistic implications of science. Yet her girlish study of minerals and flowers was not without effect on Emily's mind. It taught her to look closely at the object before her, to record her observations unchanged, to respect facts. This was an acquirement of more importance than the bits of scientific lore that became lodged in her memory and were worked into the fabric of her poems, years later.

Literary expression was as vital a part of education in the 1840's as scientific attainments. The more ambitious college students not only submitted to the discipline of rhetorical exercises throughout the four years of their course, but strove to advance their skill in speaking and writing by taking part in the programs of rival literary societies and of the Greek-letter fraternities. They even organized, in addition, small private groups to hear and criticize their essays and orations. Public exhibitions were frequent and were commonly well attended.

People flocked in from the surrounding countryside to attend the free show. The Academy was quite as active as the College in this way. Its pupils were expected to write compositions once a fortnight and read them before the school at the rhetorical exercises held on Wednesday afternoons. None of Emily's compositions have survived, but one of her teachers in his old age recalled them as extraordinary for their brilliance and originality. She was not singular, however, in possessing a highly developed faculty of expression. Boys and girls vied with each other to win the approbation of their teachers and fellow-students, and whatever laurels Emily won were achieved in the face of keen competition.

A tantalizing glimpse of an examination at the Academy is preserved in the diary of William Gardiner Hammond, one of the leading scholars in the class of 1849 at Amherst College and a severe critic of his own and others' effusions:

Nov. 17. Tuesday [1846]. Got my lesson in Horace and went with Woodbridge to see the examination at the Academy. Heard several classes recite, in French, Arithmetic, etc. Some of the girls read excellent compositions, one or two would not have disgraced educated men. One of the best was on "trifles" by a Miss Howland.

Had Emily Dickinson been in school when this examination was held, we might have had a contemporary impression of one of her lost compositions.

At the summer exhibition the following August, which Hammond also attended, Emily was undoubtedly present, but all the speaking on this occasion seems to have been done by the boys, the girls' part being limited to ensemble singing at intervals during the interminable program.

To serve as music [Hammond wrote], the place of a band was most beautifully filled by a choir of young girls and several youths, led by *Emerson:* they sang most *beautifully;* and I thought the music far better adapted to a literary exhibition than the loud notes of martial music. The performance closed with a pretty fair oration, on the

"scholar's object attainable," and neat Valedictory addresses, from Sanford. Not caring to hear a prayer from Leonard Humphrey I rushed
out. . . .

Emily Dickinson, though she was a good student, dreaded
examinations and exhibitions. She had no inclination to display
her talents in public. In August, 1845, she wrote to Abiah:

> I am already gasping in view of our examination; and although I
> am determined not to dread it I know it is so foolish, yet in spite of
> my heroic resolutions, I cannot avoid a few misgivings when I think
> of those tall, stern trustees, and when I know that I shall lose my
> character if I don't recite as precisely as the laws of the Medes and
> Persians. But what matter will that be a hundred years hence?

Toward every other aspect of her school, however, Emily
was eager and even ecstatic. Her devotion to the young men
and women who were her teachers knew no bounds. She was
capable of shrewd observation and satirical comment, as her
burlesque description of one of her schoolmates who was "always whizzing about" shows. If she saw her teachers through
rose-colored spectacles, it was because she found them engaging
as well as earnest. Their personal charm enlisted her admiration quite as much as their high aims.

As a girl pupil Emily came naturally in closest contact with
the preceptresses. She has left no reference to Mrs. Caroline D.
Hunt, widow of the pastor of North Amherst, whom she first
knew in that capacity. According to a contemporary notice, Mrs.
Hunt was "entitled to the warmest thanks of every parent who
has any respect to the reputation of his daughters" for her success in improving the manners of her pupils. "While the recita-
tions in Botany . . . and intellectual philosophy, and other
branches, the excellent compositions, and the great variety of
beautiful drawings and paintings, which adorned the walls of
the hall, all which have received her unwearied attention, gave
the highest evidence of her 'aptness to teach' and a faithful
application of that happy talent." Probably Mrs. Hunt found

little to do in improving the manners of Edward Dickinson's daughters, but she initiated them into the mysteries of "intellectual philosophy" at a tender age, and no doubt impressed upon their minds, following Mrs. Alvira H. Lincoln's *Familiar Lectures on Botany*, that "the *vegetable world* offers a boundless field of inquiry, which may be explored with the most pure and delightful emotions. . . . The study of Botany seems peculiarly adapted to females," etc.

Mrs. Hunt was succeeded in 1841–42 by Miss Helen Humphrey of Southwick, the sister of her dear friend Jane and a recent graduate of Mount Holyoke, of whom Emily Dickinson wrote, "She was universally beloved in Amherst." Then after an interval of Mrs. Hunt and Miss Jennette P. Dickinson (no relation) came Emily's favorite instructress, Miss Elizabeth C. Adams, who served in 1843–44, while Jeremiah Taylor, then in his first year out of Amherst, was principal. Of "dear Miss Adams" and her "happy face" Emily could not say too much, and her delight overflowed when Mr. Taylor returned for the 1846 Commencement, while Miss Adams was again teaching at the Academy.

Oh, I do love Mr. Taylor. It seems so like old times to meet Miss Adams and Mr. Taylor together again. I could hardly refrain from singing "Auld Lang Syne." It seemed so very à propos. Have you forgotten the memorable ride we all took with Mr. Taylor, "Long, long ago"?

During Emily's last two terms (spring and summer, 1847) Miss Rebecca M. Woodbridge, daughter of the minister of Hadley, was preceptress. Her account of this young woman, who was but four years older than herself, is too ardent not to be quoted:

We all love her very much. . . . She is tall and rather slender, but finely proportioned, has a most witching pair of blue eyes, rich brown hair, delicate complexion, cheeks which vie with the opening rose-bud, teeth like pearls, dimples which come and go like the ripples in yonder little merry brook, and then she is so affectionate and lovely. Forgive my glowing description, for you know I am always in love with my teachers. Yet, much as we love her, it seems lonely and strange without "our dear Miss Adams."

Unless we keep in mind Emily's constant enthusiasm for her school and her fervent admiration for her teachers, we may easily read too much into her relationship with the young man whom she last knew as principal of the Academy. Leonard Humphrey was but twenty-three years old when he took office, greatly to Emily's satisfaction. A leading undergraduate and valedictorian of his class, he "had made the mark of a fine scholar and a gentle Christian spirit." As a member of the Alpha Delta Phi fraternity, a closely knit coterie to which Austin Dickinson also belonged, Humphrey was undoubtedly a sharer in the life of the brilliant group of young people with whom Emily then freely moved. He was one of her intimate circle to whom she looked up as her "master," but there is no indication that she was any more attached to him than to Mr. Taylor of the memorable ride.

After a year at Andover Seminary, Humphrey returned to Amherst College as a tutor. Emily mentions a call from him in company with Mary Warner, "and we had a delightful time, you well know." Then the village was shocked by Humphrey's sudden death, which occurred on November 30, 1850, while he was visiting his parents. Emily shared the general sorrow. A month later, during a moment of deep depression due to several causes, she unburdened her heart to her friend Abiah, taking the recent loss of Humphrey as her text:

. . . the hour of evening is sad—it was once my study hour—my master has gone to rest, and the open leaf of the book, and the scholar at school *alone,* make the tears come, and I cannot brush them away; I would not if I could, for they are the only tribute I can pay the departed Humphrey.

You have stood by the grave before; I have walked there sweet summer evenings and read the names on the stones, and wondered who would come and give me the same memorial; but I never have laid my friends there, and forgot that they too must die; this is my first affliction, and indeed 'tis hard to bear it. . . . I don't think there will be any sunshine, or any singing-birds in the spring that's coming. I shall look for an early grave then, when the grass is growing green.

There is a little too much of the conventional lady by the weeping-willow tree in this. Emily was sincere, I think, but in the manner of the very young. If she considered her school-master's death her "first affliction," it was because she was sensitive to the grief of the village and was willing to make it her very own. In life and fact, Emily's relation to her admired young teacher was not closer than Milton's to Edward King. Her girlish letter shows her trying with all her might to weep for the local Lycidas—"the departed Humphrey"!

> So may some gentle Muse
> With lucky words favor *my* destined urn.

There was little sadness in Emily's life while she remained a girl in school. Emily Fowler, whose father was a member of the College faculty from 1838 to 1843 and who remained in close touch with the village until her marriage to Gordon L. Ford in 1853, has left a vivid but confused record of the young people of her girlhood, their "laughter and ability and sighing" remembered after forty years. The earliest of her reminiscences relate to the period around 1842 when both Emilys were students at the Academy, but mingled with these early impressions are others that must be dated at least as late as 1857. It is from Mrs. Ford that we learn of Emily's reputation as the wit of the school and of her contributions to a manuscript magazine called *Forest Leaves* which the girls passed around. I shall return to her early writings in a later chapter.

For our present purposes the special value of her recollections is that they show us an Emily Dickinson totally distinct from the secluded and unapproachable being of later years, a girl fond of country rambles, participating eagerly in the simple and spirited amusements of the village, and "a free talker about what interested her"—which did not include small-town gossip. We hear of excursions to Mount Norwottuck, sugaring-off parties at Sunderland, picnics where the men caught fish and concocted a delectable chowder, dances surreptitiously organized when the elders were out, valentine gatherings where verses were hilariously compounded of misfit quotations, a Shakespeare club where the girls defeated the young men's proposal to read from Bowdlerized texts, an essay club known as the "Unseen Trap," and of various other entertainments devised by young men and women whose brains were ceaselessly and creatively active. "Emily was part and parcel of all these gatherings, and there were no signs, in her life and character, of the future recluse. . . . She mingled freely in all the companies and excursions of the moment, and the evening frolics." For the latter the "First President's House" where the Fowlers lived was a favorite rendezvous.

Several of the young women with whom Emily was closely associated during her Academy days were four or five years older than herself, and all were distinguished by character, intelligence, and charm. Their effervescence of high spirits, their propensity to "elevate the ancient Henry," as a contemporary invitation to a party of high jinks put it, was prophetic of a surplus energy soon to be applied in earnest to the business of life. Among them Emily successfully held her own. Her wit was memorable, and her demure manner "brightened easily into fun when she felt at home." She shared their fervor as well as their frolics. "She loved with all her might," wrote Mrs. Ford, "there was never a touch of the worldling about her, and we all knew her truth and trusted her love." The temper of mind acquired through daily intimacy with the lively and utterly unsophisticated companions of her girlhood could never be satisfied to rust unused.

Like most of her friends Emily passed many hours in gardening, practising on the piano, and acquiring the prickly art of housekeeping in all its branches. She was not by inclination a domestic spirit, but she learned to do her part. The neighborly custom of the village demanded that fruit and flowers be exchanged in season, and that jellies, desserts, and other dainties should be sent about at all times as "attentions" to friends. Emily became an adept at such exquisite cookery, but she was a past mistress of bread-making as well. At the annual Cattle Show of 1856 a loaf of her "rye and Indian" took the second prize. Edward Dickinson to the end of his life professed to care for no bread that was not of her baking, and she saw to it that he was not disappointed. Then too, as she remarked to Higginson, "people must have puddings." Emily made them. But other housewifely duties irked her. Sewing was an exasperation, and as for cleaning the house her attitude was summed up in saying, "I prefer pestilence." Lavinia devotedly took over the grosser tasks.

The garden, however, was Emily's special province. She possessed a natural affinity for flowers and always had them about her. Like Mrs. Samuel Bowles, of whom an enthusiast reported, "it was almost impossible for a plant to die, even a woodland plant, when she had once taken it under her care," Emily had an uncanny knack of making even the frailest growing things flourish under her hands. She was successful, as few in Amherst were, in cultivating the English violet out of doors. "Miss Emily's garden had a touch that no one else's had," as one who remembered it wrote. "I think that others planted gardens with lemon verbena, jockey club, sweet clover, and Star of Bethlehem, because Miss Emily had these in her garden." Lilies too were great favorites with her. When her schoolmates nicknamed her sister the Pond Lily, Emily quickly exclaimed, "Then I am the Cow Lily," alluding to the orange lights in her hair and eyes. The day lily was almost an Amherst flower, not so often cherished in other places. Miss Emily once put two day lilies in the hand of a stranger as her "introduction." Others, noting her delicate and fastidious ways, compared her to the daphne odora of her sun-parlor.

Her nearest approach to a merely ornamental accomplishment was the piano playing of her girlhood. It was no more than that, and in later life was discontinued. She was enraptured when her father bought her a piano, and with the help of Aunt S—— quickly learned to play such songs as the popular "Maiden, weep no more" and a few show pieces, among others "The Grave of Bonaparte" and "Lancers Quickstep." Eventually she rose to the heights of "The Battle of Prague." Beyond this there was no one to guide her. It is hard to realize now how untrained the musical taste of most Americans was a century ago. At one of Ole Bull's recitals a man in the audience set up a demand for "Yankee Doodle"—and the violinist with a smile complied. Emily had attended two concerts in Boston in the autumn of 1846, but they interested her less than the Chinese Museum. Five years later the whole Dickinson family, except Austin who was away from home, drove through a tremendous thunderstorm to hear Jenny Lind in Northampton. Emily was deeply impressed by the singer's personality, but did not fancy her performance. Some marvellous coloratura effects excepted, she preferred plain Yankee singing. Her description of her father's sardonic attitude on this same occasion makes curious reading.

In only one respect was Emily conscious of a difference between herself and the majority of her schoolmates. The "world" still held a predominant place in her affections, but all around her friends were renouncing it for the service of a heavenly master. She witnessed repeatedly the joy of Christian conversion as it illuminated the life of one or another of her companions. Mary Humphrey, Abiah Root, Eliza Coleman were "pious"; all three subsequently married clergymen. Abby

Wood, the "particular friend" of Emily and Abiah, was to join her lot with an Amherst missionary and to depart for far-off Syria. Mary Warner was to work no less self-sacrificingly at home, married to a stalwart Christian on the College faculty. It was not easy to resist the tremendous appeal exemplified with the fervor and grace of youth in the shining lives of her contemporaries.

I am not unconcerned, dear Abiah, [wrote Emily] upon the all-important subject to which you have so frequently and so affectionately called my attention in your letters. But I feel that I have not yet made my peace with God. I am still a stranger to the delightful emotions that fill your heart. . . . I do not feel that I could give up all for Christ, were I called to die. Pray for me, dear Abiah, that there may be room left for me in the shining courts above. . . .

In electing to stand apart Emily was vaguely troubled. But she was Edward Dickinson's daughter. She could not bring herself to merge—not even with God. The year at Mount Holyoke Seminary now opening before her was to decide her fate. Would she "find grace," or would she remain "one of the lingering bad ones"?

Mount Holyoke Female Seminary

I T IS easy for us to misinterpret the situation of men and women a century ago who lived habitually in the atmosphere of evangelical piety. We wonder also how deep-sea fish, under the weight of half a mile of water, can feed and spawn as unconcernedly as creatures of the shallows, until we recall that the pressure is inside them pressing out as well as outside pressing in. Piety permeated the lives of normal people of the 1840's in a way that seems to us morbid and intolerable, yet they went about their everyday affairs much as we do. Preachings and prayer meetings they took in their stride. This must be borne in mind when we attempt to estimate the influence of Mount Holyoke Seminary on an eager scholar of the class of 1849.

We shall inevitably go wrong if we try to reconstruct the background of Emily Dickinson's year at the Seminary from the official or semi-official records. The early annals of Mount Holyoke were written by intensely pious ladies and were aimed at equally pious readers. In their view the fact that a single girl had "expressed a hope that she had found Christ" was a matter of supreme interest and called for extended comment. It outweighed the fact that over two hundred other girls were at the same time mastering their lessons, doing the housekeeping of the "family," roaming the fields, and entertaining callers from Amherst College or Williston Seminary. This normal routine of the institution, so little stressed by its historians, went on as usual even during periods of religious revival. At such times there was indeed a noticeable solemnity and tenderness during religious exercises, the "impenitent" were prayed and wept over and urged to enter into the joy of the Kingdom, but there was no infringement upon the hours appropriated to study, domestic work, or recreation, and these constituted the bulk of the day. The superficial impression that Mount Holyoke was a place where youth was cramped, curbed, and repressed in every natural desire or impulse is simply untrue. The corollary that Emily Dickinson was in revolt against her environment there does not tally with her words. "I love this Seminary," she wrote, "and all the teachers are bound strongly to my heart by ties of affection." Our conception of one of the first of women's colleges in the days of its founder should not emphasize to the exclusion of all else the aspect of its regimen which has fallen out of fashion, even though that was the aspect of greatest moment in the eyes of many contemporaries.

It will help to remove false impressions if we first see the Seminary from an entirely secular point of view, as fortunately we are enabled to do through the diary of an Amherst sophomore. William Gardiner Hammond, whose account of Amherst Academy I have already quoted, learned in the spring of 1847 that the daughter of family friends was a student at Mount Holyoke. He had never seen the girl, and he went to call upon her with the mixed emotions that a modern undergraduate would feel in keeping a "blind date." He also expected to find the young ladies guarded like nuns. Here is his uncensored account of his reception.

Tuesday 18th. [May, 1847] . . . got a horse and carriage and started for Sou. Hadley to visit Ellen Holman. Took Ide with me. Had a very pleasant ride over: conversation as usual mostly of the *girls*. Poor Ide is *"smashed"* with Jeanie Gridley. Was charmed with the road over the mountains: it runs along a sort of terrace cut in the steep mountain side: altogether very romantic and just the place to ride with a young lady. Reached S. H. about 4½ P.M.: a passable little village (a very little one) not unpleasantly situated. The seminary is a large brick building with double portico in front. Ide would not go over with me so I left him at the hotel. Rang the bell in great terror, for fear of Miss Lyon and the assistant dragonnesses: a very plain young lady came to the door, and to my great astonishment on asking for Miss Holman I was shown into the parlor without any inquisition preparatory! This was a huge apartment sumptuously furnished with a rusty stove, cherry table, and multitudinous cane bottomed chairs. Never having seen Nellie I feared some embarrassment but my fears vanished like the wind when she entered with a smiling face, hands outstretched and "So this is Willie!" Was even unexpectedly pleased with her. She is very pretty, lively, and intelligent: more piquant and original than her sisters, yet not deficient in grace and sweetness. . . . She got a teacher to accompany us through the building, that being the requisition: rather an agreeable plain young lady, S. Fisk[e]'s sister. We saw all that was to be seen: the pleasant recitation rooms: the pleasanter chapel, or what corresponds to such: the little library and reading room where all but the strictly religious periodicals are carefully put away from Saturday till Monday: the huge dining room with its all but score of tables, and huger kitchen where the young ladies of the Seminary all labor an hour daily. We went through the long space-ways meeting any number of plain young ladies, and catching sly peeps into their little boxes of sleeping rooms: said *"beautiful"* at every eligible window, and did all the other things right and proper in *viewing the building.* Reflecting at last that I had nine miles to drive, and that Ide was probably dying of *ennui* at the tavern, I reluctantly broke away, with most sincere promise of soon repeating my visit, and still sooner writing. At the hotel we got a nice tea, in true country style: then *put* for home, and that not slowly. Had a glorious ride, both feeling excited and full of the d---l.

Hammond was not slow in redeeming his promise to come again. On June 9 he drove to South Hadley, taking with him a junior named Pomeroy, who had a fair cousin at the Seminary. They were cordially received and "had a most delightful call, two or three hours long." On this occasion Hammond caught his first glimpse, under somewhat peculiar circumstances, of Miss Mary Lyon.

As we passed through the outer parlor I was almost *petrified*, to see Ide & Shepard, with faces half a yard long, talking to the old she-dragon herself. They had come, as I learned afterwards, out of sport, on purpose to see Nelly H.: they asked for a young lady they knew was not there, and then for Miss Lyon: and when she came, went in to her with the utmost *coolness* on the score of their father's & mother's old acquaintance! waiting to see us as we came out: it was most inimitably done.

Shortly after leaving, Pomeroy and Hammond joined forces with the two scamps and arranged to borrow the "team" they had come in, so that each might take his lady for a drive. Unfortunately Nellie had become involved with "two country cousins, raw lads from Easthampton school," who had just come to visit her, and so could not go for fear of offending "general principles." Hammond, therefore, "went back to the hotel, and waited a long time for Pom.: he and his lady did not return till after 9 P.M.! they had been across the river, and drank tea at a hotel!" This does not sound as though youth were being curbed.

A month later to the day Hammond was back again, and this time confided to his diary that he had "enjoyed the pleasantest visit I ever have made there yet: and that's saying much." With most of the Amherst undergraduates he had ridden to Northampton very early in the morning to hear Rufus Choate and Daniel Webster deliver opposing pleas in the famous Oliver Smith Will case, and had stood for several hours in the packed and stifling courtroom. Early in the afternoon he walked to South Hadley, crossing the river by Hockanum ferry. By special invitation he sat at Miss Lyon's table for the evening meal, then returned to Amherst on foot, having covered something over

twenty-five miles in the course of the day. Among other incidents:

Saw some of the young ladies exercise in Calisthenics a species of
orthodox dancing in which they perambulate a smooth floor in various figures, with a sort of sliding, stage step; not unlike children's
plays, all except the *kissing* part, which is probably omitted as not likely
to prove interesting where *all* are of the same sex: the whole movement is accompanied by singing, in which noise rather than tune or
harmony seems to be the main object. By a species of delusion peculiar
to the Seminary, they imagine that all this [is] very conducive to
health, strength, gracefulness etc. Had a capital chance to look at the
girls during the evolutions, and especially when they *defiled* before us
out of the room hand in hand, just as children play "twist tobacco,"
facing us, and advancing crab-fashion, sideways. Saw one or two
pretty girls there: but the majority of *transcendent* ugliness. Then
went to tea by special invitation: or to speak more accurately went to
water: for nothing more *ardent* is allowed. Sat at Miss Lyon's *Prae-
torium* and partook hugely of a queer sort of hasty pudding, with
cream and sugar, which formed the chief *delicacy.* Tea over, the
young ladies all turned to face our seat (how I did blush: the only
comfort I had was to catch the eye of someone in the crowd, and *wink*
at her.) the *exceptions* were taken, and the evening devotions performed: then while the crowd went by, I waited in utter loneliness,
as kindly directed by Miss Whitman, till Nelly appeared from her
own seat, in the farthest corner of the room: then we adjourned to the
parlor again and had another good long chat. Nelly told me how Miss
Whitman had made many inquiries regarding my frequent visits, and
finally professed herself perfectly satisfied with my appearance etc.!
... "Tempus" will "fugit": so much earlier than I wished, and later
than I ought, I started at half past seven for Amherst. No incidents
diversified my long, lonely, dark walk: and by half past ten I was once
more in my room. Thus passed an *Amherst holiday.*

On July 15, while most of the Seminary girls were enjoying
an excursion to the mountain which gives the College its name,
Hammond and Pomeroy improved the occasion by taking their
friends buggy-riding.

Miss Whitman gave most gracious permission, and off we went. It

is needless to say we had a glorious ride: for everything, even to the
weather, the scenery, and the *team*, was all we could have wished. We
rode down by the falls of the Connecticut. . . . Soon after our return
Pom. & Miss T. went to ride: and while they were gone, Nellie and
I walked out to visit "young Niagara" a pretty mill-fall in the neighborhood, very much admired by the romantic young ladies of the Seminary: unfortunately however the mill was not in operation! Had a
very pleasant walk, nevertheless: and then came back, and chatted over
[Longfellow's] Hyperion, and studies, and impulsiveness etc. most
merrily. . . . Pom. and Miss T. did not return till nearly 8 P.M. and
soon after we left, though much loth. Nellie made me promise the
first letter, though she rightfully owes it. The ride home was pleasant:
and once more in Amherst, we returned to the sober realities of life,
and remembered we had had no *supper*.

Hammond's last visit of the year was on the occasion of the
final examinations, which he attended with his father. He was
already a connoisseur of such exercises, and his comments are
those of a professional critic.

I found a place among some students, near Pomeroy, and also quite
near Nellie H. though I had to content myself with gazing at her in
silence.—A class in Virgil were on the floor when I came and the little I could catch was highly creditable to their scholarship. Then the
first four books of Euclid: very well done: the teachers gave out the
captions, and then the girls drew their own figures and demonstrated
them without the use of letters. Then a class in Botany, of which
Nellie formed a part, very interesting to me and honorable to herself:
then History and one or two other things of the kind, very good and
very dull: then Calisthenics, in which Nellie *ought* to have taken a
part, but to her own great joy, and my sorrow, was excused: all very
much as when I saw them before: everyone dressed in white, with
green wreaths for this special occasion.—Then music from the piano,
and singing: very fair: then five compositions: very good indeed,
though rather for style than ideas: even in the style it was often easy
to detect traces of some popular author. Then more music, and the performance closed: I went into the parlor, and chatted a few minutes
with Nellie. Prof Snell [of Amherst] by chance came in, and "grinned
horribly a ghastly smile" to see what I was doing. Could stay but a

few minutes: so, not "wi' mony a vow and locked embrace" but with many a kind and heartfelt word of constant friendship, we parted.

Here too we must take our leave of the engaging Hammond. It is a thousand pities that Emily Dickinson is never mentioned in his vivacious diary, but he has served a good purpose if his jottings have convinced us that Mount Holyoke Seminary was a very human place, even in the days of "the old she-dragon."

Two months after the anniversary just described Emily Dickinson became one of the two hundred and thirty-five students that crowded the Seminary to its utmost capacity. Since numbers made impossible the ideal that each girl should have a room of her own, she was assigned as roommate to her cousin, Emily L. Norcross, of Monson, a senior and an utterly colorless figure. All that we know of her is that she owned a shoe-brush and blacking. She was the kind that would. Most of Miss Lyon's cherished young ladies came from New England or New York, daughters of professional men, small merchants, and farmers, but there were five from Canada, three from the South, and several from the raw West—Missouri, Ohio, Illinois, Iowa, and Wisconsin. The reputation of Mount Holyoke in its eleventh year was already nation wide.

Miss Mary Lyon, its founder and first principal, was then in her fifty-first year, a very tired woman nearing her end, but still ceaselessly contriving to perfect the college of her vision. Her energy, insight, sympathy, and humor seemed as inexhaustible as ever. Around her she had gathered a devoted group of teachers, most of them still in their twenties, all of them trained in the Seminary and eager to consecrate three to ten years of their lives, or even more, to the cause of higher education for women. They did not look forward to a career of scholarship, as their successors have come to do. They were simply making active use, as Mary Lyon designed, of the years before marriage, years that for many young women were often empty and objectless. Only three of the teachers Emily Dickinson knew remained unmarried.

In leaving home for the first time Emily evidently felt some misgivings. She dreaded, though quite needlessly, the examinations she must take in order to enter, for many applicants were found insufficiently prepared and at sixteen she was among the youngest. Gossip declared also that the rules of the Seminary were unbelievably strict, that many of the girls were crude and unmannerly, and that the food prepared by the students themselves in "pie circles" and cooking squads was scanty and unpalatable. She was agreeably surprised to find conditions the reverse of what she had feared. Her letters to Abiah Root and to her brother Austin, after her first severe homesickness had passed, thrill with little exclamations of satisfaction. "Everything is pleasant and happy here. . . . Things seem much more like home than I anticipated, and the teachers are all very kind and affectionate to us." "Miss Lyon and all the teachers seem to consult our comfort and happiness in everything they do." Her domestic work, that most controverted feature of the Mount Holyoke system, she did not find burdensome, and the meals were wholesome, abundant, and varied. She enclosed a sample menu. Best of all, "there are many sweet girls here." She was content.

The Seminary "family," as Miss Lyon loved to call it, was divided into senior, middle, and junior classes, and the three classes again into "sections," each in charge of a teacher who was to act as what is now known as faculty adviser. Emily Dickinson, who was not admitted immediately to advanced standing as a member of the middle class, was apparently assigned to a junior section led by Miss Rebecca W. Fiske, the same "agreeable plain young lady" who had guided Hammond on his tour of inspection. She was the sister of Samuel Fiske, a lively Amherst senior, who as a member of Austin Dickinson's fraternity must have been well known to his family. Here was a link with home. Emily came to know Miss Fiske early and likewise found her agreeable. "I love her very much," she wrote to Austin, "and think I shall love all the teachers when I become better acquainted with them and find out their ways, which, I can assure you, are almost 'past finding out.'" Her extant letters, however, make no further mention of her teachers, except of Miss Mary C. Whitman, the associate principal, who had general charge of the middle class to which Emily was soon promoted. In contrast to Miss Lyon, who with wisps of radiant auburn hair and cap strings flying was always bustling about, poking her head into the Rumford oven, mothering a homesick girl, pausing to solve a knotty point in Butler's *Analogy,* and the next moment gazing with clear blue eyes straight into the soul of a delinquent, Miss Whitman was tall, cool, and remorselessly competent. On her fell the burden of routine discipline. There is a hint that toward the middle of the year she admonished Emily Dickinson to check a tendency toward "rebellion and an unsubdued will," to the delight of both Emily and Austin. On a later occasion when Miss Whitman refused her permission to go home for a Sunday with her family, Emily quietly submitted.

The reason for Miss Whitman's rebuke, if it deserves so strong a term, may be conjectured. At some time during the year—family tradition places the incident about Christmas time —Emily Dickinson signalized her independence by refusing her assent to an otherwise unanimous vote of her schoolmates. Her action has been quite absurdly represented as a defiance of Miss Lyon's authority, but it was in fact nothing more than a simple case of conscience. Here is the anecdote as recorded by a trustworthy listener who heard it from Emily herself.

Miss Lyon, during a time of religious interest in the school, asked all those who wanted to be Christians to rise. The wording of the request was not such as Emily could honestly accede to and she remained seated—the only one who did not rise. In relating the incident to me, she said, "They thought it queer I didn't rise"—adding with a twinkle in her eye, "I thought a lie would be queerer."

We must allow for slight inaccuracies in the anecdote as here reported. Miss Lyon's request would surely not have been made of the whole school, since most of the girls were already professing Christians. It might, however, have been made with point at a meeting of the impenitents, some seventy in number. Also, as we shall see later, Emily Dickinson wanted with all her heart to be a Christian. But her words, as quoted, give us the clue to the true nature of the incident, which in a garbled form calculated to appeal to cheap sentiment has unfortunately obtained a wide circulation. The last thing she ever wished was to make herself conspicuous, and it was no doubt to her utter consternation that she found herself "one with God" against the majority. But she could not honestly say that her convictions were altered by that fact, and she did not do so. The shrewd, humorous, great-hearted head of the Seminary would not have been what she was had she not possessed sufficient insight to comprehend the girl's point of view and to respect her transparent honesty of mind. We have it on loving authority that Emily Dickinson was "the idol of the school and its Preceptress." Miss Whitman, however, may have thought that a few remarks on a decent respect for the opinions of mankind were in order. So interpreted the incident does violence to the character of none of those concerned.

Were it not for the testimony just quoted to her popularity at South Hadley and for the recollection of a schoolmate who told Mrs. Todd that Emily "was always surrounded by a group of girls at recess, to hear her strange and intensely funny stories, invented on the spot," we should be apt to think of her as rather shy and remote from the activities of others. Early in the autumn when a menagerie came to town and almost all the girls, under the escort of "Daddy Hawks," went to see the bears and monkeys perform, Emily stayed away and "enjoyed the solitude finely." She neither sent nor received valentines, though a number of her friends successfully eluded the injunction of the authorities against "those foolish notes." She may have had her daguerreotype taken by an artist who opened a studio in South Hadley for a few weeks, but her name is not among those of the party who scaled Mount Holyoke in June and registered at the summit. She liked to be outdoors and delighted when spring permitted her "to walk out in the green fields and beside the pleasant streams in which South Hadley is rich." But apparently these strolls were solitary. If like Nellie Holman she had callers from Amherst other than her brother, the fact is not recorded, save for mention of the "treacherous" friend whose report that she was ill with a bad cold led to her being brought home much against her will before the end of the spring term.

The truth is that she was studying hard. The program for a specimen day which she wrote out for Abiah indicates that she had few leisure moments, and those she was likely to spend in writing letters to her family and her absent friends.

At 6 o'clock, we all rise. We breakfast at 7. Our study hours begin at 8. At 9. we all meet in Seminary Hall for devotions. At 10¼ I recite a review of Ancient History in connection with which we read Goldsmith & Grimshaw. At 11, I recite a lesson in "Pope's Essay on Man" which is merely transposition. At 12, I practise Calisthenics and at 12¼ read until dinner, which is at 12½ & after dinner, from 1½ until 2, I sing in Seminary Hall. From 2¾ until 3¾ I practise upon the Piano. At 3¾ I go to Sections, where we give in all our accounts for the day, including Absence—Tardiness—Communications —Breaking Silent Study hours—Receiving Company in our rooms and ten thousand other things, which I will not take time or place to mention. At 4½, we go into Seminary Hall, & receive advice from Miss Lyon in the form of a lecture. We have Supper at 6, & silent study hours from then until the retiring bell, which rings at 8¾, but the tardy bell does not ring until 9¾, so that we don't often obey the first warning to retire. Unless we have a good & reasonable excuse for failure upon any of the items, that I have mentioned above, they are recorded &

a *black mark* stands against our names. As you can easily imagine, we do not like very well to get "exceptions" as they are called scientifically here.

Thanks to an excellent training in Latin received at Amherst Academy, Emily was able to complete in less than a year the normal studies of the middle class. The system at Mount Holyoke, inherited from Mary Lyon's experiments at Ipswich Academy, divided the year into four periods known as "series," in each of which a student pursued two subjects intensively. At the conclusion of a series came a thorough testing, which in March and August took the form of public examinations. During the first series Emily was occupied in reviewing History and English Grammar, junior year subjects. On her seventeenth birthday she passed an examination on the first four books of Euclid, "without a failure at any time." She then commenced the studies of the middle class with Chemistry and Physiology, besides carrying on a rapid review of Algebra. The end of the second series brought the dreaded examinations, "more public than in our old academy, and a failure would be more disgraceful"; but she survived them. In January she was writing two compositions a month, each of them, if we may trust tradition, "an epoch for those who heard." Her studies of the third series are not accounted for, but during the fourth she completed Astronomy and Rhetoric, "which take me through to the Senior studies." The last remark is comprehensible if we suppose that Latin and Natural Philosophy were the missing subjects of the third series, and that she was excused from Botany in view of her proficiency in that subject.

Intellectually her year at the Seminary was a period of hard mental discipline under stimulating conditions. Emily proved that she could more than keep abreast of her companions in Latin and such "English branches" as were then taught in the leading colleges for men, while in addition singing in one of the two choirs and keeping up her practice on the piano. She achieved something of a success as a writer of compositions which her schoolmates were unwilling to forget. And she was brought into daily contact with one of the great personalities of her time. Superficially she may seem to have absorbed little from Mary Lyon. The life of seclusion that she later led was ostensibly the very reverse of the life of public service that Miss Lyon counselled. But it was not a life of inactivity. "Do what no one else is willing to do—go where no one else is willing to go," was the watchword of the Seminary. Many fulfilled it literally in the mission field. In a more subtle way Emily Dickinson also obeyed the militant injunction.

> To fight aloud is very brave,
> But gallanter, I know,
> Who charge within the bosom
> The cavalry of woe. . . .

The first of the huge negations that separated her from the accepted forms of action in her time, and by so doing forced her into individual activities of her own, occurred while she was at the Seminary. There she discovered, finally and irrevocably, that she could not share the religious life of her generation. One outlet was forever closed to her, not because she lacked religious feeling, but because she could not confine her religious feeling to the channels that were marked out for her. For better or worse, she felt impelled to turn aside from the way of truth as her contemporaries understood it, and gropingly seek out her own path. Hers was to be a career of exploration, not of far-off islands, but of the desert places in the human soul.

Some passages from the Seminary journal, supplemented by a few surviving letters, give the background for this episode in Emily's spiritual drama. We must bear in mind in reading the journal that its writer was an intensely devout woman, soon to become a missionary, who used the technical language of religious psychology with the same abandon that teachers of "progressive" tendency display nowadays in employing the terminology of current mental science.

Religious activities commenced almost as soon as the students were assembled with the taking of a census of the converted and the unconverted. Nowhere at that time was such information considered a matter of purely private concern.

[October 2, 1847] This P.M. the names of the professors of religion, those who have a hope, and those who have not were taken. I cannot tell you how solemn it was, as one after another class arose. I saw more than one weep as her name was put down *"no hope."* There is a large class of this character—will it be so at the end of the year?

[October 11] Our religious meetings commenced yesterday. The praying circles met at 7½ in the evening. The impenitent at 4½ in Sem. Hall.

By the middle of December there was observed a quickening of "interest," the first signs of a possible revival. Some of the impenitent were becoming "tender."

[December 13] Our house was unusually still yesterday. There are some indications of the spirit's presence. There is among some Christians more feeling, also among some of the impenitent. Miss Lyon's meeting last eve was solemn. She spoke of the necessity of the Spirit to teach & make us feel the reality of Bible truths.

[December 16] This A.M. at devotions Miss Lyon spoke to us upon the doctrine of Dependence on God. . . . There has been almost fixed attention for the last three mornings. Oh! for the Spirit's presence & I think there are some indications of it.

[December 20] Miss Lyon's meeting with the impenitent yesterday was one of interest. There is attention & some awakening but little *deep* feeling yet. She spoke to them more solemnly than at any previous meeting. She addressed them in regard to the salvation of their own souls, of seeking it in earnest & now.

On this same Sunday the preacher, Mr. Belden of the Second Congregational Church of Amherst, invited the prayer circles of the Seminary to join his people in observing a fast on the coming Friday, December 24. After quietly feeling out the sentiment of her community and finding it favorably disposed, Miss Lyon accepted the invitation. She appointed as usual a meeting of the impenitent who had decided to observe the day of prayer, and more than fifty of the girls voluntarily attended. There was hope that at least one soul would be led into the fold.

[December 24] The day has passed. The house has been very still, quite as much so, as on the Sabbath. . . . After our return from church, Miss Lyon met with all the impenitent as on the Sab. . . . There are 25 of the present Middle Class without hope. We can but feel solicitous for the morrow, lest the feeling of today shall be dissipated. Oh, we need more of the Spirit's presence. How he was with us one year ago. I do think Christians are in a better state than a week ago, but we are not yet where we should be, low at the foot of the cross.

[December 25, Christmas Day] Attended to our usual business to day. There has been a good degree of quiet. I have hardly heard one "Merry Christmas" this morning.

Readers of Samuel Sewall's *Diary* will recognize the traditional Puritan antipathy to the celebration of Christmas, which was only just beginning to be relaxed. In 1847 not a college in New England allowed its students to go home for the day.

If Emily Dickinson had wished not to observe the fast on the day before Christmas, she was entirely free not to do so. The custom on such occasions was to request silence of all in order that the religious exercises might not be disturbed. Otherwise the students might do as they wished. The idea of compelling a girl to pray against her will would have shocked these ardent Protestants. Since Emily cordially disliked Mr. Belden, she may not have been moved to join in a day of prayer with his congregation.

The first Monday in January was regularly observed as a fast-day. Again the house was hushed, and again Miss Lyon labored to reclaim the impenitent.

[January 3, 1848] She commenced after singing & prayers, by inviting all who could answer the following questions affirmatively to meet with her at 7 o'clock this Eve. Does it *seem* to you that you want religion? Do you feel that *now* is the time to seek it? Does it seem to you that you are willing to give up the world? Does it seem to you that you are willing to attend to it, even though ridiculed by your best friends for it, even if you knew *you* must be alone in seeking it? Does it seem to you that you want your will bowed to *God's?* Do you want all your portion in God? Do you want to be entirely employed in the service of God? Do you want that religion, that shall make you care for souls? These were the questions, upon each she dwelt. . . . She then went on to speak to the other class, those who could not then decide, more particularly. Mentioned the various excuses made by sinners, for not *now* seeking salvation, & submitting to Jesus. And showed how vain they were, how vain they would seem in the light of Eternity. The closing remark was, "How vain to resist God. Did you ever see the little insect fall into the flame, see it struggle and strive to escape? how vain—Just so you are in the hands of *angry* God! What if you do resist? Which are *you,* a feeble worm of the dust? Oh! how vain! how much better to submit."

After this blast of Jonathan Edwards, nearly sixty attended the meeting at seven. On January 6 and 7 Miss Lyon spoke at morning prayers on the subject of regeneration. She dwelt particularly upon the greatness of the change, and upon the certainty that all might share in this new birth if they would.

[January 10] I think it was a good day to many of our family. . . . The meeting at 4. was one of great solemnity. Before commencing her remarks Miss L. invited to a meeting at 7 o'clock, all those who had a fear, who felt pained at the thought that this work might cease & they be passed by. Her subject was Jesus Christ and Him crucified. I would love to tell you much that she said, but you know how *she* would speak upon that subject. There were about 40. wrote notes to attend the meeting in the eve.

[January 11] We met this eve as last week in the Sem. Hall. at the time of recess meetings. . . . The meeting was fully attended, only those came who chose. God is still with us. This week will be one of importance.

Of Emily Dickinson's state of mind during this time of increasing tension we have direct evidence. On January 11 Emily Norcross, her cousin and roommate, wrote to Mrs. Andrew Porter of Monson, a motherly woman who had recently visited the Seminary and taken part in the religious meetings, a discouraging report.

Emily Dickinson appears no different. I hoped I might have some good news to write with regard to her. She says she has no particular objection to becoming a Christian and she says she feels bad when she hears of one and another of her friends who are expressing a hope but still she feels no more interest.

On January 17 Mrs. Porter's niece, Sarah Jane Anderson, mentioned Emily in a letter to her aunt, and again the report was unfavorable: "She still *appears* unconcerned."

But under the surface more was happening than Sarah Jane Anderson realized. Sunday, January 16, according to the Seminary journal, "was a *beautiful* day. It was like Spring." Reverend Mr. Blodgett of Greenwich, a minister deeply beloved, preached two sermons not unworthy of the day. His morning discourse from the text: "There is therefore now no condemnation to them which are in Christ Jesus, who walk not after the flesh, but after the Spirit," commended itself particularly to the teachers of the Seminary. "It was worth more than all the sermons we have had this whole term." "It was just what we needed." The journal continues:

At the meeting in the P.M. Miss L. spoke from the passage in Joshua "Choose ye this day whom ye will serve" &c also in Cor. "To day if ye will hear his voice." At the close she invited all who had decided that they would to day to serve the Lord, and those who had to day felt an uncommon anxiety to decide to a meeting in her room. This you see would include all who are particularly anxious. There were seventeen present.

In writing to Mrs. Porter shortly afterward, Miss Whitman alluded to this meeting in Miss Lyon's room. "Seventeen attended a meeting in the evening for those who felt unusually anxious to choose the service of God that night, and it was a very solemn meeting." Then, knowing Mrs. Porter's interest in Emily Norcross and her roommate, she added: "Emily Dickinson was among the number."

We may not cross the threshold of the room where Mary Lyon and her brilliant pupil knelt side by side. For the older woman religious faith, attested by a spiritual rebirth, was the keystone of completely mature personality. Her own convictions were the unfolding of a strong and happy nature. After preliminary struggles, she had felt a moment of revelation descend upon her like a Pentecost, out of doors, among the Buckland hills. Just so the sense of dedication had fallen upon Wordsworth one summer morning. But Mary Lyon was never tempted like the English poet to "rest in nature, not the God of nature." Her strong practical sense taught her to believe that good citizenship in a Christian nation must be patterned on citizenship in a spiritual kingdom. She was accustomed to expound the duties and privileges of that citizenship to the young ladies of the Seminary, treating them as adult minds able to judge for themselves. Many who were "out of hope" were swayed by her fervent logic. Emily Dickinson came to the very point of yielding, then recoiled.

Four days later the winter vacation began. Emily went home for two weeks. When she returned, the spell was broken.

[February 7] A meeting was appointed at 7 P.M. for those who have indulged a hope this year. If any one who attended a meeting of the same kind before vacation, felt that she ought not to do so now, she was to write a note, or if any who had not attended, felt that they now have some hope, they too were to write a note. Five new ones attended, one was not there, who had been before. She wrote no note however.

We can only guess who the one was. Two fragments of letters written about this time, however, show that Emily was profoundly shaken. Her language is very different from that of the girl who had "no particular objection to becoming a Christian."

Abiah, you may be surprised to hear me speak as I do, knowing that I express no interest in the all-important subject, but I am not happy, and I regret that last term, when that golden opportunity was mine, that I did not give up and become a Christian. It is not now too late, so my friends tell me, so my offended conscience whispers, but it is hard for me to give up the world.

. . . .

I am one of the lingering *bad* ones, and so do I slink away, and pause and ponder, and ponder and pause, and do work without knowing why, not surely, for this brief world, and more sure it is not for heaven, and I ask what this message *means* that they ask for so very eagerly: *you* know of this depth and fulness, will you try to tell me about it?

Emily knew well what conversion meant in terms of character. She had just witnessed the great change in her friend Abby Wood: "religion makes her face quite different, calmer, but full of radiance, holy, yet very joyful." But the meaning of meanings? The ultimate secret? Neither Mount Holyoke nor its vigorous principal could tell her that. She became indifferent to completing her course. A year or two before she had looked forward to the Seminary as the pinnacle of her hopes, but now she professed herself "cheered" by the thought that she was not to return. Was it simply the fact that home was very dear to her that led to this change of heart?

In Amherst during the winter vacation she had found a new preceptor, a friend who spoke to her of books and nature, and who seemed to open to her charmed vision a road to immortality infinitely more alluring than that marked out by Calvin and paved with adamantine blocks by Jonathan Edwards. She was eager to learn all that he could teach her.

PART TWO

TUTORS AND SHEPHERDS

Later Years

An Amethyst Remembrance

R EADERS of Emily Dickinson who wish to know the most intimate facts of her personal history need offer no apologies for indulging in what is a perfectly natural and legitimate curiosity. Apologies should come, rather, from those who hold that after her secretly cherished poems have been for half a century before the public, and after three conflicting versions of her supposed love-story have been printed, it is still possible to discountenance an interest in the crucial event of her life on the ground that "Emily Dickinson never wished her romance probed." This plea became irrelevant the moment her stature as a poet was made evident. If her family had wished to protect her private life from scrutiny, there was only one way to do it, a way clearly marked out for them by her own lifelong refusal to publish her poems. They chose instead to publish, and in so doing forfeited once for all the immunities previously attached to her "barefoot rank." Now that she has taken her rightful place in company with Wordsworth and Keats and Browning, the quality of her life is no less a subject of general interest than theirs.

And rightly so. Poems of high distinction are not picked up like nuggets by the chance discoverer; they are the fruits whereby a distinguished way of living is known, the secret and pure essence of a unique personality. It follows that the commentary which best deepens and enriches their significance is the biography of the poet. There may be those who are content merely to savor the beauty of a poem as a lady might dally with a plucked flower. The true lover of poetry, however, is like the horticulturalist who delights no less in the flower, but who must see the whole plant and dabble in the dark earth about its roots to learn the manner of its growth. In the case of Emily Dickinson the extraordinary intensity and compression of her writing were not unrelated to the deprivations which turned her nature inward upon itself. "Precisely an existence" was what she paid for her uncanny sensitiveness to the sweetness of unheard melodies. It will not do to gloss over the experiences that molded her being. Though we cannot hope to penetrate to the hidden springs of genius, that is no excuse for refusing to examine the psychic topography which determines the direction of its flow.

In addition to these general considerations there are three special reasons why the most private aspects of Emily Dickinson's life should be investigated without reserve. The first and most obvious is that a large section of her poetry deals ostensibly with her love for a man whom she could not marry and with the way in which she met the frustration of her hopes. As her poems were printed posthumously, and as they now stand, these lyrics are presented in no intelligible order. Consequently what might be a great sequence of love poems, comparable to Dante's *Vita Nuova* or any other in existence, is broken into scattered fragments and its design lost. Shakespeare's *Sonnets* have suffered the same loss of coherence through unsupervised publication. Would any one who discovered a clue to the identity of the Dark Lady consider the heart of that mystery too sacred to be plucked out? It may never be possible to determine the approximate dates of Emily Dickinson's poems, but a knowledge of her story would permit us to arrange them in some sort of comprehensible order.

Furthermore if we could collate the poems with their basis in fact, we could form a truer idea of Emily Dickinson's powers of invention and dramatization. In various poems she has described a visit to the ocean which never took place, her own deathbed sensations, and her feelings as she rested in the grave. Were her love poems, like these, figments of the imagination, or were they reports in verse of what she had actually experienced? The question is important in forming a sound estimate of Emily Dickinson's personality and of her quality as a writer. If Mrs. Browning's *Sonnets from the Portuguese* had been written before Robert Browning ever called in Wimpole Street, we should not feel about them as we do today.

The third reason is that Emily Dickinson was the subject of irresponsible gossip during her lifetime. The legends that distort and vulgarize her story cannot be dispelled until the exact truth is known. Unfortunately several of them have been recently revived and given a wide circulation. We can hardly blame "outsiders," however, for giving credence to sensational reports when we are told that "many a hot or quaint tale" emanated from a source very close to the poet herself. It is a needful service to Emily Dickinson's memory, therefore, to insist that she was telling the literal truth when she wrote: "My life has been too simple and stern to embarrass any," and to clear her record of any implications not in harmony with her words. There are still gaps to be filled in the story of her relations with the several men in whose dear and valued friendship she found inspiration and a partial relief from loneliness, but enough information is available to make the nature of these relationships plain.

Every one connected with Amherst between 1850 and 1880 was vaguely aware of the mysterious love-affairs attributed to Squire Dickinson's peculiar daughter, though these rumors were not openly repeated. Nevertheless they circulated underground, losing nothing in the telling, but changing shape and borrowing details from each other as is the common way of legends. When the first collection of Emily Dickinson's poems was published, guarded allusions to her supposed "love-story" began to appear, and versions highly colored by neighborhood gossip have been coming out of the ground ever since.

All the legends are reducible to two basic types. The first has to do with an early attachment to an eligible young man, whose attentions were forbidden by Emily's father on the ground that the suitor's prospects were not sufficiently hopeful. Gossip specifies a lovers' meeting in the garden interrupted by lantern light, a stern father ordering the young man off the premises, a defiant Emily promising never to leave her home until her lover could claim her and to wear nothing but white for his sake, and a broken-hearted lover dying after a few years of agonized separation. The second story asserts that Emily fell deeply in love with a married man, usually a clergyman, whom she met in Washington or Philadelphia in the spring of 1854; that he reciprocated her love and urged her to elope with him, but that she negatived the proposal; that he removed to a distant city and there dragged out the remainder of a disappointed life while she shut herself up from the world in her father's house. I have known former residents of Amherst who would die to defend the truth of one or the other of these stories. Miss Lavinia, or Mrs. Austin Dickinson, "told my mother."

Both the legends, though well on their way to becoming folktales, have a basis in fact. The first refers to Emily's friendship with a law-student in her father's office during and immediately after her year at Mount Holyoke Seminary. The second refers to what she called an "intimacy of many years" with a prominent clergyman whom she did meet in Philadelphia in the spring of 1854. She was fervently devoted to both these friends, and to the second especially she attached herself with all the intensity of her nature; but that either of them was ever her "lover," in any sense of the word that the world understands, there is not one scintilla of evidence, and in the second case not even a probability. The trouble with the legends, aside from the violent distortions of detail that each contains, is that they impose a cheap and commonplace interpretation on what was in reality a subtle and highly individual relationship. They reduce the pioneering of a soul in matter to the stale formulas of Hollywood romance and Greenwich Village psychology. In this and the following chapter I shall attempt to describe Emily Dickinson's friendships in her own terms, resisting as far as may be the temptation to color the discoverable facts by intimations borrowed from her poems. In a later chapter we shall consider what she made of her experiences for purposes of poetry.

Emily Dickinson, as we have seen, was an eager schoolgirl, with a craving for vital knowledge that no formal institution could satisfy. Books were of course a frugal chariot for the exploring soul, but better than books was intercourse with minds that she regarded as superior to her own. From her Mount Holyoke days to the end of her life there were few times when she did not regard herself, more or less playfully, as somebody's "scholar." In seeking out and attaching herself to the men whom she selected as her tutors, she displayed an adventurousness quite at variance with her accustomed shyness. Her thirst for intellectual and spiritual guidance was not to be denied. It was the master-passion of her life.

In her second letter (April 25, 1862) to Thomas Wentworth Higginson, who was the last of her chosen mentors, she summarized in characteristically pedagogical language her relations with the men who had been his predecessors. Her statement demands the closest attention, since brief as it is, it constitutes the longest account of her early attachments that she was ever to render to any one.

I went to school, but in your manner of the phrase had no education. When a little girl, I had a friend who taught me Immortality; but venturing too near, himself, he never returned. Soon after my tutor died, and for several years my lexicon was my only companion. Then I found one more, but he was not contented I be his scholar, so he left the land.

Her words make it clear that at least two men had profoundly influenced her mind. One was the friend of her girlhood who taught her "Immortality." The other was the "one more" who in leaving the land had left her without a master. Both were now lost to her. The correct identification of these two friends will give us the key to the crises of Emily Dickinson's life.

Who was the man that Emily Dickinson recognized as her "earliest friend" and preceptor? His identification was not made possible until in 1933 an unpublished letter of the greatest significance appeared in the catalogue of an autograph dealer. The information supplied by this letter put an end to all speculation on the subject and opened a new chapter in the poet's biography.

On January 13, 1854, Emily Dickinson wrote from Amherst to the Reverend Edward Everett Hale, then pastor of the Church of the Unity, in Worcester, to ask for his assurances about the last moments of a man who had been dear to her. Like others brought up in the Puritan faith she held the belief that God's elect, as the solemn moment of dissolution approached, would reveal by hopeful signs their confidence in their soul's eternal welfare. It made a difference that they should be "willing to die." This belief in which she was nurtured, and not sentiment or morbid curiosity, was the reason for Emily's lifelong interest in deathbed details. It was for such evidences of the spiritual state of her friend that she wrote to Hale.

> I think, Sir, you were the Pastor of Mr. B. F. Newton, who died sometime since in Worcester, and I have often hoped to know if his last hours were cheerful, and if he was willing to die. . . . You may think my desire strange, Sir, but the Dead was dear to me, and I would like to know that he sleeps peacefully.
>
> Mr. Newton was with my Father two years, before going to Worcester, in pursuing his studies, and was much in our family. I was then but a child, yet I was old enough to admire the strength, and grace, of an intellect far surpassing my own, and it taught me many lessons, for which I thank it humbly, now that it is gone. Mr. Newton became to

me a gentle, yet grave Preceptor, teaching me what to read, what authors to admire, what was most grand or beautiful in nature, and
that sublime lesson, a faith in things unseen, and in a life again, nobler
and much more blessed.

Of all these things he spoke—he taught me of them all, earnestly,
tenderly; and when he went from us, it was as an elder brother, loved
indeed very much, and mourned and remembered. During his life in
Worcester he often wrote to me, and I replied to his letters. I always
asked for his health, and he answered so cheerfully that, while I knew
he was ill, his death indeed surprised me. He often talked of God, but
I do not know certainly if he was his Father in Heaven. Please, Sir, to
tell me if he was willing to die, and if you think him at Home. I
should love so much to know certainly that he was today in Heaven. . . .

This is no perfunctory letter of pious inquiry. Emily's words
throb with a scarcely restrained emotion. They leave no doubt of
Newton's importance to her at the most impressionable period
of her life. Moreover, the friend who taught her "a faith in
things unseen, and in a life again, nobler and much more
blessed," can hardly be other than the "friend who taught me
Immortality" of her letter to Higginson. The man to whose
early instruction Emily Dickinson so warmly acknowledged her
indebtedness deserves a prominent place in any account of her
life.

Benjamin Franklin Newton was born in Worcester on March
19, 1821. I have been unable to learn anything relating to his
early years. He is not known to have visited Amherst before
he became a student in the office of Dickinson & Bowdoin in the
winter of 1847–48. He was not a college graduate, and at the
age of twenty-seven was somewhat behind the young men of
his generation in entering a profession. At the time of his coming Emily Dickinson was at Mount Holyoke Seminary. She
does not mention her father's new student in the long letter that
she wrote to Abiah Root describing her Thanksgiving vacation,
but there is an apparent allusion to the beginning of their intimacy in a letter written "on a snowy Sunday morning in
1848" to Susan Gilbert: "I've found a beautiful new friend and

I've told him about dear Susie and promised to let him know you so soon as you shall come." The Dickinson house at this period was full of young men, cousins, law-students, class-mates of Austin's, and tutors from the College, and with many of them Emily was on terms of affectionate intimacy. But her letter to Hale leaves no doubt that of them all Ben Newton became particularly dear to her. He was the guide of her taste and the awakener of her mind. When he left at the end of two years she thought of him as an elder brother, "loved indeed very much and mourned and remembered." For the short re-mainder of his life their friendship was continued by corre-spondence.

Late in 1849 or early in 1850 Newton returned to Worcester, where his family had lived for three generations, to complete his legal studies in the office of Benjamin F. Thomas, a grand-son of Isaiah Thomas and an extremely successful lawyer, who had recently resigned as Judge of Probate to enter upon a large and for those times lucrative practice. There was nothing ex-traordinary in this move. Law-students often served their ap-prenticeship in more than one office, and probably considered it an advantage to do so. In the course of the year Newton was admitted to the bar and set up for himself.

Any suspicion that he had left Amherst a disappointed lover must be reconciled with the fact that on June 4, 1851, he was married to Miss Sarah Warner Rugg, a woman twelve years his senior. She may have been, however, more nurse than wife, for at the time of his marriage Newton was already an ailing man, stricken by pulmonary tuberculosis. He kept on with his legal work, nevertheless, and in May, 1852, upon the division of the old Southern District, he was appointed State's Attorney for the Middle District (Worcester County). Less than a year later, on March 24, 1853, he died.

The resolutions adopted by the Worcester County Bar the day following his death show that Newton, in his brief professional career, had won the full confidence and esteem of his colleagues. He was regretted as a man generally beloved. An obituary notice, after speaking in laudatory terms of his character and abilities, makes it clear that he was active to the end and was busily engaged in winding up his affairs:

> He was out on Wednesday, the day previous to his decease, and called on several persons to whom he was indebted. He wished to settle his accounts now, he said, as he did not anticipate a much longer continuance of his life. He spoke calmly of his death; and seemed anxious that this event, so solemn to him, should cause no one any loss or trouble. He died peacefully, calmly, and hopefully at the early age of 32 years.

Had Emily Dickinson seen this account of her friend's death she might not have needed to write to inquire about his last moments, but she probably read in *The Springfield Republican* for March 26 the bare announcement of it, three sentences which spoke chiefly of an unexpired insurance policy. She was not prepared for the blow. Only a week before, as we shall see, Newton had written her a letter hinting his true condition so gently that she had not understood, a letter, now like a message from eternity, full of confidence in her extraordinary powers and of earnest hope for her future. As the shadow of her loss darkened the coming April days, she brooded over the unruly ways of death, but there was no word in her lexicon to solve that mystery. Earth could not answer, and after ten months she felt impelled to write to the Reverend Mr. Hale to know if her friend were indeed in heaven.

She had good reason to be grateful to Ben Newton, for he had put her in touch with new and stimulating currents of thought beyond the range of her orthodox upbringing. More than that he had awakened in her stirrings of young ambition, if not of young love. He had told her that she had the power to be a poet and had praised her early verses in terms that she never forgot. All this may be gathered from passages widely scattered through her letters.

Books and reading often formed a subject of conversation at the Dickinson house. Edward Dickinson's library was well stocked with classics. His personal taste, according to Emily, was for "*lonely* and *rigorous* books." She also told Higginson that he preferred to have his children read nothing but the Bible, perhaps forgetting to add "on Sundays." There are signs that he kept a close eye on what his daughters were reading. He could not object on moral grounds to their darling "Ik Marvel," but he could and did make disparaging remarks about "somebody's rev-e-ries." These "modern literati," meaning Dickens and Mrs. Stowe, he considered greatly inferior to the authors of his youth. There were also strange and unsettling books abroad which he did not wish to have introduced into his family. As late as 1862 Emily wrote: "He buys me many books, but begs me not to read them, because he fears they joggle the mind." To books in general Emily was accustomed from earliest childhood. She had merely touched the fringes of the radical literature of the day, however, and its scope and implications were unknown to her. When Newton, a Unitarian and evidently something of an advanced thinker, entered her circle in 1848, he brought with him heady breaths of fresh air.

Others besides Newton took an interest in the literary education of the Dickinson girls. Their brother Austin seems to have smuggled Longfellow's *Kavanagh* into the house in spite of parental disapproval. Elbridge G. Bowdoin, the junior member of the firm, was responsible for introducing them to *Jane Eyre* and other works of the Brontë sisters. But Newton provided an even more exciting diet. In her first interview with Higginson (1870) Emily related how, when she and Lavinia were "little things in short dresses," one of her father's students expressed surprise that they had never heard of Mrs. Lydia Maria Child. He "used to bring them books and hide [them] in a bush by the door." The first taste of forbidden fruit, according to tradition, was Mrs. Child's *Letters from New York*, and to understand why Emily after reading it thought in ecstasy: "This then is a book! And there are more of them," we must be reminded of its effect on contemporary readers. Higginson has elsewhere described the *Letters from New York* as a "new sensation," which he thus particularized:

Their tone also did much to promote the tendency, which was showing itself in those days, towards a fresh inquiry into the foundations of social science. The Brook Farm experiment was at its height; and though she did not call herself an Associationist, yet she quoted Fourier and Swedenborg, and other authors who were thought to mean mischief; and her highest rhapsodies about poetry and music were apt to end in some fervent appeal for some increase of harmony in daily life. She seemed always to be talking radicalism in a greenhouse; and there were many good people who held her all the more dangerous for her perfumes.

There were young men and maidens, also, who looked to her as a teacher, and were influenced for life, perhaps, by what she wrote. I knew, for instance, a young lawyer, just entering on the practice of his profession under the most flattering auspices, who withdrew from the courts forever—wisely or unwisely,—because Mrs. Child's book had taught him to hate their contests and their injustice.

Here was a book to "joggle the mind" indeed, and it is not difficult to see why some subterfuge was necessary to get it into the house of a cautious and conservative village lawyer. But Newton did not stop with Mrs. Child. The quality of his influence can be gauged by the fact that soon after he left Amherst he sent Emily a copy of Emerson's *Poems*. She spoke of her pleasure in the gift and in the letter that came with it when she wrote to Jane Humphrey on January 23, 1850:

I had a letter—and Ralph Emerson's Poems—a beautiful copy—from Newton the other day. I should love to read you them both—they are very pleasant to me. I can write him in about three weeks—and I *shall*.

This was many years before Emerson was accepted by orthodox New Englanders as saint and sage. In fact there were few people in Amherst then who did not regard him askance. But for the rare souls in whom the urge of the Puritan seeker was not stifled—and Emily Dickinson was one of these—Emerson was a fountainhead of living waters.

With Ben Newton's help Emily first surveyed a wider horizon than her father's house could show her and sent her mind adventuring in the exciting world of ideas that the new vision disclosed. There is direct evidence also that Newton discovered her faculty for poetic composition, confirmed it by his praise of her early verses, gave her confidence in her powers, and urged her to dedicate all her energies to the cultivation of her great gift.

When Emily wrote on June 7, 1862, to thank Higginson for his approval of the poems she had sent him, she began her letter by telling him that she had already known the intoxication of having her promise as a poet recognized. He was to understand that she was no tyro, greedy for praise, but a serious artist who wanted straightforward criticism.

Your letter gave no drunkenness, because I tasted rum before. Domingo comes but once. . . .

My dying tutor told me that he would like to live till I had been a poet, but Death was much of mob as I could master, then.

The tutor here referred to can be no one but Ben Newton, who as we have seen was slowly dying of tuberculosis, but was active to the last and was anxious to settle his earthly concerns. What more natural, as death closed in on him, than that he should write a letter of farewell to the ardent little friend in Amherst with whom he had earnestly and tenderly spoken of books and nature and things unseen? That he actually did so, and that it was this letter which gave Emily her first taste of "rum," may be inferred from another chance allusion in her correspondence with Higginson.

My earliest friend wrote me the week before he died, "If I live, I will go to Amherst; if I die, I certainly will."

Emily did not at first realize that this cheerful promise to visit

Amherst was her friend's way of announcing his approaching death, and was tantamount to saying that his spirit would attend her always. But twenty-three years later she still recalled these words from the letter written the week before he died. She also remembered that her dying tutor had wished to live to see her become a poet. May we not assume that both passages were contained in the same momentous letter? Newton, then, was the first to put in words a wish to which the secret bent of her nature responded with a thrill of high excitement, so that she never forgot that supreme concentration of her forces. "Domingo comes but once." For her it was equivalent to the moment when the shade of Virgil pronounced Dante henceforth crowned and mitred over himself. Her sponsor too, even as he spoke the inciting words, had gone to join the white-robed company.

So far we have been able to trace with some precision the ways in which Ben Newton stimulated the growth of Emily Dickinson's mind. But she was a woman as well as a poet. What of her womanly feelings? Can we affirm with assurance that Newton never assumed the rôle of the young lover that legend, with whatever wild exaggerations, pictures? Did he not leave Amherst because Edward Dickinson refused to countenance him as a son-in-law? The evidence is inconclusive. Newton was poor and consumptive and held advanced views—one could understand why Emily's father might consider him no suitable match for her. On the other hand, Newton's marriage little more than a year after his leaving Amherst does not seem to indicate that his heart was deeply engaged there. From all we can learn his was not a shallow nature.

There is nothing to show that Emily Dickinson, though she loved Newton as an elder brother, ever considered him as a possible husband. He was always her "tutor." She seems to have taken his companionship somewhat for granted while he was with her and not to have found out how much he meant to her until after his departure. Then indeed she missed him greatly. Her loneliness and depression are discernible in her letters, in spite of a gallant attempt to maintain a playful tone. Furthermore, the year that began with her parting from her gentle yet grave preceptor ended even more sadly with the sudden death of her admired teacher, Leonard Humphrey. Emily wrote to Abiah of this event as her "first affliction," but some phrases in the letter sound as though she had another sorrow in mind, though its nature is somewhat obscure.

> . . . I am *selfish* too, because I am feeling lonely; some of my friends are gone, and some of my friends are sleeping—sleeping the churchyard sleep. . . . I will try not to say any more—my rebellious thoughts are many, and the friend I love and trust in has much *now* to forgive.

In the poem beginning "Your riches taught me poverty" (137, xxi), which we may guess was written about this time as a tribute to a friend no longer with her whose mind she considered dazzlingly superior to her own, there may lie a clue to the state of her feelings. The last two stanzas imply that she blamed herself for not knowing how to appreciate her friend's true worth until he had slipped away from her.

> At least it solaces to know
> That there exists a gold,
> Although I prove it just in time
> Its distance to behold!
>
> It's far, far treasure to surmise,
> And estimate the pearl
> That slipped my simple fingers through
> While just a girl at school!

There cannot be much doubt that Emily was thinking of Newton. Some years later, we cannot be sure just when, she sent this poem to her sister-in-law with the words: "You see I remember." Sue would know what.

The news of Newton's death surprised her at a moment of recovered gaiety, and the shock was all the more lasting. In March, 1853, hearing that her brother had been trying his hand at poetry, she wrote in her most sprightly vein to warn him off what she even then considered her particular province.

And Austin is a poet, Austin writes a psalm. . . . Now Brother Pegasus, I'll tell you what it is. I've been in the habit *myself* of writing some few things, and it rather appears to me that you're getting away my patent, so you'd better be somewhat careful or I'll call the police.

These words, breathing a happy confidence, were written, I believe, in the brief interval between the receipt of Newton's last letter and of the notice of his death. Emily was treading the clouds. She was writing eagerly. She was to be a poet. Then the friend who had taught her immortality ventured too near himself, and brightness fell from the air. The change in the tone of her letters to her brother is striking.

Somehow I am lonely lately. I feel very old every day, and when morning comes and the birds sing, they don't seem to make me so happy as they used to. . . . I feel very sure lately that the years we have had together are more than we shall have. . . .

Her thoughts were turned to problems of time and eternity that she could not solve. As she wrote afterward, recalling these months, "Death was much of mob as I could master, then." Evidently her first efforts to write poetry were interrupted for a time by the death of the man who had encouraged them. That she did take Newton's death deeply to heart is certain. She was still mourning for him, and struggling to comprehend the inexorable fate that consigned golden lads like Newton and Humphrey to dust, when she wrote to Hale. Several of her poems, written when she had returned to her writing with a deeper intuition, also speak feelingly of the "two I lost."

A few other allusions in her poetry, we may suspect, were prompted by recollections of her earliest friend.

> A book I have a friend gave,
> Whose pencil, here and there,
> Had notched the place that pleased him,—
> At rest his fingers are.
>
> Now, when I read, I read not,
> For interrupting tears
> Obliterate the etchings
> Too costly for repairs.

More uncertainly still, he may be the "moldering playmate" elsewhere recalled. After her grieving was "softened by Time's consummate plush" she returned to the theme of the "lost jewel" and rewrote it to suit her later taste. In the earlier version her simple thought had been to honor her friend by lavishing upon him all the gorgeousness that her vocabulary could furnish, and she had produced an elaborate mélange of geography and gems, a diffuse and overstrained poem that said more than she meant, a verbal counterpart of the Albert Memorial. Since then she had learned the value of severe economy, it is instructive to note with what effect.

> I held a jewel in my fingers
> And went to sleep.
> The day was warm, and winds were prosy;
> I said, " 'Twill keep."
>
> I woke and chid my honest fingers,—
> The gem was gone;
> And now an amethyst remembrance
> Is all I own.

Her dying tutor had wished to see her a poet. Very well, her last and best tribute to his memory would be to show that she had become one.

Rowing in Eden

THE AMETHYST afterglow of her friendship with Ben Newton was still gently fading when Emily Dickinson found in another quarter the light she was seeking. It was like a dazzling moonrise, glamorous and unreal, and it was followed by midnight clouds and storm, and eventually by the closing in of a vault of solid darkness overhead, scarcely relieved by the sparkle of a distant star. In such terms she might have described the consequences to herself of finding the "one more" whom she considered the dearest of her friends and whose going left her desolate. He was the "bright absentee" of her early devotion, the "dim companion" ever present in her thoughts, the perfect lover whom she was never to know save "in vision and in veto." Lacking him she lacked all. To those who understood she was accustomed to speak of her private grief as "that old nail in my breast."

We need not doubt for a moment that Emily Dickinson's poems record minutely and truthfully a love and a sorrow deeply felt by a most sensitive nature. It is one of her triumphs that they do so with matchless poignancy. But in dealing with the biography of the writer of these vividly personal lyrics we must guard against the temptation to make her life fit the pattern suggested by her poems. From time out of mind poets have been privileged to round out the imperfect arcs of fact. Between the unfulfilled romance deducible from Emily Dickinson's love poems and the story that may be pieced together from external evidence there lies a region of some obscurity. In at least one important particular, moreover, the facts of record do not support the assertions of the poems. Unfortunately inventions appropriate to poetry have not always been kept distinct from biography.

What do the poems tell us? They recur again and again to a momentous interview between two star-crossed lovers, a meeting pictured most completely and movingly, with a solemn procession of religious images, in "There came a day at summer's full" (133, xiii).

> Each was to each a sealéd church,
> Permitted to commune this time. . . .

Other poems amplify certain details of this fateful interview. The transport of the woman's self-dedication to the man whose life she could not share is recorded in "I gave myself to him" (139, xxii) and "He put the belt around my life" (144, xxxii). Memories of the anguish of renunciation were associated with physical objects; there was one angle of the floor that she had to train herself in later years to disregard,

> Where he turned—so—and I turned how—
> And all our sinew tore.

Three poems imply that the lover besought her to join him and that she refused:

> It was a quiet way
> He asked if I was his.
> I made no answer of the tongue
> But answer of the eyes. . . .
>
> . . . .
>
> I rose because he sank—
> I thought it would be opposite,
> But when his power bent,
> My Soul stood straight. . . .
>
> . . . .
>
> "Would I be whole?" he sudden broached.
> My syllable rebelled. . . .

There was a moment when she "groped upon his breast," a kiss, and then "each bound the other's crucifix" in a final parting. The impalpable bar between them is sufficiently explained in "I had not minded walls" (361, cxlviii).

All these poems are written from the woman's point of view and in the first person, but let us not heedlessly disregard Emily Dickinson's warning that the speaker is not herself but a "supposed person." Her romance was not created out of nothing, and the supposed person may often be considered as identical with the author to the extent of voicing her real feelings. But we should not expect to find in fervid love poems an exact statement of actual circumstances. Whatever nuggets of fact they might contain would under stress of emotion be hammered out "like gold to airy thinness beat." Where this subtle expansion has been wrought the poems imply that the lovers' passion was mutual and fully acknowledged; that the man desired to follow its promptings and urged an elopement which she declined. The tragedy of renunciation is thus complete, with the woman playing the heroic part. It is the ungrateful duty of a responsible biographer not to accept this story at its face value.

Elsewhere in her poems Emily Dickinson gives a different and we may believe a truer version of her emotional history. "When I hoped, I recollect" (368, clxiv) is full of circumstantial details, but one all-important detail is omitted—the lover is not even mentioned. Three special days stand out in the memory of the woman speaking: a day when she hoped, a day when she feared, and a day when she despaired. Of the last she recalls only the chaos of her feelings, but the first two are associated with what seem like actual settings. On the day when she hoped she remembers that she was standing "in a chamber facing West" and that the weather outside was wintry.

> Hope it was that kept me warm—
> Not merino shawl.

On the day when she feared, though there were "icicles upon

my soul," the world outdoors was swimming in the sun and the air was filled with birds' songs. This hot summer day, we may guess, is none other than the "day at summer's full" again, but now stripped of dramatic elaboration and remembered only on account of the unexplained terror that it brought. If we may trust the quieter poem, it would appear that Emily's romance was not confined to a single supreme moment, as has sometimes been stated, but developed gradually through a series of emotional crises, the first separated from the second at least as far as winter from the ensuing summer. The actual situation, also, would seem to have consisted far more of purely inward drama, a woman's unsatisfied hopes and unspoken fears, than of outward events such as a proposal and a renunciation involving both man and woman.

Plain hints that Emily Dickinson was aware of her powers of dramatic invention are not wanting. As we have already noted, she wished to dissociate herself from the heroine of her poems. But she was surely speaking for herself when she commented objectively on her mental procedure:

> I play at riches to appease
> The clamoring for gold.

Another poem is even more explicit on this subject:

> The vision, pondered long,
> So plausible becomes
> That I esteem the fiction real—
> The real, fictitious seems.
>
> How beautiful the dream!
> What plenty it would be
> Had all my life but been mistake
> Just rectified by Thee!

It is a tribute to Emily Dickinson's artistry that she made her poetic fictions so plausible as to mislead many, including one member of her family who did not know her very well and who was not temperamentally inclined to value a life "too simple and stern to embarrass any."

We may return from the realm of poetry and invention to sober biography by establishing a precise date, one of the few that can be connected with the love poems. On June 7, 1862, Emily sent to Higginson "There came a day at summer's full" with the characteristic request to know if she had "told it clear." By that time evidently the climax of her supposed love-affair was over, and was so far behind her that she could write of it with some detachment and could even confide what she had written to an honored stranger. The experiences that occasioned her love poems must have occurred, therefore, between 1854 and 1862, though many of the poems were undoubtedly written later than the second of these dates.

If we ask what friendship she most cherished during those eight years, and indeed for the remainder of her life, there is only one possible answer. Much as she mourned for Newton, much as she later admired and respected Higginson, the man who of all others became her support and comforter while he lived, and when he had died her "Heavenly Father," was the Reverend Charles Wadsworth, pastor of the Arch Street Presbyterian Church of Philadelphia. He was a man of God of the old school, filled with the vital message of his ministry, a tower of strength to the wavering and the distressed. At the time of their first meeting, in May, 1854, he was just forty years old, at the height of his great powers, happily married, and immersed in the multifarious concerns of his pastorate. She was twenty-three, and not yet inured to loneliness.

Her own words leave little doubt that she found in Charles Wadsworth the "atom [she] preferred to all the lists of clay." In her letters to his friends James D. and Charles H. Clark, written during the last four years of her life, she characterized him as "the beloved clergyman," her "shepherd from 'little girl'hood," and her "dearest earthly friend." He was the "fugitive, whom to know was life." Any circumstance concerning him was forever precious. She treasured like sacred relics the book of his sermons which James Clark had privately printed and the autograph letters which he also sent her. The latter were "like Immortality," "gifts from the sky, more precious than the birds, because more disembodied." She inquired with tremulous interest for particulars about Wadsworth's sons. Mention of the Adirondacks in a letter from Maria Whitney recalled his love for that region "before the woods were broken." To James Clark she wrote: "He was a dusk gem, born of troubled waters, astray in any crest below." And again: "I do not yet fathom that he has died, and hope I may not till he assists me in another world."

Nor is this all the evidence of her absolute devotion to Wadsworth's memory. In letters, as yet unpublished, to a friend who was aware of her intimacy with the Philadelphia clergyman, she somewhat guardedly revealed the depth of her feelings after his death. This event, so momentous to her that the date was etched upon her mind, occurred on April 1, 1882. In the autumn of that year she wrote: "It seems sometimes as if special Months gave and took away. August has brought the most to me—April robbed me most—in incessant instances." In December, standing by themselves at the end of a letter, are the four words: "Is God Love's Adversary?" As the first anniversary of Wadsworth's death approached: "All other surprise is at last monotonous, but the Death of the Loved is all Moments—*now*. Love has but one Date—'The first of April'—'Today, Yesterday, and Forever.'

'*Can* trouble dwell with April days?'
'Of Love that never found its earthly close, what sequel?'

Both in the same Book—in the same Hymn. Excuse your mourning Emily." (March, 1883.) And finally, after her own illness in the spring of 1884 she wrote: "The crisis of the sorrow of so many years is all that tires me. As Emily Brontë to her Maker,

I write to my Lost, 'Every Existence would exist in thee.' "

Such expressions are conclusive. They compel us to believe
that Charles Wadsworth was a friend of supreme importance in
Emily Dickinson's life. They do not, however, oblige us to
assume that she was of supreme importance in his, though that
assumption was not unnaturally made by members of her family
and by others who were close to her. But the supposition that
any sort of lovers' understanding, no matter how attenuated,
ever existed between them is inconceivable in view of his known
character. He was not the kind of man to tolerate faithlessness of
spirit in himself, nor is there the least hint to indicate that he
was other than deeply attached to the beautiful and gracious
woman who was his wife. Wadsworth's whole career was lived
as strictly as Milton's, ever in his great Task-master's eye. He
never spared himself, and died at sixty-eight utterly spent in
the Lord's service.

In the opinion of qualified judges his only peer as a pulpit
orator was Henry Ward Beecher, but the two great preachers
were entirely unlike in their methods. While Beecher went out
to meet his audiences, travelled widely, took cognizance of
timely topics, and was both clergyman and publicist, Wadsworth
remained at home, based his preaching on an undeviating conception of his spiritual message, and never conciliated any one.
His business was to preach Christ and Him crucified to all who
would hear him. In the pulpit he used few gestures and scrupu-
lously avoided any tricks of manner. He adhered closely to the
carefully written manuscript of his sermon, almost reading it
aloud. Nevertheless his sheer moral intensity penetrated the
most sealed and obdurate hearts, and his congregations were
shaken as if by a whirlwind. As Emily Dickinson put it, he
wrought upon his hearers gradually, then with increasing ham-
mer strokes, and when the stupendous moment came, dealt "one
imperial thunderbolt that scalps your naked soul."

Notwithstanding his great powers Wadsworth remained a

self-effacing man. Though cordial, frank, and often full of humor among his special friends, he was ordinarily diffident and reserved. At the Arch Street Church his pulpit was so arranged that he could enter and leave it through the basement and thus avoid greeting his congregation. He would cross the street to escape an encounter that might lead to casual chat. His morning hours were strictly reserved for his study, where he read and meditated, wrote his sermons, and no doubt prayed for guidance. At other times he was at the service of his parishioners. When his sympathies were touched, he could be beautifully tender. He held a fiery temper in firm control, though a few minatory flashes sometimes escaped him. On such occasions there was apt to be a noticeable clearing of the air.

The portrait in a gold frame that hung in Emily Dickinson's bedroom we may venture to believe was a portrait of Wadsworth. A daguerreotype taken in early manhood shows him with flowing black locks and remarkably piercing black eyes behind heavy glasses. Determination rests in the mouth and chin. His was a plain, homely face in repose, but energetic and decisive; a face capable of wonderful mobility and a wide range of expressiveness. His deep voice and sturdy frame—he was five feet ten inches tall—confirmed his appearance of dynamic power. To many he seemed to possess a strength that was not of this world only.

Emily, in calling him "my shepherd from 'little girl'hood," used a phrase which would allow us to suppose that she had known him before she visited the Colemans in Philadelphia on her return from Washington, but there is no record of any earlier meeting. If Lavinia, who was Emily's almost constant companion, never saw him, Emily herself cannot have met him very often. We know of only three meetings in all, though there are shadowy intimations of a possible fourth. It is probable, therefore, though not proved, that she first saw him in the pulpit of the Arch Street Church.

The stress of mind that led Emily to seek his closer acquaintance may be inferred from her letter to Hale. In January, 1854, she longed to know surely if her lamented friend Ben Newton were in heaven. We do not know in what terms Hale replied nor whether his letter brought her the assurances she craved, but no conventional words could have stilled her troubled spirit. Her perturbation must have been noticed in the Dickinson household, and it may have been in the hope of giving her the alleviation of a change of scene that her father induced her to visit him in Washington. She met noted men, she went to Mount Vernon, she heard the Germanians sing "like brazen robins"; but there was no answer to her insistent questionings. Then she "experienced honor" for a deep-hearted clergyman and appealed to him. It would not have been difficult for her to arrange for a private interview through her host Mr. Coleman, formerly the principal of Amherst Academy, who was a leading member of the Arch Street Church. Wadsworth must have recognized her emergency and helped her somehow to find peace. Thenceforth his congregation included an invisible worshiper. Emily gave him her heart in gratitude and reverence. For some years to come his friendship and guidance were her chief reliance. Then he "left the land."

A woman is never so susceptible as when she has just risen from her knees. Experienced clergymen know this, and are on their guard. But Emily Dickinson had gone back to Amherst. How could the Reverend Mr. Wadsworth divine what effect his kindly letters of spiritual counsel were having? That he did correspond with her we may safely infer. One of her poems refers to "the box in which his letters grew," and the fact that he came to see her in Amherst after some time had elapsed can hardly be explained except on the assumption that what Emily characterized as their "intimacy of many years" had become firmly established between 1854 and 1860. In the absence of dates for certain indicative poems it is impossible to say when

Emily Dickinson began to imagine what her life would be like if she had such a companion as Mr. Wadsworth, but little by little she grew to think that she was dedicated to him. Before she was aware the cherished fancy took firm possession of her mind. Eventually it was to assume alarming proportions, like the genie from the fisherman's bottle, obscuring the sky.

Wadsworth did not come to Amherst to preach at the College nor to visit his classmate at Union, Professor Edward Tuckerman, who held the chair of botany. He came to the neighboring town of Northampton to see James Dickson Clark, with whom he had been on intimate terms for a long time. Emily had met Clark, a "scholarly stranger" introduced to her by her father probably in the late 1850's, at any rate before she knew that he was acquainted with Wadsworth. She wrote him in 1883 that, with the exception of her sister, she had never spoken to any one but himself of her "dearest earthly friend." It was little more than an hour's drive from Northampton to Amherst, and while he was staying with Clark, Wadsworth took the opportunity to pay a call on his distant parishioner.

Emily Dickinson tells us that when he first came to see her he was wearing mourning for his mother, who had died on October 1, 1859. The meeting probably occurred in late February or early March, 1860, when Lavinia was visiting the Norcross cousins in Boston. Emily noticed the black with his hat and exclaimed, "Some one has died?" In her heart of hearts the man before her was her chosen one. May we not guess that she half expected to hear other words than his deep-toned "My mother"? "Did you love her?" asked Emily. Paper and ink do not tell us where the accent fell.

It is just possible to suppose that the second's interval between her first question and his answer was made forever memorable to Emily by the wild, illicit hope which suffused her bosom, and that she later recalled it for purposes of poetry. In her poem she recollected a day when she hoped, a day of frost and sleet when she stood "in a chamber facing West." When Wadsworth entered the Dickinson parlor on a February or March day he was in mourning—possibly a widower. The speculation is a tempting one.

In Emily Dickinson's letters there are no other recollections of Wadsworth that can surely be attached to this particular visit, unless this was the only visit that he made before he left for California in the spring of 1862. But it is by no means certain that he did not come again, though the evidence is shadowy. There is no external proof that he was near Amherst in the late summer of 1861, but there is much to lead us to surmise that he paid Emily a second visit at that time. Her letters do not sound as though she had met him only once between 1854 and 1880, but rather as though she were recalling bits of conversation from several meetings. Her poems, too, though not to be taken literally, repeatedly emphasize a momentous interview on "a day at summer's full," which I have taken to be the same as the day when she "feared." It is difficult to believe that this interview had no basis in fact. Something must have happened to account for Emily's statement to Higginson (April 25, 1862) that she had felt "a terror since September, I could tell to none." This terror that could not be shared even with her sister must have been connected with the most closely guarded secret of her heart. It is not too much to postulate, therefore, that Wadsworth came again.

He may have been considering a remove from Philadelphia as early as August, 1861, though he probably did not receive the call from San Francisco that he eventually accepted until the following winter. It was a dark moment. Every one's nerves were on edge. The dreaded specter of Secession had materialized in April, and the Civil War had dragged through five months. The overconfidence of the North had been sobered by Bull Run. No one could see the end. Wadsworth had not a trace of the reformer in him. He knew well that the South was fighting for

its life. He loathed the war as an exhibition of cruelty and un-
reason. Some people thought him a very lukewarm Union man.
He may have begun to feel out of sympathy with his surroundings in Philadelphia, though his congregation was devotedly
loyal to him and sought by every means to prevent his departure.

Emily Dickinson remembered some alarming things that he
said to her at a time not specified. We may guess that he said
them at this time of strain. To her he was always a mystery.
She adored him, or rather she adored the image in his likeness
that her mind created, but the actual man she did not really
know. He was "fathomless," a "Man of Sorrow." "Once when
he seemed almost overpowered by a spasm of gloom, I said,
'You are troubled.' Shivering as he spoke, 'My life is full of
dark secrets,' he said." He told her also that he was "liable at
any time to die." If when he came to see Emily late in that
tragic summer he was gloomy and restless, if he spoke darkly
of the future and intimated that he might go away or might
even die at any time, would she not have felt an instant concern
amounting to terror for the friend she so cherished and so
dreaded to lose? There were doubtless tears, and if her friend
in attempting to console her slightly overdid the fatherly part,
she may easily have misread the sympathy in his dark eyes as an
answer to her inmost feelings. "The time was scarce profaned
by speech"—and the possibilities of misunderstanding were cor-
respondingly large. But we need not push conjecture as far as
this. Once before Emily Dickinson had gone through a parting
with a man whom she held dear, and he had gone away to die.
Now the inexorable nexus of circumstance seemed to be coiling
back upon itself and displaying a similar pattern, even more
huge and hopeless to conceive than before. She had reason to be
afraid.

"And the day that I despaired"? The blow she was fearing
fell in the spring of 1862, when she heard from Wadsworth—

he would certainly have included her when he wrote his letters of farewell to friends in the East—that he was actually on the point of leaving for California, then a three weeks' voyage by the Panama route. In Philadelphia she could in a sense "see his lifetime," but not in unknown San Francisco. Between them was to be "just the door ajar that oceans are," or overland the breadth of a continent torn by civil war ("they thwarted us with guns"). It is true that Wadsworth did not sail from New York until May 1, six days after Emily had written to Higginson about the "one more" who "left the land," but this discrepancy need not disturb us. She always anticipated her disasters, and from the moment that she received word of his impending departure, she would have counted him lost to her. He was already in thought far away in distant California, minister of Calvary Church. Was it a mere coincidence that led Emily to call herself "Empress of Calvary"?

When Ben Newton left her, years before, she had turned to her lexicon for companionship. She was seeking relief in preparing herself to be the poet he wished her to be. The prospect of Wadsworth's loss was an infinitely deeper distress, but she met it in the same way. All through the winter of 1861–62 she was writing desperately to keep her head above disaster: "I sing, as the boy does of the burying ground, because I am afraid." It seemed to her that she had never written poems before, or only one or two. Some of her finest lyrics were a part of this outpouring, and others may be added conjecturally because they reflect the extreme tension of her fears.

"My life closed twice before its close" (45, xcvi) is one. The date of this poem is not known, but every word is comprehensible if read as an expression of Emily's mood in the spring of 1862. She had then known the anguish of two momentous partings, one with Newton, who had died, and one still more recent and painful with Newton's successor, whom she thought she would never see again. The tender concern that she had felt to know if her first friend were in heaven, the sharp torment of apprehension and realization of a second and greater loss—these two facts lay side by side in her consciousness like two figures on a tomb. Was she not discriminating one from the other with a fine inward perception when she wrote the concluding lines?

> Parting is all we know of heaven,
> And all we need of hell.

In another and even better known poem (174, xl) she returned to the same theme, but with a difference. This time she spoke of two bereavements by death, and of a third loss which may or may not be of the same kind.

> I never lost as much but twice,
> And that was in the sod.

The ambiguity occurs in the second line, which may be read: "And that [also] was in the sod," or: "And that was in the sod, [this is not]." If we follow the second reading, then Newton's death may be one of the two losses mentioned in the first line, and possibly Leonard Humphrey's, her "first affliction," the other. The third loss, which was not "in the sod," was her parting with Wadsworth. In the light reflected upon the past by this supreme disaster every previous loss was magnified and accentuated. Newton, who taught her immortality, had ventured too near; Humphrey, who might have taken Newton's place, had died soon after; and now the "one more," not content that she be his scholar, had left the land, expecting never to return. Was it a conspiracy of "the redoubtable God"? Or would God relent?

> Burglar, banker, father,
> I am poor once more!

sighed Emily—and wrote to the Reverend Mr. Higginson, whom she did not know, to ask if he would become her instructor. And once more the banker member of her Trinity saw to it that her draft was honored.

It was not the first time she had thrown herself upon a clergyman who was a stranger. She had appealed in distress to Hale, then to Wadsworth. Fortunately Higginson, though absorbed in recruiting and training a regiment, was not too busy to answer the odd little note that he found in his mail. It is perhaps significant of what she was passing through that her second letter to him was written from her pillow while she was recovering from an unexplained illness. Later she told him that he had saved her life. If he did not, poetry did. It was her one outlet. She gave it all her energy, cutting herself off more and more from the outside world in order that she might have time for the work she was carrying on in secret. In projecting her intensest feelings on paper she was finding a form of relief in action; she was, in Emerson's phrase, "grinding into paint" her burden of despair. So she was enabled to fulfill the prescript of her generation for utter rectitude of conduct, which for her meant the stifling of hopes, and yet to keep the bitter waters from stagnating in her breast. Though her mental balance was unsteady for some years to come, she achieved and held it. By mastery of her suffering she won a sanity that could make even grief a plaything.

Twenty years passed before she saw again and for the last time the friend whose loss had cost her so much. He had returned, late in 1869, from San Francisco to Philadelphia. Their correspondence, if it was broken off while he was in the West, was resumed during the seventies, Emily always sending her letters enclosed in notes to a friend who directed the envelopes to Philadelphia. Quite unexpectedly, one summer evening in 1880, Wadsworth called. Emily and her sister were with their lilies and heliotropes when the servant answered his ring. Lavinia, usually the one to face callers, exclaimed in surprise, "The gentleman with the deep voice wants to see *you*, Emily," and disappeared. To her seeming he spoke like an apparition. "Where did you come from?" she asked. "Why didn't you tell me you were coming, so I could have it to anticipate?" "Because I did not know it myself. I stepped from my pulpit to the train." She clutched at the nearest straw of commonplace—how long had it taken him to make the journey? "Twenty years," said he, with inscrutable roguery. In the course of their conversation he told her that his younger son reminded him of her, and when he rose to go he was speaking of the youngster's interest in frogs. Emily said that she had always thought of them as her watchdogs. With his smile at that they parted. It is not stated that Emily knew the color of the sky, but perhaps it was at last tinged with amethyst.

Emily Dickinson's friendship with Wadsworth, unlike her earlier friendship with Ben Newton, was not primarily an intellectual affair. It taught her all that a woman can learn who gives herself spiritually and imaginatively to the man of her choice, and more than she needed to know of suffering. But since she considered Wadsworth, however archly, one of her tutors, we may briefly examine the quality of his influence upon her mind. In the absence of letters on either side, we can only gauge it in general terms.

If we may judge from the three volumes of sermons published after his death, Wadsworth did not possess an adventurous intellect. It is a little surprising that he should have passed among his contemporaries for an independent thinker. His mind was mortised and tenoned in eternal verities. All the accepted doctrines of Calvinism were to him such living truths that they admitted of no argument. He set his face like flint against whatever might weaken them. Life on earth was a probation for the life to come. The humanitarianism that would soften the lot of prisoners and paupers was but a "mawkish and mongrel sensibility" which "would turn our prisons for criminals into luxurious hospitals . . . and even take the children's bread and cast it unto dogs." Worldly prosperity was a normal reward and sign of godliness; it was not for man to interfere with God's distribution of property. The great law of gravitation rounding dew-drop and star alike he considered a divine ordinance, for he had assimilated Newtonian physics; but the more recent findings of biological science that controverted the authority of the Bible he contemptuously dismissed as "Huxley's blasphemies." He could rejoice in the "songs of Zion," meaning Watts, but he had no taste for the "fashionable agonies that the world calls music."

In such ways as these Wadsworth failed to transcend the opinions of his age. But on the other side he emphasized most consistently a positive gospel of joy. He had no use for self-torturing asceticism and held that God intended the good things of this world for the pleasure of His children. For those who missed life's banquet there lay beyond life the everlasting recompense, the bright city of palm trees, an immortality of active and joyous fulfillment. In speaking of this sublime hope Wadsworth became a poet of apocalyptic vision, earnest and compelling in his insistence on the raptures of eternity. This was a language that Emily Dickinson well understood and often employed herself. The Book of Revelation was her favorite book of the Bible. Its imagery was ingrained on her mind from her earliest years. When she wrote as a schoolgirl:

> I hope the father in the skies
> Will lift his little girl,—
> Old-fashioned, naughty, everything,—
> Over the stile of pearl!

and still playfully:

> The smallest "robe" will fit me,
> And just a bit of "crown";
> For you know we do not mind our dress
> When we are going home;

and when she wrote as a woman who had known sorrow and loss:

> I shall know why, when time is over,
> And I have ceased to wonder why;
> Christ will explain each separate anguish
> In the fair schoolroom of the sky,

she was speaking as a poet of Doctor Wadsworth's "school." Many of his ideas and opinions she fully shared. At times the similarity of expression, even allowing for a common source in religious literature, is so close as to be striking.

Between her twenty-fourth and her thirty-first years Emily was most ardently Wadsworth's "scholar." The sternness of his creed would not have repelled her. It was no more than what she was used to, for Amherst too was a citadel of orthodoxy. But by 1862 she was conscious that she could no longer share the beliefs that her family accepted. "They are religious, except me," as she put it to Higginson. The crumbling of her childhood faith, which she was too honest not to admit, must have disturbed her deeply at times, for her nature was more religious than she knew. In her hours of uncertainty, when the God of her fathers looked very much like "an eclipse," Wadsworth could offer her soothing counsels and the peace of vicarious certitude. In that haven, for a time at least, she could moor her tempest-shaken bark. His darkly fervid teaching confirmed the Puritan mysticism which at moments she could almost make her own. If she relied more constantly on other angles of vision, it was not from him that she learned them.

Literary Friends

THE WINTER of 1861–62 was the sharpest psychic corner in Emily Dickinson's life. Her dream-palace was suddenly left tenantless. In desperate earnest she began to write poems, and though no man could ever be to her again what her departed master had been, she appealed to Higginson to sustain her confidence. From about this time may be dated her withdrawal from the world. One narrow path was marked out for her; she would follow it to the end. She would live only for her writing. Perhaps as a poet she could find the fulfillment she had missed as a woman.

So far her course is entirely comprehensible. Only a few years later Helen Hunt, after the tragic loss of a husband and two sons, turned to poetry as an occupation and a solace. But there the similarity ends. Mrs. Hunt eagerly accepted the obligations of a literary career, sought opportunities to publish her work, and sparkled through later life on a wave of popular acclaim. Emily Dickinson, on the contrary, elected to sink deeper and deeper into seclusion and steadily declined to let her poems be printed. Her indifference to publication is a point of apparent abnormality that demands careful attention. Authors do not ordinarily behave in that way.

Some authors, however, have considered it beneath their dignity to take money for their writings. Was Emily Dickinson deterred from publication by such ladylike scruples? One or two of her poems seem to indicate that she held views of this kind. Did she not shrink from notoriety?

> How dreary to be somebody!
> How public, like a frog
> To tell your name the livelong day
> To an admiring bog!

Did she not loathe the least taint of commercialism?

> Publication is the auction
> Of the mind of man,
> Poverty be justifying
> For so foul a thing.

> Possibly,—but we would rather
> From our garret go
> White unto the White Creator,
> Then invest our snow. . . .

To the friend who wrote the unsigned obituary notice of "Miss Emily Dickinson of Amherst," printed in *The Springfield Republican* for May 18, 1886, it seemed a mark of almost incredible virtue that a poet of unique utterance should have resisted the urgings of editors and literary friends. Such self-denial could betoken only a refinement of fastidiousness in keeping with the great maxim of the Genteel Tradition that "a woman's hearthstone is her shrine." It gloriously distinguished Emily Dickinson, that "soul of fire in a shell of pearl," from the inky women who shamelessly vended their wares in the public mart.

Gentility nonsense such as this possessed for Emily Dickinson's generation a value difficult to comprehend at the present time. It held up for admiration the fugitive and cloistered virtue whose whiteness, in Milton's downright phrase, is but an "excremental whiteness." If Emily was too much a lady to submit her verses to the test of publication, we can no longer cite the fact in her praise. But fastidiousness was never her leading motive. She was so perfectly and beautifully to the manner born that it could not have occurred to her to be uneasy about her status. On occasion she could be utterly scornful of gentlefolk and their insincere conventionalities:

> What soft, cherubic creatures
> These gentlewomen are!
> One would as soon assault a plush
> Or violate a star. . . .

"Dimity convictions" would no more have restrained her from publishing her poems, had she realized the necessity of publication, than they restrained Helen Hunt and Emily Fowler Ford. We must look more searchingly for the real reasons why her poems were so long withheld.

One of them was undoubtedly the fact that Emily Dickinson needed no other incentive to write than the satisfaction afforded by the creative act itself. Poetry was her only playmate through years of loneliness. In the seclusion of her father's house, while she tended her flowers or performed her share of the household routine, she watched with breathless intentness the motions of her mind, so curiously a part of her and yet aloof. When it circled her garden she noted its recurrent phosphor-flashes; when it penetrated heaven, its starry twinklings. It was now home, now tomb. She searched her lexicon for words, and at night in the polar privacy of her room her hand wrote them. Of the hundreds of tiny poems she amassed, some were pencilled on odd scraps of paper, the back of an envelope or the margin of a newspaper, and left just as they shaped themselves when some rhapsody of expression seized upon her. Others, revised with anxious care and neatly copied on sheets of notepaper with alternative readings at the foot of the page, were sewed together in little fascicles and hoarded in her bureau. These last she may have regarded as her "letter to the world," some day—a long way off—to be delivered.

A number of her best poems were certainly in existence in the early sixties: among them, "Safe in their alabaster chambers," "A bird came down the walk," "There came a day at summer's full," "Some keep the Sabbath going to church," and "Success is counted sweetest." For the rest of her life she was steadily adding to them, working as though the days were not long enough for her to record her teeming brain. The rewards of authorship were an unconsidered by-product. Yet there are many small but significant indications that Emily Dickinson felt the natural desire for communication that every true artist must feel. A little note written before 1856 to her brother's intended wife speaks of the satisfaction it would be if she could some day make her dearest relatives proud of her. The implication is that she hoped to win distinction by her writing. "I cannot dance upon my toes," she wrote about 1862,

> But oftentimes, among my mind
> A Glee possesseth me
> That had I ballet Knowledge
> Would put itself abroad
> In Pirouette to blanch a troupe
> Or lay a Prima mad.

Mrs. Ford thought that some of the peculiar habits of her later life originated in a suppressed and ungratified desire for poetic recognition. Certainly Emily was not averse to having her poems read, though she did not permit them to be read indiscriminately, even in her family. It was not applause that she craved, but a discerning response. In the subtle ways dear to her she found out readers and critics who could give her that, and in their eyes she established the "fame petite" that sufficed her need.

The list of those other than her kindred to whom she sent poems included Samuel Bowles, Josiah Gilbert Holland, Thomas Wentworth Higginson, Helen Hunt Jackson, Thomas Niles of Roberts Brothers, all people with a professional interest in literature. If we examine their early opinions of Emily Dickinson's work, we may be led to suspect a second reason why she was content to postpone the question of publication. The public which cared for poetry at all in the sixties and seventies was not prepared to meet her on her own level. Its conception of poetry was almost the antithesis of hers. No wonder then that like Emerson's Uriel she was "doomed to long gyration in the sea of generation" before the world was ready to acknowledge her. The quality of her achievement can be measured by the almost total failure of her literary friends to perceive it. Let us consider some revealing instances.

Samuel Bowles, a lifelong friend of the Dickinson family and a great favorite of Emily's, may serve as first exhibit. Though not himself a poet, Bowles was alert to poetry as to most matters and possessed a cultivated taste. Two of the three poems which, as far as has yet been discovered, were all that appeared during Emily Dickinson's lifetime were printed in his paper. The first need not detain us, since it was merely a nonsense valentine and its publication was probably intended as a joke on the writer. But it was a different matter when Emily's lines on the snake, beginning "A narrow fellow in the grass," were betrayed into print in *The Springfield Republican* for February 14, 1866. The poem that eluded her vigilance was no girlish *jeu d'esprit*. Did any one of the several thousand subscribers to the country's leading provincial newspaper, reading

> The grass divides as with a comb,
> A spotted shaft is seen;
> And then it closes at your feet
> And opens further on,

realize that a writer who could so exactly observe and render the texture of experience was a master of the writer's craft? Could any reader of the following stanza miss its quaint wizardry of precision, or fail to perceive that nothing at once so homely and so unexpected, so accurate in image and so unpredictable in its aptness, had yet appeared in American poetry?

He likes a boggy acre,
A floor too cool for corn,
Yet when a boy, and barefoot,
I more than once, at noon,
Have passed, I thought, a whip-lash
Unbraiding in the sun,—
When, stooping to secure it,
It wrinkled, and was gone.

We are not left to surmise. Samuel Bowles's comment on this very stanza has been preserved in Dickinson annals. He spoke with a country editor's knowledge of agricultural matters: "How did that girl ever know that a boggy field wasn't good for corn?" If Emily's tiny masterpiece excited any further comment at the time of its first publication, the fact has not been placed on record.

Bowles undoubtedly possessed a more genuine appreciation of Emily Dickinson's gifts than his chance remark would lead us to suppose. He at least showed an eagerness on several occasions to bring her work before the public. It is inexplicable, however, that two seasoned writers like Higginson and Holland, both of whom had read a considerable number of her poems in manuscript and had had full opportunity to judge their worth, should have concluded that publication was out of the question. Neither of these admirable men failed to recognize the singular intensity and individuality of her writing. Holland was a professional editor on the lookout for new writers; Higginson was devoted to the advancement of women. But if they realized that they were confronted by poetry of the first caliber written by a woman, neither of them knew what to do about it. They were dazed.

Yet there is much to be recorded in Higginson's favor. He responded at once to the queer appeal for guidance that Emily sent him out of a clear sky, in 1862, at a time when he was immersed in urgent business. He praised her verses with gener-

ous kindliness, and after a few attempts to bring her to conformity wisely left her to pursue her independent flight. He
went out of his way to visit her in Amherst, and from first to
last gave her the constant support of a large-hearted, brotherly
sympathy. But his critical perceptions were not equal to the
occasion. He was capable at the same time of profound insights
and incredible lapses. Both together occur in the one letter from
him to her which has survived, a letter which dates from the
late sixties. After speaking with the sincerest admiration of the
"strange power" of her verses and letters and the "fine edge"
of her thought, Higginson continued:

It is hard for me to understand how you can live so alone—with
thoughts of such rarity coming up in you and even the companionship
of your dog withdrawn. Yet it isolates one anywhere to think beyond
a certain point, or have such flashes as come to you—so perhaps the
place does not make much difference.

Had he written nothing else about Emily Dickinson we should
have to credit him with one of the most discerning minds of his
generation, but he instantly cancelled this fine stroke of understanding by pressing her to attend a meeting of the Boston
Woman's Club.

After visiting her in Amherst in 1870, Higginson recorded
among the impressions jotted down for his wife: "I never was
with any one who drained my nerve power so much. Without
touching her she drew from me. I am glad not to live near
her." But even a direct experience of her personal quality did
not prevent him from assuming a patronizing tone when, after
a second interview three years later, he wrote to his sisters:

I saw my eccentric poetess Miss Emily Dickinson who *never* goes
outside her father's grounds and sees only me and a few others. She
says, "There is always one thing to be grateful for,—that one is one's
self and not somebody else," but Mary [Mrs. Higginson] thinks this
is singularly out of place in E. D.'s case. . . . I'm afraid Mary's other
remark, "Oh, why do the insane so cling to you?" still holds.

Still later the phrase becomes "my partially cracked poetess at Amherst." Did the score of poems then in his possession mean nothing to him?

The truth was that a woman poet was a woman poet to Higginson, and even Emily Dickinson was nothing more. He advised her in his first letter to read the works of his Newburyport protégée, Harriet Prescott (Mrs. Spofford). He bracketed her with his sister Louisa when he lectured to the Woman's Club of Newport in 1875 on "Two Unknown Poetesses." Feminine genius was all of a piece to him, whether manifested by a Lucy Stone, an Anne Whitney, an Emily Dickinson, or a Queen Victoria. He approved it in the lump in a warm blur of chivalrous devotion, giving his allegiance to Woman in the abstract as he had previously given it to the Negro Slave. This temper of mind did not make for critical discrimination.

Higginson admitted with perfect candor his limitations. In *The Atlantic* for October, 1891, he printed an article embodying many of Emily Dickinson's poems and letters, and he then took occasion to confess his inability to comprehend her.

> The impression of a wholly new and original poetic genius was as distinct on my mind at the first reading of these four poems as it is now, after thirty years of further knowledge; and with it came the problem never yet solved, what place ought to be assigned in literature to what is so remarkable, yet so elusive of criticism. The bee himself did not evade the schoolboy more than she evaded me; and even to this day I still stand somewhat bewildered, like the boy.

When this essay was reprinted in *Carlyle's Laugh and Other Surprises* (1909) the author altered the words "thirty years" to "half a century," but made no other changes. Apparently it did not occur to him that the existence of "a wholly new and original poetic genius" was a fact of any particular moment, nor that criticism had a duty to mediate between such a mind and the uncomprehending public. For twenty-five years he advised that these remarkable poems be kept under cover, and he lent his name and authority to the first selection published only after many misgivings. When Emily Dickinson's *Poems* (1890) caused a literary sensation, he was as much surprised as he was delighted. These facts speak volumes of the low estate to which poetry had fallen. Emily Dickinson's first question: "Mr. Higginson,—Are you too deeply occupied to say if my verse is alive?" was the last question that current criticism was prepared to face. It could not be answered by a man who was willing to stand bewildered for half a century, doubtful of what place ought to be assigned in literature to poems which transcended most that he had read by living authors.

Higginson, however, was not alone in doubting whether such poetry could succeed. Doctor Holland, who with his wife was an intimate friend of the Dickinsons and had known Emily since her teens, also considered that her poems could not be published: "they really are not suitable," he said, "they are too ethereal." He was speaking to Mrs. Ford, Emily's friend from her earliest days and the author of two volumes of verse. Some fifteen years later, after the first two books of poems by Emily Dickinson had been published, Mrs. Ford recalled the conversation and her subsequent reflections:

I said, "They are beautiful, so concentrated, but they remind me of orchids, air-plants that have no roots in earth." He said, "That is true,— a perfect description. I dare not use them"; and I think these lyrical ejaculations, these breathed out projectiles sharp as lances, would at that time have fallen into idle ears. But gathered in a volume where many could be read at once as her philosophy of life, they explain each other and so become intelligible and delightful to the public.

Mrs. Ford was acute in remarking that Emily Dickinson's poems were more effective if taken together than if read singly, but she neglected to draw the inference that this could not possibly be true of "air-plants" with no roots in a common ground of experience. We do not know which poems Doctor Holland had before him, but among those which Mrs. Ford had known

for many years was "Some keep the Sabbath going to church,"
containing among its twelve lines:

> With a bobolink for a chorister,
> And an orchard for a dome.
>
> .   .   .   .
>
> And instead of tolling the bell for church,
> Our little sexton sings.
>
> .   .   .   .
>
> God preaches,—a noted clergyman,—
> And the sermon is never long.

It would be hard to conceive a poem more permeated with New
England imagery, associations both of landscape and of local
custom; or, for that matter, one more strikingly expressive of
the essence of New England Protestantism, albeit with an individual twist peculiar to its author. To consider such a poem, or
Emily Dickinson's poems in general, ethereal and unrooted in
the soil betrays a helplessness of judgment beside which Higginson's honest bewilderment appears almost brilliant. Yet two
intelligent contemporaries who knew the poet's environment and
something of her story entertained that opinion, and it has been
unthinkingly echoed many times since.

One woman, however, possessed the courage of convictions
which Higginson and Holland lacked. Of all Emily Dickinson's
literary friends Helen Hunt was the most persistent in urging
her to publish her poems and the most ingenious in her attempts
to overcome the poet's diffidence. We cannot say exactly when
the assault on the ivory tower commenced. According to Lavinia
Dickinson, Helen Hunt stayed at the Dickinson house for two
weeks at a time vaguely described as "after Major Hunt's
death"; she was constantly closeted with Emily, and a number
of manuscripts were sent off. Major Hunt was killed in 1863,
however, and it was not until 1865–66 that the literary career
of "H. H." began. She was travelling in Europe from 1868 to
1870, and her first book, *Verses*, was published in the latter

year. Since Lavinia's report implies that Mrs. Hunt was an experienced author when she visited Emily, I am inclined to place their literary conference between 1870 and 1874. At that time Mrs. Hunt was engaged upon the first series of *Saxe Holm's Stories*, in many of which she made use of circumstances, characters, and settings drawn from Amherst and the surrounding region. She may have wanted Emily to refresh some of her memories. She may have hoped that Emily would allow certain of her poems to be used in one story in particular. But there is no evidence that Emily was willing to go as far as that.

In 1876, the year when *Mercy Philbrick's Choice* appeared in the "No Name Series," Mrs. Jackson, as she had then become, again flashed through town and, as Emily dutifully reported to Higginson, besought her for contributions. "It was not stories that she asked of me." Presumably Helen asked for poems to be included in the anthology of unsigned verse called *A Masque of Poets*, published in 1878. Emily seems to have declined after some hesitation, and the circumstances which led to the inclusion of "Success is counted sweetest" in the book remain obscure. But if Helen took an unwarranted liberty in publishing her friend's poem without permission, Emily readily forgave her. She records a "sweet forenoon" with Mrs. Jackson and her husband just before *A Masque of Poets* appeared, and her admiration for "Helen of Colorado" was never more exalted than in the years immediately following.

With Thomas Niles, the publisher of the "No Name Series," she entered into correspondence. He seems to have joined with Mrs. Jackson in urging her to publish, for we find her writing to him about 1883, "The kind but incredible opinion of H. H. and yourself I would like to deserve." Was she about to yield? Mrs. Jackson made a final effort. "What portfolios full of verses you must have!" she wrote on September 5, 1884. "It is a cruel wrong to your 'day and generation' that you will not give them light." She asked to be made Emily's literary executor, and continued, "I do not think we have a right to withhold from the world a word or thought any more than a *deed* which might help a single soul." The appeal came too late. Emily had already been overtaken by a nervous collapse from which she never fully recovered. The following August Helen Hunt Jackson died.

But if Mrs. Jackson failed to bring Emily's poems before the world, she managed on two occasions—once in the *Saxe Holm's Stories,* which she never acknowledged as hers, and again in the anonymous *Mercy Philbrick's Choice*—to make palpable use of her friend's story. Also she worked into the narrative, in each instance, poems of her own more or less closely modelled on Emily Dickinson's. Since the two women were on terms of close friendship and saw each other occasionally during the years when these stories were written and published, it is impossible to suppose that Emily was unaware of what Helen was doing. She must have given at least tacit consent to the exploitation of her secret romance under the disguise of fiction.

"Esther Wynn's Love-Letters," the last of the six *Saxe Holm's Stories* (1874), tells of the discovery by a highly sentimental uncle and niece of a bundle of old documents mysteriously hidden under the stairs. These turn out to be letters and poems with "the whole soul of a woman" in them, written fifty years before by the unknown Esther Wynn to a lover whom she could not marry. After exploring this forgotten romance with many delicious thrills, uncle and niece piously burn the letters, but not before the niece has copied four of them with the poems enclosed. The situation between Esther Wynn and her lover—"He was a married man we felt sure"—is startlingly close to that assumed in Emily Dickinson's love poems.

Esther like Emily considered that she "had no beauty"; the bond that united her to her lover was one of mind and spirit alone. She was little more than a child when they first became acquainted.

It was evident that at first the relation was more like one of pupil and master. . . . It was not until years had passed that the master became the lover; we fancied, Uncle Jo and I, as we went reverently over the beautiful pages, that Esther had grown and developed more and more, until she was the teacher, the helper, the inspirer. We felt sure, though we could not tell how, that she was the stronger of the two; that she moved and lived habitually on a higher plane; that she yearned often to lift the man she loved to the freer heights on which her soul led its glorified existence.

. . . It was plain that some cruel, inexorable bar separated her from the man she loved; a bar never spoken of—whose nature we could only guess,—but one which her strong and pure nature felt itself free to triumph over in spirit, however submissive the external life might seem.

. . . .

It was evident that there had been the deepest intellectual sympathy between them. Closely and fervently and passionately as their hearts must have loved, the letters were never, from first to last, simply lovers' letters. Keen interchange of comment and analysis, full revelation of strongly marked individual life, constant mutual stimulus to mental growth, there must have been between these two. We were inclined to think, from the exquisitely phrased sentences and rare fancies in the letters, and from the graceful movement of some of the poems, that Esther must have had ambition as a writer. . . .

If it is not obvious that we have here an exact reflection of the romance that Emily Dickinson imagined herself to be living, all doubts are dispelled by the letters and poems which follow. The first is a close imitation of such a letter as Emily might have written, full of meadows, breeze, butterflies, clover, bobolinks, and bees. Once or twice the writer almost catches the cadence of Emily's speech, but the tension and fine surprise of her wit were beyond Helen Hunt's power to reproduce. The difference between them may be made evident if one places the accompanying "clover song" beside any of Emily's nature poems.

> I wonder what the Clover thinks?—
> Intimate frend of Bob-o-links,

Lover of Daisies slim and white,
Waltzer with Butter-cups at night;
Keeper of Inn for travelling Bees,
Serving to them wine dregs and lees,
Left by the Royal Humming-birds,
Who sip and pay with fine-spun words;

. . . .

Symbol of Nature's magic zone,
One out of three, and three in one;

. . . .

Sweet in its every living breath,
Sweetest, perhaps, at last, in death!
Oh, who knows what the Clover thinks?
No one! unless the Bob-o-links!

A subsequent letter contains a dream-allegory of love's happy fulfillment not different in kind from the dream of gathering roses related in one of Emily's letters to Mrs. Holland. The last three poems, one of them sent with a pomegranate blossom, bear the same relation to Emily's love poems that the clover song just quoted does to her poems on nature. The more intricate stanza forms that Helen Hunt delighted in have been substituted, however, for Emily's simpler measures. Two examples will illustrate their quality. The first is taken from the end of a sonnet:

Can new pain
Teach me of pain: Or any ecstasy
Be new, that I should speak its name again?
My darling, all there was or is of me
Is harvested for thine Eternity!

The second is the last part of an elaborate poem called "Three Kisses of Farewell."

We shall reach until we feel each other,
Past all of time and space;
We shall listen till we hear each other
In every place;

The earth is full of messengers,
    Which love sends to and fro;
I kiss thee, darling, for all joy
    Which we shall know.

The last kiss, oh, my darling,
    My love—I cannot see
Through my tears, as I remember
    What it may be.
We may die and never see each other,
    Die with no time to give
Any sign that our hearts are faithful
    To die, as live.
Token of what they will not see
    Who see our parting breath,
This one last kiss, my darling, seals
    The seal of death.

We can only guess what hushed conferences must have preceded the composition of this intimate revelation. What part Emily played in the shaping of the story we cannot even guess. But the friend who held the pen must have divined all her secret and must have seen some of the poems that she guarded from other eyes.

Mercy Philbrick's Choice, published two years later, is not a fictional biography of Emily Dickinson, but rather a novel into which have been inserted some traits of appearance and character borrowed from her and some allusions to her actual history. So plain were some of these references that the writer of an unsigned article in *The Springfield Republican* for July 25, 1878, was inclined to attribute the book, not to Helen Hunt Jackson, but to another Amherst writer, no names being mentioned. The supposition that Emily Dickinson wrote all or any part of *Mercy Philbrick's Choice*, however, has been thoroughly investigated by Mrs. Todd and decisively negatived. Lavinia stated that Mrs. Jackson asked Emily's help on a novel which she had already projected and begun to write, and that when

Emily either could not or would not contribute her share, her friend mischievously put her into the story. This account seems to be borne out by internal evidence; on page 22 Mercy is described as "a woman of slight frame, gentle, laughing, brown eyes, a pale skin, pale ash-brown hair," while on page 172 she has become "that girl with fair hair and blue eyes." The latter description is probably a relic of the conventional heroine that Mrs. Jackson originally conceived, but the first description might pass for a close portrait of Emily Dickinson, except that her hair was a vivid Titian. Mercy's character like Emily's is marked by an uncompromising love of truth. She hides herself from unwelcome callers lest she be forced to speak or act a social lie in greeting them. Her ailing mother, a "comparatively helpless, aged child," awakens "all the deep maternal instincts of her strong nature." In these respects Mrs. Jackson's heroine resembles Emily Dickinson, but she also resembles her creator in that she is represented as a young widow who after passing through fires of suffering becomes a famous poetess.

There can be no doubt, however, that some circumstances in Emily Dickinson's life are quite literally transcribed. Her friendship with Ben Newton, for example, is paralleled in the brief account of Mercy Philbrick's relations with the young minister Harley Allen.

Mr. Allen, who had been Mercy's teacher for three years, had early seen in her a strong poetic impulse, and had fostered and stimulated it by every means in his power. . . . Intellectually, he was, in spite of his superior culture, far Mercy's inferior. He had been brave enough and manly enough to recognize this, and also to recognize what it took still more manliness to recognize,—that she could never love a man of his temperament. . . . He taught her and trained her, and developed her, patiently, exactingly, and yet tenderly, as if she had been his sister; but he never betrayed to her, even by a look or tone, that he could have loved her . . . he compelled all his home-seeking, wife-loving thoughts to turn away from Mercy; and, six months after her departure, he had loyally and lovingly promised to be the husband of another. In Mercy's future he felt an intense interest; he would never cease to watch over her, if she would let him; he would guide, mould, and direct her, until the time came—he knew it would come—when she had outgrown his help, and ascended to a plane where he could no longer guide her.

Like Emily Dickinson again Mercy Philbrick encounters a second teacher in the person of Parson Dorrance, a former clergyman considerably older than she. Though Mrs. Jackson has carefully altered details, the Parson obviously stands in relation to Mercy as Charles Wadsworth to Emily. He was interested at first in her poems, "which had surprised him much by their beauty, and still more by their condensation of thought," so that he found it hard to associate "this slight, fair girl, with a child's honesty and appeal in her eyes" with writings more masculine than feminine in tone. For a page or two Mrs. Jackson appears to be drawing from life, albeit with some coloring from a romantic imagination.

It was a turning point in Mercy's life when she met Parson Dorrance. Here at last was a man who had strength enough to influence her, culture enough to teach her, and the firm moral rectitude which her nature so inexorably demanded. During the first few weeks of their acquaintance, Mercy was conscious of an insatiable desire to be in his presence: it was an intellectual and a moral thirst. Nothing could be farther from the absorbing consciousness which passionate love feels of its object, than was this sentiment she felt toward Parson Dorrance. . . . She questioned him eagerly. Her old doubts and perplexities, which Mr. Allen's narrower mind had been unable to comprehend or to help, were now set at rest and cleared up by a spiritual vision far keener than her own. . . . Parson Dorrance in his turn was as much impressed by Mercy; but he was never able to see in her simply the pupil, the questioner. To him she was also a warm and glowing personality, a young and beautiful woman. . . . Long before he dreamed of such a thing, he might have known, if he had taken counsel of his heart, that Mercy was becoming to him the one woman in the world. There was always this peculiarity in Mercy's influence upon all who came to love her. She was so unique and incalculable a person that she made all other women seem by comparison with her monotonous and wearying. Intimacy with her had a subtle flavor to it, by which other flavors were dulled. The very impersonality of her enthusiasms and interests, her capacity for looking on a person for the time being merely as a representative or mouth-piece, so to speak, of thoughts, of ideas, of narrations, was one of her strongest charms.

After she has refused Parson Dorrance's love because her heart is engaged elsewhere, and after he has died, Mercy is drawn closer to him by a growing perception of their spiritual affinity.

Slowly the whole allegiance of her heart transferred itself to the dead man's memory; slowly her grief for his loss deepened, and yet with the deepened grief came a certain new and holy joy. It surely could not be impossible for him to know in heaven that she was his on earth? As confidently as if she had been wedded to him here, she looked forward to the reunion with him there, and found in her secret consciousness of this eternal bond a hidden rapture, such as has been the stay of many a widowed heart through long lifetimes of loneliness.

The passages in which Mrs. Jackson seems to be dealing with Emily Dickinson's affairs are only occasional. No known episode in Emily's life corresponds to the story of Mercy Philbrick and Stephen White, the self-indulgent lover who proves himself morally unworthy of her. It is with a characterization of Stephen White that the novel opens, and we may confidently assume that Mrs. Jackson had invented him and the outline of the plot in which he figures before it occurred to her to individualize her heroine by features borrowed from Emily Dickinson. That Emily did not resent the liberty has already been made clear. It is almost impossible to believe that the liberty was taken without her knowledge.

In view of "Esther Wynn's Love-Letters" and *Mercy Philbrick's Choice* the publication of one of Emily Dickinson's poems under Mrs. Jackson's auspices in *A Masque of Poets* cannot be taken as an isolated incident. Twice in fiction Mrs. Jackson had sketched the shadowy outline of a figure like Emily Dickinson and had stressed the poems written in secret by a woman of unique genius. Then an authentic poem was laid before the public. Was she hoping to prepare an audience for a literary discovery? The management of such a campaign would have exactly suited Helen Hunt Jackson, but we can only guess at intentions that were never fulfilled. In 1879 or 1880 she became absorbed in Indian affairs and for five years was occupied in writing *A Century of Dishonor* and *Ramona*. But for this interruption it is conceivable that she might have succeeded by some ingenious and mystifying device in getting more of Emily's poems into print. Helen Jackson was a hard person to resist.

Still, in spite of her admiration for Emily Dickinson, it is doubtful whether she realized the distinction of her friend's poems. She could not resist the temptation to "improve" the stanzas that she sent to press. Higginson's copy of *A Masque of Poets* bears testimony to her meddling. At the top of the page that carries "Success" he wrote Emily Dickinson's name and added, "altered probably by Mrs. Helen Hunt." Then with pen and ink he restored the original readings in two places. Where Emily had written:

> To comprehend a nectar
> Requires sorest need,

Helen Hunt had preferred: "Requires the sorest need," though the emendation spoils the vigor of the grouped accents. And again when she encountered:

> The distant strains of triumph
> Break, agonized and clear,

she changed the line to: "Break, agonizing clear," on the ground that, though the defeated hero might be *agonized*, the strains of triumph could only be *agonizing*. But niceties of logic are not the finer breath of poetry. Later editors have fortunately agreed with Higginson in preferring the poem as it was written.

After "The Snake" had been printed and "defeated too of the third line by the punctuation,"and after "Success" had appeared with Helen Hunt's corrections, Emily Dickinson might have foreseen what would inevitably happen to her poems if she left them for posthumous publication. But her attitude toward her writings remained that of a novice. In all innocence she regarded publication as an adventitious act, not an essential part of the process of creation, but something merely "ostensible." Trained to regard the art of poetry with extreme reverence, she was too modest to think that her productions could be worthy of recognition. Her thoughts seemed "numb" when she "put them in the gown." What indeed could they amount to in comparison with the work of Mr. Emerson or Professor Lowell or dear Doctor Holland? Still they were her very own. She had put her lifeblood into them, and she would not have them, in their simple homely angularity, run the risk of being considered ungainly, "the only kangaroo among the beauty."

This was as near as Emily Dickinson ever came to the perception that her poetry was of a different order from that of most of her contemporaries, and she lacked the assurance to suppose that the difference could be in her favor. Higginson, in whose judgment she confided, though he felt himself in the presence of a new and strange power, was too soaked in Cambridge to imagine that a literary revolution could start in Amherst. He could only advise her not to publish, and from a prudential point of view he was perhaps right. Even as late as 1890 there were many readers of poetry who failed to appreciate the vigorous economy and austere functional beauty of her lines.

In the decades following the Civil War vigor was not the dominant note of American poetry. The bards of the moment were engaged in playing a thin, incongruous obbligato to the bustle of life, when they were not turning away from it altogether. The virile if crude energy that was expanding cities, building railroads, developing industries, snatching and dissipating incredible wealth, the imagination that was perfecting thousands of mechanical inventions, rarely found expression in literature. Poetry stood aloof from the sordid spectacle, meager and virginal, nor had it any corresponding life of its own. It might dally with sentiment and aspiration, it might deal with tragic circumstance, but only if it could do so neatly. The refinement of received ideas, the decorating and upholstering of experience, comprised its function.

Many poets expressed their dissatisfaction at the weakness of contemporary verse. The air was full of outcries of disgust and of prophecies of a stronger race of singers. "When the true poet comes, how shall we know him?" asked Richard Watson Gilder, melodiously. He will have "manners like other men," but

> His speech not musical, but harsh and broken
> Shall sound at first, each line a driven spear.

We need only change the gender. Among all the jig-saw architects of airy rhyme Emily Dickinson was the one artist-engineer. She had faced the problem of putting her spiritual house in order, giving to the task the supreme concentration of energy that others were giving to mechanical organization. Her poetry in its precision and structural integrity was an achievement comparable, in its way, to the building of the Brooklyn Bridge. What was to be done with poems that avoided pyrotechnic displays and flew like bullets straight to the mark? It is clear that her literary friends did not know. Is it any wonder then that publication remained, as she told Higginson, "as foreign to my thought as firmament to fin"?

Society in Solitude

EMILY DICKINSON in her later years has so often been pictured as a kind of New England nun that an exaggerated impression of her retirement has been created. It was neither abruptly begun nor was it at first abnormal. From the time of her return from Mount Holyoke until her death she lived quietly in her father's house. Her sister Lavinia followed the same course, and so did hundreds of other unmarried gentlewomen. If no husband claimed them, they had hardly an alternative unless need forced them to teach dame school or to keep a shop. Only a few strong-minded females like Mary Lyon broke through the silken net of convention. The common destiny of a New England spinster was to live self-effacingly at home.

Emily did not at once become a recluse. During her twenties she moved in village society, an introspective, wittily demure young woman, rather apt to do exactly as she pleased. She was sensitive to stares in church, shy of casual meetings, and impatient of formalities. Her family indulged her, and when she decided not to attend public functions or to receive visitors, they respected her whim. She was fond of solitary walks with her big brown dog Carlo, a shaggy ally and protector provided by her father, but she also went with friends on horseback rides and carriage drives, joined occasionally in the amusements of the younger set, and generally recognized her social obligations as Squire Dickinson's elder daughter. When a young Amherst merchant brought home a bride to the "First President's House" that he had purchased from Professor Fowler, Emily was among the earliest to call, and the visiting card that she left is still extant. Gradually, however, she chose to leave such matters to her mother and sister. Still she looked forward eagerly to visits from such intimate friends as the Hollands, and as late as 1861 she was wearing "a brown dress with a cape if possible browner," and carrying "a parasol of the same!"

It is not clear just when Emily Dickinson began to dress invariably in white and to invest herself in an atmosphere of "hallowed mystery" that her garments symbolized. By 1862 her retirement from the world had become marked but was not absolute. Higginson reproached her for shunning men and women, and she admitted that a chestnut tree in blossom, encountered on her walk, was better company. But she was ready enough to go to Boston for the care of her eyes in the summer of 1864, and for a longer period during the following year. At these times she lived in a Cambridgeport boarding-house with her Norcross cousins, and a chance remark would lead us to suppose that she fled the company of the other boarders. She expected to go again in the spring of 1866, "but father objects because he is in the habit of me." Through the sixties she still appeared to greet her father's guests at the annual Commencement teas when the Dickinsons entertained the academic world. By 1870 her seclusion had become a conscious resolution: "I do not cross my father's ground to any house or town." A preference for privacy deepened into a morbid dread of prying eyes. For the last fifteen years of her life the village knew Emily Dickinson only as a white figure flitting about the garden in the summer dusk, as a voice from the dimness of the hall startling visitors in the Dickinson parlor by spectral interjections, or as a presence responding to occasions for congratulation or condolence by neighborly gifts of flowers and dainties accompanied by little notes pencilled in an odd hand and phrased in orphic idiom. The village at first considered her an invalid and latterly pronounced her "gifted but queer." Friends of the family thought her an exquisite touch-me-not and considerately avoided any intrusion on Miss Emily's privacy.

Her voluntary isolation seems to have been at first little more than a preference for company of her own choosing. Whatever it may have become after years of indulgence, it did not begin as a phobia. New England women were capable of violent withdrawals from the world: Hawthorne's mother, from the time of her husband's loss at sea, shut herself up with her grief and for the rest of her life scarcely saw the members of her own family. Emily Dickinson's seclusion was plainly not of this type. She did not shun the human race to brood over an overwhelming disappointment. Her relations with her family and intimate friends remained normal.

Nor did she withdraw into a cave of romantic sensibility, though in her girlhood the notion of the poet as a beautiful soul standing apart from the crass occupations of life was widely accepted. Emily must have heard many times from tutors and college students the doctrine propounded in the following passage from *The Amherst Collegiate Magazine* for October, 1854. The writer, Hasket Derby of the class of 1855, was one of her friends among the undergraduates.

Solitude, remarks an elegant writer, is the school of Genius, but it is not the solitude of monasticism . . . nor is it the solitude of the hermit's mossy cell. . . . Such solitude is a sundering of the ties of humanity and choosing a single spot to be miserable in. But he who retires to the seclusion of his chamber and there in communion with the spirits of the mighty dead through the medium of books, works out the great problems of philosophy, science, and politics; he who after long reflection in his closet forms the vast schemes to be realized in future life, he who marks out a consistent course of action based on fixed principles, he it is that truly makes solitude the school of genius, and through it paves the way to fame.

If the seclusion of the study makes the philosopher and man of science, equally is the sublimity of Nature the school of the poet and artist. . . . They have entered into the mysteries of nature, realized the truth and deep meaning of her manifestations to man, and in a thousand different ways they have taught their lessons of beauty, strength or grandeur to their uninspired brethren. The poet, the sculptor, the painter, have come forth from hidden caves, inspired by an unseen God.

The poet is a secret agent. He shuns the crowded forum and mingles not in the stir of political life. The retirement of his secluded villa begets enough of zeal and fire, and his own imagination must create another world for him to move in. . . .

Stripped of their magniloquence, these words might pass for a statement of a theory of poetry in accordance with which Emily Dickinson shaped her life. She would have agreed entirely with the conception of the poet as an interpreter of nature's mysteries. Was there not "a noiseless noise in the orchard that I let persons hear"? But her retirement had no anti-social implications. There are traces of this kind of romantic aloofness in Thoreau's retreat to his Walden cabin, though he was also impelled by the practical desire to find time to write a book. Emily Dickinson valued her individuality no less than Thoreau, but there is not a hint that she courted solitude in order that she might be more completely a law unto herself. Loneliness was a burden that she set herself to bear. Far from considering her individual notions superior to the general sense of mankind, she was continually begging the men she most admired to guide and instruct her. Though she was not always able to take their advice, she considered that the defect was hers.

Doubtless her habit of seclusion was facilitated in part by the fact that during her fourth decade she was overstrained and far from well. She had never been robust, and the prolonged nervous tension brought on by falling in love with a man whom she could not marry was almost too much for her. In March, 1859, she wrote to Louisa Norcross: "I've had a curious winter . . . for I haven't felt well much, and March amazes me." By 1863 she was dangerously near the breaking point, as a note apologizing to the same cousin for postponing a visit indicates:

The nights turned hot, when Vinnie had gone, and I must keep no window raised for fear of prowling "booger," and I must shut my door for fear front door slide open on me at the "dead of night," and I must keep "gas" burning to light the danger up, so I could distinguish it—these gave me a snarl in the brain which don't unravel yet, and that old nail in my breast pricked me; these, dear, were my cause.

To Higginson she wrote during the summer of 1864 to say that she had been ill since the previous September and in Boston for a physician's care since April. "He does not let me go, yet I work in my prison and make guests for myself." The following year, again in Boston, she complained that the doctor had forbidden her to use her pencil. By 1869 she could report improvement but not complete recovery to her Norcross cousins: "I am not so well as to forget I was ever ill, but better and working." The relatively small number of poems and letters that can be dated in the later sixties would seem to show that Emily was then passing through a time of lowered vitality.

What she minded most about her periods of ill health was that she lost precious moments that might have been given to her work. The Puritan strain in her revolted at the dissipation of her gift of life. She had more poems to write than she could find time to write them in. At home she had her share of the housekeeping to do; her father preferred to eat no bread but hers, and there were always puddings to make, Aunt Libbie dropping in for a dish of homestead Charlotte Russe, and "julep cookery" to be concocted in return for neighborly attentions. Occasional intervals snatched during the day and a few hours stolen from sleep at night were all she could count on for poetry. The plainest reason, then, why she limited her society to that of a few chosen friends was that she had no time to spare. Her work must at no cost be neglected. If there were people who failed to understand her determined isolation and made merry over her as a "partially cracked poetess," she had more important things on hand than to defer to their opinions. She was not the sort of person to do things by halves.

If Emily had broken down and acknowledged her secret disaster, her family might have saved her from assuming an attitude that came to have in it elements of pose and even of morbidness. But they were helpless in the face of her gallantry. Lavinia worshipped the ground she walked on and would never have dreamed of thwarting her least wish. Her father, in spite of his austerity, idolized his brilliant and willful daughter. Her mother could only flutter. A few sensible friends refused to respect the cocoon of aloofness that she was weaving about herself. Vital Mr. Bowles, when Emily would not come down to receive him, bounded up the stairs shouting for his "rascal," and adding to her scandalized delight an adjective that needed to be "washed." Mrs. Daniel Bliss, the Abby Wood of Emily's schooldays, returned from Syria in 1873 to find her former crony enmeshed in a mysterious seclusion, "inaccessible to all but an elect few, who were admitted to the sanctuary with appropriate preliminaries and ceremonies." She good-naturedly refused to approach the Sibyl until she could be received on the old basis. But such friends were all too rare. The cocoon tightened year by year until it became a psychic prison. Only a Robert Browning could have released the Lady of Shalott, and no Robert Browning came her way.

So for the latter years of her life Emily Dickinson immured herself behind the hemlock hedges. The grove of oaks in back of her home remained a "Gibraltar remnant" where she could walk in impregnable seclusion. Her outward existence henceforth was almost devoid of incident. It was a long interval of sameness so absolute that the arrival of a new month was like a guest's coming and the closed vans of a circus passing her window at night seemed to her an Arabian experience.

The chief events that punctuated the monotony were the

deaths of her kindred and cherished friends. In spite of the fact that her family circle remained unbroken until her forty-fourth year, Emily had come to know the meaning of bereavement at an early age. Even as a child she was taken to funerals. A number of girls that she had loved at Amherst Academy died when barely out of their teens; their admired master Leonard Humphrey followed. At first she had "run home to awe" with a child's bewilderment, but the great mystery haunted her. "That bareheaded life, under the grass, worries one like a wasp." Ben Newton died with the best of life before him, and she felt that death was rioting over helpless mortality. "Heaven hunts round for those that find itself below, and then it snatches." She was in full rebellion.

The national agony of the Civil War coincided with her deepest trouble of heart, but brought no alleviation of it. War seemed to her "an oblique place." Soon the village was in mourning. In October, 1861, came news of an Adams boy dead of fever; in December his brother died of a wound received at Annapolis. Lieutenant Frazar A. Stearns, son of the President of Amherst College, fell gallantly at Newbern in March, 1862. His body was brought home for burial, and the muffled drum beats echo in Emily's letters. "Sorrow," she wrote, "seems more general than it did, and not the estate of a few persons, since the war began; and if the anguish of others helped one with one's own, now would be many medicines." Though her brother Austin, then a young husband and father, felt no call to arms, the family did not escape without a share of sadness. Mrs. Dickinson's sister Lavinia had died in 1860, and the beloved cousins Louisa and Fanny Norcross were doubly orphaned by their father's death in 1863. Like Browning, whose wife was lately dead, Emily felt that she "sang off charnel steps."

> Safe in their alabaster chambers,
> Sleep the meek members of the resurrection,
> Rafter of satin, and roof of stone. . . .
> Untouched by morning and untouched by noon,

In this and many succeeding poems Emily reviewed the panoply of death and reconnoitered every aspect of mortality. It is no wonder that Howells wrote after reading the first published selection from her writings: "Such things could have come only from a woman's heart to which the experiences of a New England town have brought more knowledge of death than of life."

She was granted a few years' respite before the sudden death of her father, in June, 1874, benumbed her anew. After that she needed no guide in dusty ways; she had traced them all. When the first Mrs. Higginson died, she wrote to her bereaved friend: "The wilderness is new to you, Master, let me lead you." From June, 1875, to November, 1882, her mother was an invalid in her daughters' care, first recovering slowly from a paralytic stroke, then confined to her bed by a fractured hip. "When father lived I remained with him because he would miss me. Now, mother is helpless—a holier demand." The burden of nursing and keeping up the spirits of the dying woman left Emily small time for anything else. She saw occasionally a few close friends—Judge Lord, Mr. Bowles, her father's clergyman. "Little wayfaring acts," she told Higginson, comprised her pursuits, "and a few moments at night for books, after the rest sleep." Was there still room for poetry? he asked. She answered, "I have no other playmate."

One by one the sustaining friends passed away. Samuel Bowles, whose physiognomy read "because I live, ye shall live also," died exhausted in 1878. He, alas, "was not willing to die." Doctor Holland followed in 1881; the Reverend Charles Wadsworth in 1882; her favorite cousin William Hawley Dickinson of Worcester in 1883; Judge Lord in 1884; Helen Hunt Jackson in 1885. These were but the more signal of the inroads on her peace.

She became expert in the management of grief. Blossoms and books she knew for solaces of sorrow, but it is clear that religious consolations were no more to her than an intermittent support, always in danger of collapse. Since she had outgrown the "faith of the fathers," which as she put it wore brogans and carried blue umbrellas, her immediate reliance on Providence was a matter of exalted moments only. Helpful messages from her great friend in Philadelphia could give her assurance, and in crises of mutual sorrow she invariably voiced her sympathy in the tender language of Christian belief. Yet there were many times when her "low feet staggered." To Charles H. Clark she wrote in 1883: "Are you certain there is another life? When overwhelmed to know, I fear that few are sure." It was essentially the same question that she had asked of Hale thirty years before. Through life she tossed like a small boat outside the breakers; firm land lay just ahead, yet somehow no harbor was to be found. It was not for her to know the confirmed peace of the Christian mystic.

What upheld her best was the indomitable pride of individuality, the stoical fortitude that she inherited from her father, and an unquenchable joy in existence that was her own peculiar gift. Nothing could defeat a nature that welcomed every harshness that life could invent with an insatiable thirst for experience, and that found delight in refusing any compromise with destiny. These traits were fundamental in Emily Dickinson from first to last. A brief anthology of her sayings during the last fifteen years of her life reads like a chapter from Marcus Aurelius, with an added touch of Ariel's ecstasy.

> It is delicate that each mind is itself, like a distinct bird.
> We must be less than Death to be lessened by it, for nothing is irrevocable but ourselves.
> I suppose the pain is still there, for pain that is worthy does not go soon. The small can crush the great, however, only temporarily. In a few days we examine, muster our forces, and cast it away.
> To relieve the irreparable degrades it.
> The time to live is frugal, and good as it is a better earth will not quite be this.

To have been made alive is so chief a thing, all else inevitably adds. Were it not riddled by partings, it were too divine.

The "happiness" without a cause is the best happiness, for glee intuitive and lasting is the gift of God.

I find ecstasy in living; the mere sense of living is joy enough.

A withdrawal from the world conducted in this spirit is not an admission of defeat, nor was her mind focused exclusively upon her own affairs. During her years of deepest seclusion she read the daily paper with relish, and few things that interested the world failed to interest her. She sent incessant messages of affection to her kinsfolk and absent friends, and even made new acquaintances by correspondence, as with Thomas Niles and with Professor Chickering. She kept in eager touch with the news of the village. Not a family in the Dickinsons' wide circle of neighbors that did not receive her tiny notes on any occasion of joy or sorrow, and sometimes on no occasion at all. Many of these little "bulletins from Immortality" have been included in her published letters, but a large number still remain uncollected. She must have sent them abroad, day after day, like filaments to bridge the airy gulf between soul and soul. Thus she kept in communication with the life about her long after she had ceased to participate in it.

Her letters and poems belie the impression of monotony that the quiet chronicle of her later years conveys. Behind the inscrutable hedge an intense inward energy was active. Her grounds were ample; like Thoreau she had travelled widely in her native village. In the course of seemingly eventless days her mind was constantly filled with events, with momentary ecstasies set in motion by home and garden incidents, with deep and candid intuitions of her own states of consciousness, with speculations on the timeless mysteries of love and death suggested by her reading, by her quick imaginative sympathies, and by her own piercing memories. Of very few people can it be said as truly as of Emily Dickinson that nothing she did was of the least consequence while little that she thought and wrote failed to attain momentousness.

The letters that she composed during her years of seclusion are like her poems, distinguishable from them only by their greater length and variety. Often her spontaneous thought broke into meter and rhyme, as if she could not put pen to paper without transcribing the pulse-beats of her mind. Some of the pieces included in her *Poems* were, in fact, bits of letters written as prose. But prose is a misnomer for the words that she projected upon paper, one or two to the line. Only a sentence or two and she was singing. Though the vigor of her later handwriting is lost in print, something of the high-pitched, tense staccato of her style may be conveyed if one of her notes is printed line for line as it stands:

> Sweet Nellie,
>   Blossoms,
> and Cakes,
> and Memory!
> "Choose ye which
> ye will serve"!
> *I* serve the
> M e m o r y.
> Blossoms will
> run away,
> Cakes reign
> but a Day,
> But Memory
> like Melody,
> Is pink
> Eternally.
>   Emily.

A letter seemed to her to possess a spectral power. It was the disembodied mind, walking alone. She put into her own whatever was newest and dearest to her at the moment, whatever would best express herself, an epigram, a memory, a portrait, a ripple of wind on the meadow, a slant of light on the apple trees, the tumbling of a bee in the lilac bush. Seldom did she have anything of ostensible import to communicate. She wrote, as Pepys wrote in his diary, to impound an overflow of delight in happy phrases. Without effort, seemingly, she attained repeated instants of bliss, any one of which would have betrayed the toiling Faust to the devil. If the joy of spring was in her heart, she must hasten to share it with her Norcross cousins. (I omit only her little messages of remembrance and affection):

Dear Children,—I think the bluebirds do their work exactly like me. They dart around just so, with little dodging feet, and look so agitated. I really feel for them, they seem to be so tried.

The mud is very deep—up to the wagons' stomachs—arbutus making pink clothes, and everything alive.

Even the hens are touched with the things of Bourbon, and make republicans like me feel strangely out of scene.

Mother went rambling, and came in with a burdock on her shawl, so we know that the snow has perished from the earth. Noah would have liked mother. . . .

Pussy has a daughter in the shavings barrel.

Father steps like Cromwell when he gets the kindlings.

Mrs. S—— gets bigger, and rolls down the lane to church like a reverend marble. . . .

The letter ends with the news that Mrs. J—— has "fledged her antique wings" in a better world, and the poem beginning:

> Great streets of silence led away
> To neighborhoods of pause.

Not uncommonly Emily's communications leap from point to point of her perceptions with an agility that must have left many of her correspondents gasping. She liked to embody her meaning once for all in a phrase as inevitably condensed and flashing as a dewdrop. But on the rare occasions when she had a scene or an event to describe she was capable of sustained vividness. The fire that, early in the morning of July 4, 1879, swept away over half the business section of Amherst occasioned one of her most graphic pages:

We were waked by the ticking of the bells,—the bells tick in Amherst for a fire, to tell the firemen.

I sprang to the window, and each side of the curtain saw that awful sun. The moon was shining high at the time, and the birds singing like trumpets.

Vinnie came soft as a moccasin, "Don't be afraid, Emily, it is only the fourth of July."

I did not tell that I saw it, for I thought if she felt it best to deceive, it must be that it was.

She took hold of my hand and led me into mother's room. Mother had not waked, and Maggie was sitting by her. Vinnie left us a moment, and I whispered to Maggie, and asked her what it was.

"Only Stebbins's barn, Emily;" but I knew that the right and left of the village was on the arm of Stebbins's barn. I could hear buildings falling, and oil exploding, and people walking and talking gayly, and cannon soft as velvet from parishes that did not know that we were burning up.

And so much lighter than day was it, that I saw a caterpillar measure a leaf far down in the orchard; and Vinnie kept saying bravely, "It's only the fourth of July."

When she was not fixing some winged perception in the amber of her words, her characteristic mood was sparklingly sententious. All her lyric exuberance and almost hectic brightness went into the effort to mold the axioms of her experience into perfect form. Sometimes her apothegms are so compact or so singular in their fusion of disparate ideas that they fail to "hit the nerve of feebler sight." The fault, I suspect, is not always with the reader. A wise and detached observer, Professor John W. Burgess, writing from personal knowledge of Emily Dickinson, felt constrained to emphasize the spasmodic quality of her thought:

Her letters and conversation were full of peculiarities which might almost be called oddities, and some of these were almost incomprehensible. . . . She was vacillating in her mental processes and not always interesting, but at times she seemed almost inspired, and I have heard her express more truth in a sentence of ten words than the most learned professor in the college in an hour's lecture.

The comparison does not, perhaps, seem too flattering, until one recalls the old-fashioned reverence for learning. Many of Emily's *obiter dicta* are very palpable hits. "The Bee that comes home sober is the butt of the Clover" still has its point for descendants of the Puritan fathers, while "Biography first convinces us of the fleeing of the biographied" is a saying not likely to be lost on a writer of her life. But it is understandable that clues should be needed when she remarks out of the blue: "Always begins by degrees," or "Ascension has a muffled route," or "Fathoms are sudden neighbors." Was it in perfect innocence that Emily confided to Higginson: "All men say 'What' to me, but I thought it a fashion"?

Besides the game of "guess what I am thinking" that Emily loved to play with her correspondents, she found an alleviation of solitude in watching from her window the rural pageant of Main Street. She studied it attentively, with a sense for human comedy almost as keen as Jane Austen's. Sooner or later all the inhabitants of Amherst passed by. Many were old acquaintances whose virtues and failings she knew by heart. Others were newcomers, additions to her "menagerie," tantalizing curiosity. From her sister-in-law and others she heard anecdotes of them. She noted intently their gait and gesture, and dismissed them in epigram. "Meat within is requisite to squirrels and to me," she wrote, but more than one man who unconsciously sustained her appraising gaze seemed to offer nothing more tangible than "the figure of a nut." So few people had anthracite in their veins! "I meet some octogenarians, but men and women seldomer, and at longer intervals 'little children' of whom is the 'Kingdom of Heaven.'"

Most satisfying of all were the children that played in the Dickinson yard, a band including a niece from the house next door and the minister's children from the parsonage across the street. Emily stimulated their enterprises with a childlike zest, for the child's heart in her had yielded with extreme reluctance to the woman's—perhaps had never fully yielded. She was too virginal to take an intimate delight in babies; she could only regard them with a soft awe. "They seem to me like a plush nation or a race of down." But romping children she understood completely. She abetted them in circumventing adult authority and contributed small surprises to their illicit feasts. They were aware of her generally as a hovering presence, a white figure dimly discerned behind half-closed blinds as she passed out gingerbread cookies or doughnuts. Now and then, however, they saw her plain, as one of their number has described it, kneeling on an old red army blanket to tend her beloved flowers or gazing from a western window through a vista of trees at the evening sky.

The summer of 1883 had a crepuscular glow about it. It was the last before her health failed. The long strain of attendance on her mother was over. Her dearest earthly friend too was no longer of this earth. She was free to watch the summer delicately fading. With the coming of autumn her own skies were again darkened. The last of the many losses that touched her nearly was the death of a child, her brother's younger son Gilbert. How often she had seen the little blond blessing come running from the other house on some errand of his mother's, like a small missionary with his basket. He was more than a messenger, he was the strongest spiritual link between the two households. Now after three days of delirium he was gone. This time God's "rectification of his frontier" was more than Emily could bear. By October she admitted that she was very ill. The doctor called it nervous prostration, but to her it seemed that "the crisis of the sorrow of so many years is all that tires me." Her final malady was Bright's disease.

For the remaining two years of her life she was never completely well, though there were intervals when she took her nerve by the bridle and forced herself to resume a semblance of activity. The summer of 1884 she passed "in a chair," but she was not too ill to write to her friends nor to work at her poems. In November the doctor forbade her book and thought. Again she rallied, and by August, 1885, was allowed to roam in her room and to write. She confessed her illness as little as possible, but imperceptibly her forces were exhausted. Even to members of her family she seemed remote and withdrawn. Again the leaves unfolded, and as she caught a Pisgah-glimpse of summer she sent to her Norcross cousins the sudden words: "Called back." Late in the afternoon of May 15, 1886, she passed gently from unconsciousness to death.

Three days later her body was carried across flowering meadows to the village burying ground. Higginson, seeing his strange friend for the third time as she lay in her coffin, noted the unravaged youthfulness of her face, the glory of her Venetian hair, and "perfect peace on the beautiful brow." He turned away to write in his diary: "How large a portion of the people who have interested me have passed away." Only four years before Longfellow and Emerson had died; Lowell, Whittier, and Holmes were still living.

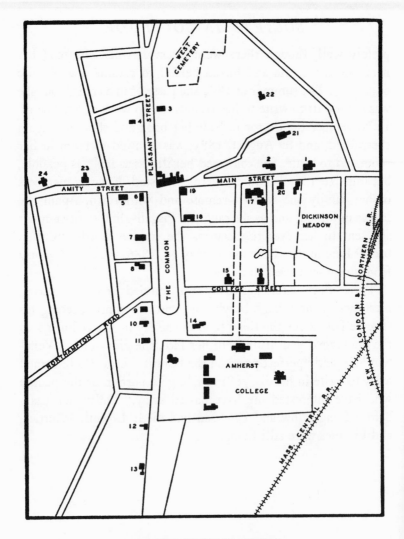

THE TOWN CENTER OF AMHERST

Redrawn from an atlas published in 1873

1. Emily Dickinson's birthplace and home, 1830–1840, 1855–1886.
2. William Austin Dickinson's house, built 1856.
3. Emily Dickinson's home, 1840–1855.
4. The Primary School.
5. Amherst Academy, 1814–1861.
6. Boltwood's Tavern, later the Amherst House.
7. The Baptist Church.
8. The "First President's House": Prof. W. C. Fowler.
9. The Meeting House, later College Hall.
10. Morgan Library (Amherst College).
11. The President's House.
12. Birthplace of Helen M. Fiske (Helen Hunt Jackson).
13. President Edward Hitchcock's house.
14. Lucius Boltwood's house.
15. Dr. Laurens P. Hickok's house.
16. President Julius H. Seelye's house.
17. The Village Church and Parsonage.
18. Grace Church (Episcopal).
19. The Town Hall.
20. Professor Richard H. Mather's house.
21. Deacon Luke Sweetser's house.
22. Professor William S. Tyler's house.
23. Professor Aaron Warner's house.
24. William Cutler's house, where Susan Gilbert lived.

PART THREE

THE SOURCES OF A STYLE

Seeing New Englandly

THE POSTHUMOUS publication of Emily Dickinson's poems at intervals from 1890 to 1936, and the great vogue that her writing achieved during the 1920's, have to a considerable degree obscured her relations with time and place. She seems so decidedly a contemporary that we need to be reminded of her position as a forerunner. The primary fact about her is that her mind was formed in what would now be called the New England hinterland during the three expansive decades before the Civil War, and thereafter was protected, as though under glass, from all shaping influences. So, though she lived and wrote during the Gilded Age, she was not of it. Her mental climate was much the same as Emerson's. What she actually represents is the last surprising bloom—the November witch-hazel blossom—of New England's flowering time.

Throughout her long seclusion she retained the distinctive outlook, as she retained the dress, of her earlier years. She was a child of the Golden Day and never lost the impress of the period. Three of its strongest currents came to a confluence in her poetry: the Puritan tradition in which she was nurtured; the Yankee or, more broadly, American humor that was just coming out of the ground; and the spiritual unrest, typified by Emerson, which everywhere was melting the frost of custom. In this and the two succeeding chapters I shall try to show how these three influences determined the quality of her poetic expression. Each was implicit in her surroundings and was absorbed from the atmosphere of her time. Blended, they gave her a style that was both original and native. A further chapter dealing with her reading will indicate that, much as she admired the writings of others, she did not choose to model her own work on that of any previous or contemporary poet.

Like most New Englanders a century ago Emily Dickinson was saturated in the Bible from early childhood. The use she made of it is a convenient index to the elements of Puritanism that were most valid for her. Biblical phrases were always at her tongue's end, and she delighted to rearrange them to suit her private occasions. Nearly every letter she wrote, except when she was writing to comparative strangers, contains one or more quotations. Words of promise or of consolation were precious to her, and there is nothing exceptional in her manner of using them. But her bump of reverence was small. Even as a schoolgirl she loved to make impish applications of familiar phrases, and more often than not a passage from the Bible lay readiest to hand. She took liberties that would have shocked an earlier Puritan. The sayings of Holy Writ were not sacred to her unless they proved true when tested by her own experience. One can almost see her poking them to make them come alive. Let the serious-minded decide where she verges on the sacrilegious.

The sunshine almost speaks, this morning, . . . and Paul's remark grows graphic, "the *weight* of glory."

Thinking of you with fresher love, as the Bible boyishly says, "New every morning and fresh every evening."

Thomas's faith in anatomy was stronger than his faith in faith.

How vast is the chastisement of beauty, given us by our Maker! A word is inundation, when it comes from the sea. Peter took the marine walk at the great risk.

If prayers had any answers to them, you were all here tonight, but I seek and don't find, and knock and it is not opened. Wonder if God is just—presume He is, however, and 'twas only a blunder of Matthew's.

Why should we censure Othello, when the criterion Lover says, "Thou shalt have no other gods before me"?

Flowers are not quite earthly. . . . Were the "Great Crowd of Witnesses" chiefly Roses and Pansies, there would be less to apprehend, though let me not presume upon Jehovah's Program.

It is only fair to say, however, that the most outrageously mocking of her poems on Biblical subjects were written in a spirit of frolic and banter for a special audience, her nephew Ned. She was evidently dramatizing the boy's resentment of over-starched piety. Such verses as those beginning:

> The Bible is an antique volume
> Written by faded men,

when encountered without explanation in her collected poems seem, and are, out of key. They were no part of her "letter to the world." Emily was merely raising the Old Harry for her nephew's benefit. Among the poems sent specifically to Ned were: " 'Heavenly Father,' take to thee," "The Devil, had he fidelity," and "Belshazzar had a letter." These are amusing *jeux d'esprit*, but they do not deserve the heavy emphasis that some critics of Emily Dickinson have accorded them in the hope of relieving her of the supposed onus of Puritanism. No special effort is needed to dissociate her from the "grizzly saints" of Hawthorne's imagining or the inhibited precisians of H. L. Mencken's invective. But for that matter very few actual Puritans can be made to fit either of these descriptions.

Certain Old Testament characters were as vivid to her imagination as any of Shakespeare's or Dickens's people. She found notable subjects for poems in Jacob's wrestling with the angel, in Moses as an old man on Nebo, and in Elijah's flaming ascent to heaven. Like David she had taken a pebble in her hand and gone out to fight the world, only in her case the giant antagonist failed to succumb. But Moses of all Biblical figures was closest to her heart; she knew what it meant to glimpse a

Promised Land that she could not enter. The New Testament gave her material for but one poem, on the repentant thief of the crucifixion, but passages from St. Paul and from the Book of Revelation were among her favorite quotations.

Emily Dickinson's familiarity with the Bible was an inescapable consequence of her New England upbringing, but her highly individual fashion of using Biblical material shows that she was dexterous in eluding the merely formal elements in her background. Whatever was vital, positive, and militant in the New England tradition she absorbed and intensified. The nerveless she discarded, regardless of its reputation. She cared for no scriptures unless they were permeated with truth; if they had that supreme quality it did not matter whether the author were God, Moses, Shakespeare, or Thomas Wentworth Higginson. To the last named she wrote: "That it is true, Master, is the power of all you write. Could it cease to be romance, it would be revelation, which is the seed of romance." In her passion for veracity Emily Dickinson was a Puritan of Puritans. If she was unable to accept the traditional Puritan belief in the verbal inspiration of the Bible, it was for the most Puritan of reasons.

Before proceeding to examine her criterion of absolute truth, let us remark her attitude toward truth in its secondary or particular manifestations. She loved the concrete fact. It satisfied her desire for certainties. Faith she considered a "fine invention" for those who are not in difficulty:

> But microscopes are prudent
> In an emergency!

Life would be a precarious wager were it not that nature employs a fact to visit us now and then. This reverence for the definite and the inescapable verity is reflected in a large number of Emily's poems. It gave her an æsthetic pleasure to get the bloom upon the mountain accurately stated or the efflorescence of a sunset reproduced in words. She enjoyed catching the bee and the humming-bird in a net of rhymes. She might have modified Whitman's boast to read: Who touches this poem touches a fact. Her emphasis on the small particular truth brings her near to the center of the Puritan tradition in literature.

Milton's epics are not, as is sometimes supposed, typical of that tradition. Their splendor tends to obscure the homelier and historically more significant aspects of Puritan writing. In literary idiom *Paradise Lost* and *Paradise Regained* are more closely related to the *Æneid* and the *Commedia* than to the kinds of literature brought into being by the spirit of the age. Æsthetically Milton turned back the clock. But men now forgotten were setting it forward by finding modes of expression that suited contemporary needs. The Puritans were essentially plain people with hard-headed, middle-class interests. What they asked of secular books was not inspiration and the ennoblement of life, but instruction and information. Poetry they could approve as a pointed method of communicating useful doctrine, but for drama and romance they had no manner of use. Sermons, political tracts, news-letters, journals, histories, travels, these they understood and valued for their practical use. In the new literature of utility the Dream was dethroned in favor of the Fact.

In coming to the American wilderness the New England colonists turned their backs on the tradition of courtly poetry. Hakluyt's *Principal Voyages*, not because it was a prose-epic of maritime adventure but because it was crammed with helpful facts, and Sylvester's translation of Du Bartas's *Week*, not because it was poetry but because its doctrine was sound, crossed the Atlantic. Spenser's *Faërie Queene*, for all its patriotic and Protestant bias, remained at home. The whole fabric of lofty romance,

> Le donne, i cavallier, l'arme, gli amori,
> Le cortesie, l'audaci imprese,

faded at once in the hard American sunlight. The attention of the colonists was necessarily focused on mundane and useful things, not without satisfaction.

> All sorts of roots and herbs in gardens grow,
> Parsnips, carrots, turnips, or what you'll sow,
> Onions, melons, cucumbers, radishes,
> Skirets, beets, coleworts, and fair cabbages.

Thus in a sturdy but limping bucolic Governor William Bradford of Plymouth celebrated the grain, vegetables, fruits, flowers, and cattle of the New World plantations, ticking them off on his fingers. Fair cabbages were more to the point than fair ladies. Two centuries were to elapse before arms and the man, exemplified by Miles Standish, could be revived by the reminiscent Longfellow. But still the earth sang to Emerson much the same tune that it had sung to Bradford:

> Bulkeley, Hunt, Willard, Hosmer, Meriam, Flint,
> Possessed the land which rendered to their toil
> Hay, corn, roots, hemp, flax, apples, wool and wood.

And a later New England poet was to make finally articulate the æsthetic appeal of truth in the homely, slighted, material fact:

> Anything more than the truth would have seemed too weak
> To the earnest love that laid the swale in rows,
> Not without feeble-pointed spikes of flowers
> (Pale orchises), and scared a bright green snake.
> The fact is the sweetest dream that labor knows.

But poetry is chronically slow to adopt new modes of æsthetic feeling. The utility of fact was only too apparent, but it smacked of the sordid. It was long before a sense of that utility as a species of beauty could find poetic expression. Meanwhile the preference for sheer utility was giving rise to some unlovely manifestations. Several generations of looking at little but the bare, unpoetized facts of pioneer experience transformed the New Englander into a small man of affairs, with an abnormally developed bump of ingenuity for dealing with practical issues.

He had no time to waste on poetry, which indeed he was right in thinking had lost connection with what vitally concerned him. The Bible, the almanac, and the newspaper comprised his staple reading. Truth, in the most literal and narrow sense, had come into its own. The ground was prepared for the extraordinary extension and application of physical science which nineteenth-century America was to witness. It looked as though poetry had no further function; the facts that the world valued could be better expressed in scientific idiom.

Two courses remained open to poets. They could, remembering poetry's former glory, wring their hands at its neglect and wonder what to make of a diminished thing. Or they could absorb the spirit of the age and stumblingly at best attempt to create an æsthetic to match it. The latter course, somewhat bumptiously formulated, was Walt Whitman's program:

> What is this you bring my America?
> Is it uniform with my country? . . .
> Does it not assume that what is notoriously gone is still here? . . .
> Can your performance face the open fields and the seaside? . . .
> Does it meet modern discoveries, facts, face to face?

Emily Dickinson with entire unconsciousneess contributed to the same result. She was very much a child of the age and she was also an instinctive artist; it was her business to find forms of expression that did not blur her sharp awareness of fact nor fail to rouse a latent beauty. Her poems were demonstrations that the simplest commonplaces of life in practical America could be vitalized and made precious to the mind.

Others besides Whitman had proposed that poems be tested by their power to meet modern discoveries face to face, and had received an indifferent answer. To conventionally minded writers the machine age brought nothing that they could assimilate. They preferred to ignore it or to recognize it only in protest. Thoreau, it is true, could take a dreamy pleasure in the hum of telegraph wires, the aeolian harp of industry, but he balked at the Atlantic cable. Whitman's voracious chants swallowed the cable—

> The seas inlaid with eloquent gentle wires—

and even sought an imaginative hold on "the strong light works of engineers," the Suez Canal and the transcontinental railroad. But his recitative faltered before the locomotive:

> Type of the modern—emblem of motion and power—pulse of the continent,
> For once come serve the Muse and merge in verse, even as here I see thee.

The invitation was not accepted. "To a Locomotive in Winter" is as lifeless as any seventeenth-century poet's itemized list of his mistress's charms. Emily Dickinson, on the contrary, wrote as simply and directly of the locomotive as of any bird in her garden. The Amherst & Belchertown Railroad, her father's darling project, gave her a new fact to tell, and her poem sparkles with her pleasure in telling it.

> I like to see it lap the miles,
> And lick the valleys up,
> And stop to feed itself at tanks;
> And then, prodigious, step
>
> Around a pile of mountains,
> And, supercilious, peer
> In shanties by the sides of roads;
> .   .   .   .   .   .
>
> Then chase itself down hill
>
> And neigh like Boanerges;
> Then, punctual as a star,
> Stop—docile and omnipotent—
> At its own stable door.

"Your true poet," says Santayana through one of his characters, "catches the charm of something or anything, dropping the thing itself." The last four words are profoundly important. They help to explain why poets in the New England tradition were well equipped to deal poetically with material fact. The born Puritan could make the outward world his plaything. He was never immersed so completely in externalities as to be unaware of a second set of facts, the data of consciousness, which often corresponded with physical facts but might on occasion diverge from them. These inward awarenesses were more real than tangible things and deserved a sharper scrutiny. Under compulsion of the Calvinistic doctrine of election the Puritan was trained to search his heart for daily evidences of God's saving grace. A precise terminology described the successive states of mind leading to the climactic experience of oneness with God, and the stages of falling from grace were equally well defined. At its most complete development the New England temperament achieved an almost perfect doubleness. The technique of introspection was carried to amazing lengths by Jonathan Edwards, who traced the natural history of the will and the religious affections with the same minute accuracy that he had shown in his early notes on the habits of the flying spider. In some degree nearly every typical Yankee possessed a shrewd ability to objectify and analyze his subtlest inward feelings. Moreover the motions of consciousness were never regarded as controlled by outward circumstance. The Puritan was no behaviorist. For him the mind was its own place, and in alliance with infinite power could surmount any tangible obstacles. "There is no object that we see," wrote Mistress Anne Bradstreet in the first article of her *Meditations*, "no action that we doe; no good that we injoy; no evill that we feele, or fear, but we may make some spirituall advantage of all."

In the power to make good come out of evil, as Professor Samuel Eliot Morison has acutely observed, the genius of Anne Bradstreet was reincarnated in Emily Dickinson. The earlier Puritan, it is true, was apt to turn her experiences to religious advantage while Emily turned hers to account in her poetry, but it was not necessary for either to shut her eyes to disaster. A finer strategy lay in facing it—and turning its flank.

> If your Soul see-saw,
> Lift the Flesh door,—
> The Poltroon wants oxygen—
> Nothing more.

Emily inherited in full measure the Puritan talent for psychic reconnaissance. Many of her poems read like clinical observations of states of consciousness. She was ceaselessly occupied in discriminating among her perceptions. If a casual thought "went up her mind," she took its fingerprints so that she could identify it when it came again. Ideas took the form of distinct entities: "Hope is a subtle glutton"; "Remembrance has a rear and front." Soon the theatre of her mind was equipped with properties and peopled with dramatic figures. But the play she watched so intently was not "the tragedy 'Man'," as the haunted brain of Poe conceived it, but a personal version of the soul's invincible "Pilgrim's Progress."

Emily could trust in her own soul, but in what else could she trust? Intense religious feelings and flashes of illumination were not equivalent to settled religious convictions. She was not a systematic thinker. The spiderwebs of Calvinistic theology did not concern her. The doctrinal sermons that she heard in girlhood did little more than give her a theological vocabulary, so that when she used such technical terms as *predestination, justification, election,* and *grace* in her poems, she used them understandingly, albeit sometimes with a mischievous twist. For the rest she made eclectic choice of such doctrines as pleased her and jettisoned those that did not. In her attitude toward sin, for example, she was thoroughly unorthodox. Apparently she hardly ever used the word; it was repugnant to her to think of human nature as "sown in corruption." Minatory sermons troubled her, but the God of wrath was not her God. She hated to have divine Love made "to seem like bears." The God who sometimes visited her came as an "old neighbor." His residence was not far from hers. Unfortunately He was often out.

At the moment when Emily came into her maturity, confidence in the truth of revelation, though still formally affirmed, had become hollow at the core. Though the fabric of Puritan belief seemed as unshakable as ever, its foundations were sapped. She detected and distrusted the insincerity of conventional formulas. If the Rock of Ages was crumbling into incoherent sand, she was too realistic to put any weight on it. The need of a faith, however, was still strong in her. In certain moods she leaned eager-eyed toward heaven; in others she became frankly skeptical and derisive. As some one has charmingly put it, she delighted in being alternately God's child and God's little rascal. I must leave it to others to discern in the pages of Anne Bradstreet even "the merest hint of that elfin, almost *gamin* attitude of Emily Dickinson to God." One would not expect to find it there. To a devout Puritan matron of the seventeenth century such an attitude would have appeared little less than monstrous. But in Emily it was a natural response to the waning validity of what she had been taught to consider the ultimate source of truth.

The New England mind, however, held with great tenacity to the corollaries of its failing convictions. Certain habits of thought long ingrained in Puritan culture retained their integrity. If the old mystic quest beyond the verge of consciousness to the feet of the Almighty was tacitly abandoned in favor of a transcendental tour of man's mental and moral nature, the explorers still expected to find oneness at the heart of things. Nature, if not God, might supply a principle of unity. Widely as the formal thinking of Jonathan Edwards differed from that of Emerson, the two men were in substantial agreement in what may be called the poetic overtones of their philosophy. Both were moralists who were led by an experience of inward sweetness to state their concept of true virtue in æsthetic terms. To

Edwards the essential quality of being lay in harmonious relationships, and fullness of being or God consisted of an infinite
"consenting together" of parts. No separate thing could exist
except in its relationship to other things; in isolation it would
have neither excellence nor reality. What we discern in particular
beings as beauty or virtue does not inhere in their particularity,
but arises from the harmony of their parts, or of the whole with
other beings, or of the whole with the sum of being. Beauty is
therefore a function of relationship, a kind of nimbus that
crowns what Edwards calls the "consent" of being to being.
Emerson likewise affirms: "Nothing is quite beautiful alone;
nothing but is beautiful in the whole. A single object is only so
far beautiful as it suggests this universal grace."

A sense of beauty less in things themselves than in their
cosmic relationships was the dynamic of much New England
poetry. It implied the blending on an ideal plane of truth,
goodness, and beauty, a blending that might be too much
presumed upon by didactic writers. The identifications of truth
with God and of truth with beauty are explicit in Emily Dickinson. In one of her earliest poems she declares:

> Truth is as old as God,
> His twin identity—
> And will endure as long as He,
> A co-eternity,
> And perish on the day
> That He is borne away
> From mansion of the universe,
> A lifeless Deity.

Not less emphatically than Keats she asserts the kinship of
beauty and truth in a poem that takes the odd form of a conversation between two persons lying side by side in their graves:

> He questioned softly why I failed?
> "For beauty," I replied.
> "And I for truth,—the two are one;
> We brethren are," he said.

And so as kinsmen met a night,
We talked between the rooms,
Until the moss had reached our lips,
And covered up our names.

"Candor," she wrote to Higginson, "is the only wile." It was
certainly the chief reliance of her art. Truth to fact, sincerity of
conviction, honesty of expression, these might constitute if they
would the beauty of her verse. At least she would begin with
integrity. "As for graces of expression," she might have said
with Thoreau, "a great thought is never found in a mean dress."
Nevertheless she took some pains to see that her thoughts were
daintily clothed.

In the technical details of her poetry she was as native as a
blueberry. She did not, like Helen Hunt, experiment with novel
and intricate verse forms, but confined herself almost entirely
to the simplest hymn-meters familiar to her from early childhood, particularly to the so-called "short" and "common" measures. These she modulated to suit the rhythms of a wide variety
of moods. The controlling principle of her technique was a
severe economy of means to ends. Whatever else her poems
might be or fail to be, they were dictated by a clear sense of
architectonic values, as far as these may be exhibited within the
small compass of a lyric. She responded most intensely to the
type of beauty that Edwards defined as "the visible fitness of a
thing to its use," a type "not entirely different from that beauty
which there is in fitting a mortise to its tenon." In other words,
she translated into poetry the instinct for sound craftsmanship
in things of use evidenced by colonial silverware and clock-cases,
New England doorways and fireplaces, and Yankee sailing
ships. She never expanded or elaborated her poems. In the few
cases where we have two versions of the same lyric, the later
version is invariably condensed.

Moreover, though the idiom of her poetry is sometimes personal to the point of oddity, it is not bookish or artificial. It

reproduces as far as is possible in verse the qualities of New England speech, laconic brevity, directness, cadence. Fond as her contemporaries were of oratory, they did not lavish their admiration on ornamental discourse. Speech to them was a useful art and a form of action; its highest manifestation consisted of "speaking to the point." The Reverend Aaron M. Colton, a minister beloved of his people, to whose sermons Emily Dickinson listened Sunday after Sunday in her teens, has left us a characterization of a gifted speaker, his father, which reads throughout like an analysis of Emily's own style:

His words were well chosen and few, and were uttered with a deliberate impressiveness seldom equalled. . . . He had a keen ear for discrimination of sounds, not in music only, but in speech as well. His modulations and cadences, in speaking and reading, were well-nigh perfect. He insisted that a fine cadence is a positive beauty and power. . . . His outward ear and his inner ear caught the most delicate shades of tone. . . . The most marked feature in his speech was its brevity, unless I should except the singular precision with which he hit just the idea he wished to convey. You never had to ask him to *repeat* a remark, that you might better understand it. He went straight to the point, and set it in sunlight. What he could not make clear, he would not essay. . . . One who knew him well, testifies of him, that "whenever he spoke, whether in church meeting or in assembly, he showed a wonderful talent of compression—of saying much in fewest words, and of stopping at the right point, which he soon reached."

When speech was wrung from Emily's friends and neighbors, their habit was to say what they meant in the shortest terms. Meanwhile their ears were keen to catch the slightest innuendo of a cadence. She absorbed their reverence for words that cut exactly to the line. She learned from daily practice to appreciate the overtones that vibrate in understatement, and to love a phrase with a neat turn of wit. She too knew that

Capacity to terminate
Is a specific grace.

And all her life she was trying to go straight to the point and "set it in sunlight." To know if she told it clear was the boon she asked of Higginson.

But let no one suppose that New Englanders were insensitive to verbal music. The reverse was true, only they did not care for melody divested of meaning. Their taste was formed on the best of models, the King James Bible. When majesty of substance was combined with beauty of utterance, they cherished the felicity of words as they cherished flowers. Deacon Colton, who spoke with habitual dry precision, expanded when he read aloud. "Some of the grand periods of the rich old Saxon, in the Psalms and in Isaiah, as touched by his voice, would come out with a melody and flow, like the sublime strains of the old masters in music. . . . The words were given out from his lips 'as beautiful coins newly issued from the mint, deeply and accurately impressed, perfectly finished, neatly struck by the proper organs, distinct, in due succession and of due weight.' " Emily Dickinson, though she preferred her daily household frock, had her singing robes also and could on occasion write pure lyrics that like her bobolink

> Carolled and mused and carolled,
> Then bubbled slow away.

Though she was conscious that her poetry emanated from ways of thinking and feeling and speaking that were characteristic of a region, she did not seek to emancipate herself from provincial traits. The whole duty of a New England poet was to realize as fully as might be the possibilities of beauty implicit in the New England tradition.

> The Robin's my criterion of tune
> Because I grow where robins do. . . .
> The Buttercup's my whim for bloom
> Because we're orchard-sprung. . . .
> Without the snow's tableau
> Winter were lie to me—
> Because I see New Englandly.

Since it was the habit of her people to admire intrinsic work-manship, she built her poems from the inside outward, follow-ing closely the form implicit in her thought. Her procedure was thus directly opposite to that of Poe, if it is conceivable that he deduced his poems from a predetermined notion of the effect he wished to obtain. His doctrine of effect, if she had ever en-countered it, would have seemed to her meretricious, as though poetry were no more than a species of stage-lighting. Nor could she recognize any such antinomy between beauty and truth as that which formed a cardinal principle in Poe's philosophy of composition. The sense of life that she expressed emphasized the oneness of all being. To talk of Supernal Beauty as though it could be isolated from other human considerations and art-fully manufactured in small packages was, if not entirely mean-ingless, a contradiction of all that gave beauty its value. Even the handful of flawless lyrics that Poe could offer in extenuation of his theory did not carry conviction. Though she must have read some of his pieces when they were reprinted in *The Spring-field Republican,* she could say in 1879: "Of Poe, I know too little to think,"—which does not sound as though she were eager to know more. She could not conceive of any one creating beauty by calculation. Beauty exists; it is not caused. Pursue it with conscious intent and it is sure to vanish:

> Overtake the creases
>
> In the meadow when the wind
> Runs his fingers thro' it?
> Deity will see to it
> That you never do it.

The loveliness of a Chinese junk with richly carved and painted stern, as Professor Gilbert Murray has remarked, is not of the same order as the loveliness of a racing yacht in swift evolution. It is not my intention to suggest that Poe would have been a sounder writer if he had been actually the "Bostonian" that he once labelled himself, nor that Emily Dickinson would have been a finer poet if she had been less a New Englander. The point is that she did not attempt to be anything but herself, and that in fulfilling the law of her own being she was expressing the essential qualities of a New England mind. From the dryness and didacticism that sometimes afflicted the poetry of the region she was saved in the first instance by her own vivid intensity. But her early efforts to write humorous prose and verse, and her contact with a native strain of American humor, were likewise not without effect in confirming the vivacity of her style.

American Humor

Next in importance to the Bible in determining the mental climate of Emily Dickinson's formative years was *The Springfield Republican*. The four-page weekly (later daily) of the 1840's was more than a purveyor of news. It was an epitome of the region, an organ of indigenous opinion, proud to bear the stamp of its locality. Besides reporting national and foreign events, it covered the happenings in near-by towns with uncommon fullness, commented on their agricultural and industrial progress, and retold their history and legend. It gave constant and loving recognition to the beauties of rural scenery through all the changes of the seasons. Its columns were open to local poets and story-writers. In many Connecticut Valley households it enjoyed an authority almost equal to that of the Scriptures. Though its owner and editor was a Unitarian and a liberal, he knew how to identify himself with the plain people.

The Republican was the lengthened shadow of a single man, the second Samuel Bowles, who gave his lifeblood to the paper his father had founded in 1824. It was his one consuming interest. His vivid personality completely dominated every member of its small staff, with the exception of the associate editor, Doctor Holland, whose confirmed vein of sentiment and gentle piety could not be enlivened. Bowles supervised every aspect of the paper, writing editorials, preparing copy, reading proofs. He was remorseless in his war on excess verbiage. "Put it all in the first sentence," was his favorite admonition. Editorials must be condensed to paragraphs, paragraphs to two-line items. He had no use for phrases that did not "make a hole in the target." *The Republican* became famous for epigrammatic sentences that snapped like a whip and sometimes cut like a knife. The style of its editorials often smacked racily of the soil, for Bowles loved the vigorous vernacular and could coin pithy phrases with any Yankee farmer.

Once for six months Bowles tried journalism in Boston, but it would not do. He was the product of a region and was born to be its spokesman. Under his handling *The Springfield Republican* became the best-known provincial newspaper in the United States.

Like every other local paper *The Republican* provided entertainment for its readers, not merely by reprinting poems, stories, and "selections" by such recognized authors as Irving, Bryant, Poe, Longfellow, Holmes, Hawthorne, Whittier, and Mrs. Stowe, but also by tapping whatever veins of humorous writing were then current. "Mrs. Caudle's Curtain Lectures" by Douglas Jerrold, for example, were copied as fast as the numbers of *Punch* arrived. Bowles was likewise aware of the rich resources of American frontier humor. He read the New York *Spirit of the Times,* which was a magazine of such material, and recommended it editorially to his readers. On occasion he chose a racy bit for his own columns. In skimming through the file for the early 1840's I have noted a typical specimen of Southern humor from the pen of Johnson J. Hooper, editor of *The East Alabamian* and author of the popular *Adventures of Simon Suggs,* a chapter from William T. Thompson's *Major Jones's Courtship,* and the perennially recurrent yarn of "Cousin Sally Dilliard." From New England sources came "Major Jack Downing" letters by Seba Smith or one of his many imitators, burlesque interviews with the ballerina Fanny Elssler by "Jonathan Slick," and jocose realistic sketches of odd characters and local customs, such as "Josiah Baker. His Turkies and his Sweetheart" and "A Military Muster Down East," the last copied from *The Yankee Blade* of Gardiner, Maine. It is not true, as Franklin J. Meine has claimed, that the early humor of the South had no counterpart in the humor of any other section of the United States. We may concede the easy preeminence of the Southern and Southwestern frontier in this type of writing, but the same sort of thing was being ephemerally produced by New England journalists.

This native humor, both North and South, depended in part on a somewhat exaggerated but realistic observation of character, in part on fantastic incident of the "tall story" variety, and in part on verbal extravagance and surprise. All three may be illustrated in brief in a paragraph which made the front page of *The Republican* in 1845:

A Secret.—"How do you do, Mrs. Tome, have you heard that story about Mrs. Ludy?" "Why, no, really, Mrs. Gad, what is it—do tell?" "O, I promised not to tell for all the world! No, I must never tell on't, I'm afraid it will git out." "Why, I'll never tell on't as long as I live, just as true as the world; what is it, come, tell?" "Now you won't say anything about it, will you?"—"No, I'll never open my head about it—never. Hope to die this minute." "Well, if you'll believe me, Mrs. Funday told me last night, that Mrs. Trot told her that her sister's husband was told by a person who dreamed it, that Mrs. Troubles oldest daughter told Mrs. Nichens that her grandmother heard by a letter that she got from her third sister's second husband's oldest brother's step-daughter, that it was reported by the captain of a clam-boat just arrived from the Feejee Islands, that the mermaids about that section wore sharkskin bustles stuffed with pickled eels toes!"

An excerpt from one of "Dow's Patent Sermons," reprinted in the following year, characterized a mean man as one who would "chase a fat mosquito through a five-mile swamp, for the sake of his suet," and an avaricious man as one who "if he had the power and could enrich himself thereby, would brush the silver stars from the firmament, snatch the golden sun from the sky and sell the moon for brass."

Emily Dickinson, like young Samuel L. Clemens, who was five years her junior, not only read such passages, but as we shall see attempted in her earliest writing to imitate them. The current newspaper humor of her girlhood, though no one thought of it as having any literary significance, was not branded as vulgar. It was only after the Civil War had swelled the output to a roily flood that it began to be associated with barrooms and barbershops. Once it was labelled "low" the best people avoided it. Higginson, for example, had never heard of Mark Twain's "Jumping Frog" until it was brought to his attention in 1872 by Charles Darwin. Emily probably read the chapters of "Old Times on the Mississippi" that appeared in *The Atlantic,* but none of her published letters contain any reference to Mark Twain's books.

Yet a very mild precursor of *Innocents Abroad* was written by a member of her own Amherst circle and originally printed in the form of travel letters in *The Republican.* The book was called *Mr. Dunn Browne's Experiences in Foreign Parts* (1857), and its author, Samuel Fiske, had been a student in Amherst Academy and had graduated from the College in 1848. After teaching school and studying at Andover, he returned to Amherst College as a tutor from 1852 to 1855. He was a member of Austin Dickinson's fraternity, and his sister Rebecca Fiske was the leader of Emily's "section" at Mount Holyoke. Samuel Fiske, therefore, must have been well known in the Dickinson family.

Professor W. S. Tyler in a biographical notice prefixed to Fiske's second and posthumous book, *Mr. Dunn Browne's Experiences in the Army* (1866), speaks of him as follows:

He was a genuine son of New England. Strong common sense, Yankee tact, shrewdness and thrift, downright honesty and plainness of speech and manners, inexhaustible versatility and fertility in expedients, formed the solid basis of his character. To these were added those more brilliant and dazzling qualities, rapidity of thought, readiness of expression, fine conversational powers, genuine mother wit, spontaneous and irresistible mirthfulness, and a fancy which reveled in puns and incongruities.

It was not then considered an incongruity that "one of the most racy, witty, and spicy of all our newspaper correspondents" should be a Congregational minister, though that was Fiske's calling. The "Dunn Browne" books came too late to serve as direct models for Emily Dickinson, but they may be used to illustrate the kind of humorous writing that was greatly admired at the time.

The disillusioned spirit in which Fiske surveyed the monuments, scenery, people, and manners of Europe and the Holy Land was not strikingly different from that of the chronicler of the *Quaker City* excursion, and like Mark Twain he was able to combine an agreeable rattle of badinage and humorous effects with factual observations of rapidly changing scenes. His intention, as stated in the introductory epistle, was "to contemplate the institutions of the Old World with the eye of a philosopher, to behold her ancient ruins with the eye of an antiquary, to view the grand objects of nature with a poet's eye and the great works of the old masters with an artist's eye, . . . in short, to keep wide open my eye financial, agricultural, commercial, architectural, legal, critical, metaphysical and quizzical. I shall also take a bird's eye view of the feathered tribes, cast a sheep's eye at the flocks and herds, and obtain dissolving views of the beet sugar crop and salt mines. . . . But I will not victim-*eyes* you any longer with this train of *eye*-deas." Once under way, his faculty for punning yields to realistic and sprightly particularization. "A lurch of the ship sent three cups of coffee, two men, (one of whom was *not* your humble servant, the other *was*,) one bowl of sugar, a woman and a baby, three plates of ham, one hair brush, six roasted potatoes, a jar of

pickles, and a wash basin of water with a soapy boy in it, all
into a corner of the cabin together." He indulges in a burlesque
rhapsody on the view from the summit of the Rigi, only to
remark at the end: "Dear me! I am not at all certain I could
have written you so poetical a description if it were not for the
clouds and mists that have concealed the reality from my
view." Customs' officials, beggars, and fleas are never long
forgotten. The "miserable, sloppy, dirty Swiss glaciers" are
not to be compared with the beauty of icebergs. "I had always
associated icebergs and glaciers together in my mind, but they
are no more alike than clean linen to dirty linen, or a boy
that has been eating molasses candy and the same boy after
his face has been washed." All the ruins of Rome, with one or
two exceptions, "aren't worth an old brick-kiln," and were it
not for the guide-books this undoubted fact would be more
generally acknowledged. Occasional bits of ironic understatement foreshadow some of Mark Twain's best effects: "The
Pope himself was borne on men's shoulders, kneeling on a
cushion before a little table on which stood a crucifix of gold,
his hands clasped as if in prayer. He is a good and venerable
looking man, and an ornament to any procession." Of all Mr.
Dunn Browne's battery of humorous devices, however, the trick
of ingenious and unforeseen verbal combinations most appealed
to Emily Dickinson. It was the unfailing resource of a young
wit.

According to her schoolmate Emily Fowler Ford, Emily
Dickinson began as a humorist. She was one of a group of
girls in Amherst Academy that started a manuscript magazine
known as *Forest Leaves,* which was kept up for two years.
Mrs. Ford's reminiscences are too confused to permit an exact
dating of the period when this venture in writing took place,
but what she says of the nature of Emily's work is probably
accurate and is of considerable interest:

Emily Dickinson and Mary Humphrey were the wits of the school, and the humorists of the "comic column." . . . Emily's contributions were often in the style of a funny little sermon, long since vanished, which went the rounds in the newspapers for two years and was recited from Lyceum platforms and declaimed in village schools, from this text: "He played on a harp of a thousand strings, sperrets of just men made perfec'," the art of which consisted in bringing most incongruous things together, such as . . . samphire and camphire (camphor); . . . ending always with the same refrain, "He played on a harp of a thousand strings, sperrets of just men made perfec'." Emily's combinations were irresistible, but I cannot recall them now. One bit was stolen by a roguish editor for the College paper, where her touch was instantly recognized; and there were two paragraphs in *The Springfield Republican.*

Burlesque sermons became a popular form of American humor as early as 1840, when "Dow's Patent Sermons" began to appear in *The New York Sunday Mercury.* Emily Dickinson's model, which seems not to have been previously recognized, was William P. Brannan's "The Harp of a Thousand Strings," which was reprinted in *The Spirit of the Times* for September 29, 1855, but was unquestionably in circulation before that date. A short extract from Brannan's travesty of the frontier sermon will illustrate the qualities that Mrs. Ford mentions:

My tex, brethren, leads me to speak uv sperits. Now thar's many kind of sperits in the world—in the fust place, thar's the sperits as some folks call ghosts; then thar's the sperits uv turpen*time;* and then thar's the sperits as some folks call liquor, and I've got as good artikel uv them kind uv sperits on my flat-boat as ever was fotched down the Mississippi River; but thar's a great many other kind of sperits, for the tex says: "He played on a harp uv a *thou*-sand strings—sperits of just men made perfeck."

But I'll tell you the kind of sperits as is ment in the tex: it's *fire.* That is the kind of sperits as is ment in the tex, my brethering. Now thar's a great many kinds of fire in the world. In the fust place, thar's the common sort uv fire you light a segar or pipe with, and then thar's camfire, fire before you're ready to fall back, and many other kinds uv fire, for the tex says: "He played on a harp uv a *thou*-sand strings—sperits uv just men made perfeck."

But I'll tell you the kind of fire as is ment in the tex, my brethering —it's *hell-fire!* an' that's the kind of fire as a great many of you'll come to, ef you don't do better nor what you have bin doin'—for "He played on a harp uv a *thou*-sand strings—sperits of just men made perfeck."

Conceivably the funny stories that Emily is said to have improvised for the amusement of her friends at Mount Holyoke Seminary may have been of this kind, with Yankee locutions substituted for the dialect of Pike County. No Connecticut Valley attic has yet given up the copies of *Forest Leaves* that may be there awaiting discovery, and in spite of painful search the two paragraphs in *The Springfield Republican* have not been identified. But the loss is not serious, since several specimens of Emily Dickinson's early humorous writing, both in prose and in verse, have survived. They are marked by sheer effervescence of high spirits, the fun consisting of an extraordinary mixture of seeming relevancy and irrelevancy, an unexpected conjunction of phrases in different keys, and a rapid invention of incongruous particulars. The earliest in date is interesting both for its style, and for the internal evidence that Emily was familiar with Douglas Jerrold's Mrs. Caudle and B. P. Shillaber's Mrs. Partington, the latter a kind of Yankee Mrs. Malaprop. She is here writing a mock-tirade to reproach her uncle Joel Norcross for his failure to write to her. After picturing the delinquent's fate in the form of a vision, she continues:

Do you take any hints, I wonder? Can you guess the meaning of things, not yet aroused to the truth? You villain without a rival, unparalleled doer of crimes, scoundrel unheard of before, disturber of public peace, "creation's blot and blank," state's prison filler, *magnum bonum* promise maker, harum scarum promise breaker—oh, what can I call you more? Mrs. Caudle would call you a "gentleman," that is altogether too good. Mrs. Partington, "a very fine fellow," neither does this apply. I call upon all nature to lay hold of you, let fire burn, and water drown, and light put out, and tempests tear, and hungry wolves cut up, and lightning strike, and thunder stun, let friends desert, and enemies draw nigh, and gibbets *shake* but never *hang* the house you walk about in! My benison not touch, my malison pursue the body that holds your spirit! Any other afflictions which now slip my mind shall be looked up and forwarded to you immediately.

Extravagant combinations of phrases and ideas formed the humor of the valentines of the 1850's, which were not bought at the local stationery store but composed by the sender. Emily Dickinson's were noteworthy for their extreme ingenuity. The quizzing letter that she sent to her brother's classmate George Gould on Valentine Eve, 1850, and which he in retaliation instantly printed in the college paper, opens with a salvo of nonsense tags, and after demanding an interview in high-flown terms, goes on:

This is strong language, sir, but none the less true. So hurrah for North Carolina, since we are on this point.

Our friendship, sir, shall endure till sun and moon shall wane no more, till stars shall set, and victims rise to grace the final sacrifice. We'll be instant, in season, out of season, minister, take care of, cherish, sooth, watch, wait, doubt, refrain, reform, elevate, instruct. All choice spirits however distant are ours, ours theirs; there is a thrill of sympathy—a circulation of mutuality—cognationem inter nos! I am Judith the heroine of Apocrypha, and you the orator of Ephesus. . . .

But the world is sleeping in ignorance and error, sir, and we must be crowing-cocks, and singing-larks, and a rising sun to awake her; or else we'll pull society up to the roots, and plant it in a different place. We'll build Alms houses and transcendental State prisons, and scaffolds—we will blow out the sun and the moon, and encourage invention. Alpha shall kiss Omega—we will ride up the hill of glory—Hallelujah, all hail!

Not only were scraps of eloquence and poetry swept up in the excitement of composition as by a whirlwind, but the language tended to fall into metrical patterns. One notes the probably unconscious verse embedded in the passage just quoted:

> Our friendship, sir, shall endure
> Till sun and moon shall wane no more,
> Till stars shall set, and victims rise
> To grace the final sacrifice.

Her 1851 valentine to Mr. Bowdoin, her father's partner, runs even more directly into verse:

I weave for the lamp of evening, but fairer colors than mine are twined while stars are shining.

I know of a shuttle swift, I know of a fairy gift, mat for the "lamp of life," the little bachelor's wife!!

The following year for William Howland, a fledgling lawyer in Springfield and former tutor in Amherst College, she spun her drollery in regular stanza form:

> *Sic transit gloria mundi,*
> How doth the busy bee—
> *Dum vivimus vivamus,*
> I stay mine enemy.
>
> .　　.　　.　　.　　.　　.
>
> Unto the Legislature
> My country bids me go.
> I'll take my india-rubbers,
> In case the wind should blow.
>
> .　　.　　.　　.　　.　　.
>
> In token of our friendship
> Accept this *Bonnie Doon,*
> And when the hand that plucked it
> Has passed beyond the moon,
>
> The memory of my ashes
> Will consolation be.
> Then farewell, Tuscarora,
> And farewell, sir, to thee.

An unnamed friend betrayed Emily into print by sending this nonsense production to *The Springfield Republican,* where it appeared in the issue of February 20, 1852, beneath an editorial headnote which intimated that further contributions from the same hand would be welcomed. Emily, it is needless to say, did not avail herself of the invitation. Quite possibly Howland himself hoped to startle his unwary correspondent by arranging for the appearance of her lines in the newspaper that she constantly read. Gould had followed these tactics when he printed Emily's valentine to himself with the bantering comment: "The author, however, has not (it is plain to see) told the half of her feelings!" He could not have guessed that a biographer one hundred years after Emily Dickinson's birth would be tempted to take him seriously.

In the playful use of the grand manner for a trivial occasion we may recognize the beginning of that willful confounding of scale to which some of her later poems were to owe their extraordinary effect. Her mischief assumes a solemn air and her earnest borrows the garb of wit. In at least one instance her assumption of portentous language so effectively masked her banter that a poem conceived purely in fun has been mistaken for a piece of serious writing. To tease her father for his insistence on the family's early rising she strung together some stanzas of resounding nonsense, beginning:

> Sleep is supposed to be,
> By souls of sanity,
> The shutting of the eye.

> Sleep is the station grand
> Down which on either hand
> The hosts of witness stand!

The mock magniloquence of this poem was sufficiently apparent to the author and her family, but when the lines are separated from their context in actuality their tone may easily be mistaken. Emily's first editors included this piece of fooling among her poems on Time and Eternity, where it remains to this day.

The habit of combining small and great was ingrained in

Emily Dickinson to such an extent that she instinctively employed it again and again in her most serious poems. When, reversing the humorous device of using the grand to express the trivial, she projected a tremendous meaning into a homely image, she not infrequently laid herself open to the suspicion of making light of sacred things or of sporting with tender feelings. But in all probability she had no thought of being flippant. A way of speaking that might afford amusement if applied to light or indifferent subjects remained her constant manner even when she dealt with her most piercing memories and profound reflections. She was able to separate any circumstance or idea at will from the sentiment normally attached to it, and thus make available for artistic use what otherwise would shock or dazzle the mind into inarticulateness.

This power of detachment, this sense of doubleness, originally fostered by the Puritan genius for introspection, was confirmed by her early saturation in humor of the frontier type. "We make a thing humorous," says Professor Cazamian, "by expressing it with a certain twist, a queer reserve, an inappropriateness, and as it were an unconsciousness of what we all the time feel it to be." This is a perfect description of the quality that Emily acquired and practised. For the joke's sake she learned to resist the impulses of sentiment as completely as Mark Twain himself. The professional imperviousness to normal feeling evident in some of his journalistic sketches, as for example in "Cannibalism in the Cars," and in the jocular treatment of horror in general may be paralleled by bits of ruthless comedy scattered through her letters:

Who writes those funny accidents, where railroads meet each other unexpectedly, and gentlemen in factories get their heads cut off quite informally? The author, too, relates them in such a sprightly way, that they are quite attractive. Vinnie was disappointed to-night, that there were not more accidents—I read the news aloud while Vinnie was sewing.

[181]

Add to this parlor bloodthirstiness a sample of mortuary merriment:

> No one has called so far, but one old lady to look at a house. I directed her to the cemetery to spare expense of moving.

This is a side of the sensitive and tenderly sympathetic Emily that is often overlooked. In many of her serious poems we may note a similar aloofness from the emotion implied, an odd quirk of incongruous association that in a less poignant connection we should unhesitatingly recognize as wit. It was Emily Dickinson's special faculty to stand undismayed in the midst of convulsions, some unshaken particle in her consciousness ready to note with ironical detachment the reeling of the brain.

Examples are not far to seek. If she encountered a painful disillusionment, she was as apt as not to picture it as the shattering of a dish "on the stones at bottom of my mind" (54, cxviii). The momentousness of death to her imagination did not prevent her from stating the anguish of bereavement in terms of broom and dustpan (166, xxii):

> The sweeping up the heart,
> And putting love away
> We shall not want to use again
> Until eternity.

In a letter of 1860–61 to her Norcross cousins Emily echoed mischievously the routine question of the clerk behind the counter, "Is there nothing else?" Not long afterward, perhaps, this trite phrase blended in unexpected coalescence with her insistent cry, "Is God love's adversary?" Her frustration merged with glee as she contrived to exhibit an indifferent Providence in the figure of a village storekeeper:

> The mighty merchant smiled.
>
> Brazil? He twirled a button,
> Without a glance my way:

"But, madam, is there nothing else
That we can show to-day?"

And, finally, her genuine reverence could not repress her
delight when she detected an apt metaphor for "God so loved
the world that he sent his only begotten Son" in *The Courtship
of Miles Standish:*

God is a distant, stately Lover,
Woos, so He tells us, by His Son.
Surely a vicarious courtship!
Miles' and Priscilla's such a one.

To prevent any such outcome as that in Longfellow's poem,
God the Divine Lover vouches that—in terms of the metaphor
—Miles Standish and John Alden are one and the same; a
move of "hyperbolic archness" on God's part.

We need not agree with an incensed clerical reader of the
1890's who characterized this last outburst as "one of the most
offensive pieces of Unitarianism ever published." Emily was
not mocking the Trinity when she ran out the parallel; she
was too absorbed in her mind's adventure to regard the niceties
of pious sentiment. What was originally a faculty of humorous
expression was transformed in these poems and many others
into a highly individual and effective poetic idiom. To grasp
the soul at white heat she needed more than ever the tongs that
wit supplied. Complete integrity in what lay too deep for tears
was possible only by indirection. And more profoundly, the
detachment implied in a whimsical turn of mind was auxiliary
to the complete independence of stereotyped sentiments that
alone makes possible the writing of distinguished lyric poetry.

If nothing larger than a World's
Departure from a hinge,
Or Sun's extinction be observed,
'Twas not so large that I
Could lift my forehead from my work
For curiosity.

Emily felt both the arrogant self-concentration of a lyric poet and the instinct for comedy that is deeply implanted in the American nature. The latter is woven into the fabric of her poems and cannot easily be separated for analysis. It startles us in an unexpected phrase or epithet and is gone before we know it, as though a bird in flight had slightly lowered an eyelid at us. A few of her poems, however, are controlled throughout by comic intention. One of the signs is an abrupt change of key, as in "Lightly stepped a yellow star" (242, lviii), where for six lines Emily revels in a luxuriance of rippling *l*'s accompanied by the moonlight suggestiveness of such words as *silver* and *lustral*. When the poem reaches its utmost effect of artful loveliness, she drops unexpectedly into a conversational tone that lets us down with a bump. The final *l*-sound of *punctual*, echoing in a totally different context all the preceding *l*'s, knits the poem together in a "musical joke."

> All of evening softly lit
> As an astral hall—
> "Father," I observed to Heaven,
> "You are punctual."

Think for a moment of the well-known passage in *A Tramp Abroad* where Mark Twain describes an enchanting young girl at the opera, lavishing on her a rhapsody of adjectives, only to puncture the shimmering bubble of loveliness by letting her exclaim: "Auntie, I just *know* I've got five hundred fleas on me!" That in coarse terra cotta is the counterpart of what Emily wrought in porcelain. The design, abstractly considered, is the same.

Some of the broader effects of American humor could not well be displayed within the compass of a lyric, yet we find Emily Dickinson occasionally approximating them. The fantastic vein of drollery that dictated the tall stories of the frontier may be matched by cosmic dislocations that occur, though rarely, in her poems.

What if the poles should frisk about
And stand upon their heads!

In a spirit of pure fantasy she describes a visit to the ocean
which, as far as we know, had no basis except in her imagination:

I started early, took my dog,
And visited the sea;
The mermaids in the basement
Came out to look at me.

And frigates in the upper floor
Extended hempen hands,
Presuming me to be a mouse
Aground, upon the sands.

The tide that threatens to swallow her "as wholly as a dew
upon a dandelion's sleeve" pursues her back to the "solid
town"; then

bowing with a mighty look
At me, the sea withdrew.

An odd fascination in the thought of burglary tempted her
to fancy the delicious creepiness of entering an unfamiliar house
by illicit means, while every knickknack in the room seems
instinct with eyes:

How orderly the kitchen'd look by night,
With just a clock,—
But they could gag the tick,
And mice won't bark;
And so the walls don't tell,
None will.

A pair of spectacles ajar just stir—
An almanac's aware.
Was it the mat winked,
Or a nervous star?
The moon slides down the stair
To see who's there.

The strangest of her inventions, however, occurs in a poem which she calls a dream, and which might easily be susceptible of Freudian interpretation:

> In winter, in my room,
> I came upon a worm,
> Pink, lank, and warm.
> But as he was a worm
> And worms presume,
> Not quite with him at home—
> Secured him by a string
> To something neighboring,
> And went along.

The captive worm then changes into a snake, "in feature as the worm before, but ringed with power," that hisses a dreadful rejection of the dreamer's faint overtures of admiration, and

> Then, to a rhythm slim
> Secreted in his form,
> As patterns swim,
> Projected him.

Flight seems indicated, and only in a distant town does the dreamer feel safe. One suspects a parable.

Even less than the hyberbolic fantasy of the tall tale could realistic observation of character be adapted to Emily's brief measures. There is a touch of actuality about the "mighty merchant" of the poem already quoted that reminds us of the occasional brief snatches of satirical observation in her letters. But her tendency was inevitably toward a concentration that is the reverse of the slow development through minute touches that the humorous character sketch demands. When she made a sardonic portrait, it was done in a flash, a caricature drawn by a single lightning stroke. There is a small gallery of studies in detestation scattered through her work and seldom remarked: witness the inflated clergyman who "preached upon 'breadth' till it argued him narrow" (31, lxiv); the "hateful, hard,

successful face" that would feel thoroughly at ease with a stone
if they could only be thrown together (46, ci); various "muslin
souls" of her own sex (29, lx; 58, cxxx; 83, xxxii); and her
quick denunciation of whatever seemed to her insincere and
pretentious, anything resembling

> a stupendous Tomb
> Proclaiming to the gloom
> How dead we are.

Even men in the mass might be rendered in summary fashion
by the same method. The training days and Fourth of July
celebrations that were a favorite subject for genre sketches by
newspaper humorists gave Emily matter for an eight-line
epigram, beginning:

> The popular Heart is a cannon first,
> Subsequent a drum;
> Bells for an auxiliary
> And an afterward of rum. . . .

Contempt, like agony, was one of her changes of garments,
but it was not her habitual wear. Life was too intoxicating to
waste in scorn. She knew the taste of a more potent Domingo
than any tavern sold. Language at its utmost extravagance,
fantasy at its furthest reach, could not adequately express the
tingling of her pulses, but she might try what she could do in
the way of grafting an "afterward of rum" on the Book of
Revelation. And try she did:

> I taste a liquor never brewed,
> From tankards scooped in pearl;
> Not all the vats upon the Rhine
> Yield such an alcohol!
>
> Inebriate of air am I,
> And debauchee of dew,
> Reeling, through endless summer days,
> From inns of molten blue.

When landlords turn the drunken bee
Out of the foxglove's door,
When butterflies renounce their drams,
I shall but drink the more!

Till seraphs swing their snowy hats,
And saints to windows run,
To see the little tippler
Leaning against the sun!

It was not a Puritan impulse that inspired Emily Dickinson to convert the sun into a celestial lamp-post. She had absorbed into her being the essence of American humor. She was feeling in her way the electric vigor of a new nation in its young lustihood, conscious of uncommitted energies and unearmarked resources; life was an ecstasy that only an untrammelled imagination could fittingly interpret. All over America the sap was rising, stimulating a quick, rank foliation of popular humor that was soon to fall and merge with the soil, but stimulating too the finer flowering of a poet's response. There in her book is the record of an era of hopes long faded, preserved for us who breathe an air that has lost its morning freshness.

Emerson

L IBERAL ideas came slowly to the Connecticut Valley. Since the abortive protest of Shays's Rebellion shortly after the Revolution, the inhabitants had settled down to a peaceful and on the whole contented existence. They were reasonably prosperous by the standards of the time, and on the farms and in the small villages they were sheltered from the doctrinal winds that swept the seacoast. Historically they were inheritors of the Congregationalism of Connecticut, a shade more tolerant and democratic than that of Boston. No overbearing theocracy had planted a tradition of resistance among them, nor had the bustle of commerce accustomed them to innovations. Hence they remained staunchly orthodox more than a generation after Boston had welcomed the Unitarian movement, and few of the reforms that were agitating eastern Massachusetts rippled the placid communities west of Worcester. The people were early converted to the Temperance crusade, which possessed an almost religious sanction, but the unpopular cause of Abolition moved them not at all. The moral energies of the region found a sufficient outlet in the support of education at home and foreign missions abroad. A Brook Farm in the neighborhood of Amherst would have been unthinkable.

Nevertheless a mild liberalism was seeping in. It was not, like the radicalism of the present day, directed to the alleviation of intolerable economic abuses, but was rather a concomitant of the increasing economic prosperity which brought with it leisure to read and reflect and nourish new aspirations. Lyceum speakers and lecturers spread the intellectual ferment, and here and there a young man or young woman was ready to listen and respond.

Through the medium of an old diary and a letter we are enabled to catch a tantalizing glimpse of the coming to Amherst of one such apostle of new ideas. Early in 1847 the eloquent but slightly unorthodox John Lord, a prototype of the modern woman's club lecturer, gave a series of talks at the College on the history of literature. William G. Hammond attended, usually as the escort of a village belle, and wrote a long report of each lecture in his journal. There was nothing controversial to a modern reader in Professor Lord's treatment of his subject, but in his preaching he stressed a "pantheistic" note that evidently offended his more rigorous hearers. Moreover Lord had been an agent for a pacifist society and was suspected of holding advanced opinions. Professor William S. Tyler, a bedrock Puritan member of the College faculty, must have written somewhat sarcastically of Lord to a recent graduate who was teaching school in Alabama, for the young alumnus replied: "I picture to myself all the grave Prof's of Am. assembled at a transcendental poetical lecture, and I am then in a very humorous state of mind to say the least." Then he added: "Miss Emily should not be absent."

Would that he had been more explicit. We cannot be sure that he was referring to Emily Dickinson, then a girl of sixteen and Professor Tyler's near neighbor. But we know from Mrs. Ford, who was also a Miss Emily at this time, that Emily Dickinson had on an even earlier occasion manifested a strong attachment to new writers whom it was the fashion of the more conservative to ridicule. "Lowell," wrote Mrs. Ford, "was especially dear to us, and once I saw a passionate fit of crying brought on, when a tutor of the College . . . told us from his eight years of seniority, that 'Byron had a much better style,' and advised us 'to leave Lowell, Motherwell, and Emerson alone.' Like other young creatures, we were ardent partisans." The tutor of this anecdote was Henry M. Spofford, whose appointment extended from 1842 to 1845. Before she was more than fourteen, then, Emily Dickinson was known to her companions as a sympathetic reader of the new literature, and she may have been the Miss Emily whose name came at once to mind in connection with a "transcendental poetical lecture."

Unfortunately we have only a fragmentary notion of what liberal writers came within Emily's reach. Were it not for a chance allusion in one of her latest letters we should not know that she had read and caught the edge of Thoreau's social criticism. Her friend Ben Newton, as we have seen, found her at eighteen eager to accept his guidance as to what books to read, and from his recommendation of Mrs. Child's *Letters from New York* we may infer that he was prepared to indoctrinate her in the advanced thinking of the moment. Lowell in the 1840's was not the figure of respectability that he later became. He was still

> striving Parnassus to climb
> With a whole bale of *isms* tied together with rhyme,

while Mrs. Child, who had already risked a promising literary career in the cause of Abolition, was in marked sympathy with the humanitarian reforms of the day and promulgated in her writings a vague and somewhat sentimentalized Transcendentalism. Emily's brother Austin had none of his father's prejudices against the new writers, and his wife was also an alert reader. There is still in existence a copy of Margaret Fuller's translation of *Günderode* which the younger Dickinsons all read soon after its appearance, and it is safe to assume that they browsed through much else that would not have received parental approval, though no record of it has survived.

Samuel Bowles was likewise a channel whereby stimulating thoughts penetrated the Dickinson hedge. A letter from Emily to Mrs. Bowles in 1859 contains a revealing remark, the implications of which have not hitherto been realized. She wrote to thank her friend for the gift of a little book specially bound in green and gold, "the *immortal* colors." She continued: "I never read before what Mr. Parker wrote. I heard that he was 'poison.' Then I like poison very well." The little book can hardly have been anything else but Theodore Parker's *Experience as a Minister* (1859), one of the most powerful charges of intellectual dynamite ever put in print by an American.

As Emerson was the poet and visionary, Parker was the scholar and thinker among the Transcendentalists. A voracious and intemperate reader with a score of languages at his command, he had plowed and harrowed the fields of German philosophy and French social theory and had reaped therefrom a harvest of forthright, subversive ideas. He preached a religion liberated from traditional and ecclesiastical authority, a faith founded on nothing but the religious instinct in the heart of man; and in consequence was ostracized even by his colleagues in the Unitarian pulpit. He preached against the abnormal desire to accumulate property, against drunkenness, against war, against slavery; and thereby offended the vested interests of government and market-place. He was tireless in unmasking the greed, cunning, duplicity, and timidity that lurk in high places and established institutions, and gave himself prodigally to the support of all generous causes. The press yapped at his heels. Disturber of the public peace, infidel, atheist, enemy of mankind, were the mildest of the epithets hurled at him. Meanwhile, to the credit of Boston, he had earned the devoted support of a group of earnest and high-minded men and women who were willing to face the truth and who saw to it that he was not muzzled. But his enormous fund of energy was too soon exhausted. In mid-career his health broke, and he was hurried off to the

West Indies with little chance of recovery. From Santa Cruz, as soon as he had a little rallied, Parker wrote in the form of a letter to his church his *apologia pro vita sua*, reviewing his career step by step and sharpening the impact of his ultimate message. Into less than two hundred pages he packed the carefully reasoned essence of transcendental metaphysics and an epitome of humanitarian reform. If this was indeed the little book that Emily Dickinson liked very well, there was no limit to her sympathy with the contemporary spirit of free inquiry.

Moreover, there was much in Parker's character to attract her. As a farmer's son from Lexington, he was, despite his vast learning, as thoroughly provincial as she. He loved simple things, plain words, homely illustrations; the lives of the common folk about him "turned into a sort of poetry, and re-appeared in the sermons, as the green woods, not far off, looked in at the windows of the Meeting House." Most of all, he was fascinated, as Emily Dickinson was likewise, by the unplumbed mysteries of the mind:

But the Universe of Human Life, with its peculiar worlds of outer sense and inner soul, the particular faunas and floras which therein find a home, are still more complex, wonderful, and attractive; and the laws which control it seem to me more amazing than the Mathematic Principles that explain the Celestial Mechanics of the outward world. The Cosmos of Matter seems little compared to this Cosmos of immortal and progressive Man; it is my continual study, discipline and delight. Oh, that some young genius would devise the Novum Organum of Humanity, determine the Principia thereof, and with deeper than mathematic science, write out the formulas of the Human Universe, the Celestial Mechanics of Mankind.

Was not this call for a scientific observation of the workings of the inscrutable being within a confirmation of her own secret poems, a statement of her program and aim? How clearly soul spoke to kindred soul. When Parker summed up the cost of his struggle in the words: "Truth has her cradle near Golgotha," he proved his title to a rank equal to that of a Queen of

Calvary. So true it is that "monarchs are perceptible far down the dustiest road!"

Emily Dickinson did not encounter anything of Theodore Parker's until she was twenty-nine, but she had been acquainted since girlhood with a liberator of the New England mind even greater than he. In view of the striking resemblances, both in thought and style, between Emerson and Emily Dickinson, her references to him are disappointingly meager; late in life she spoke of *Representative Men* as "a little granite book," mentioned the *Life* by Holmes as "sweetly commended" (a distinction that it has since lost), and in an unpublished letter referred in passing to "The Humble-Bee." Yet we know from Mrs. Ford and from other sources that she was steeped in the *Essays,* and she owned a copy of the *Poems* endeared to her by poignant associations. Finally Emerson was more than a name attached to title-pages. He had visited Amherst several times, once even spending the night under her brother's roof. There is no direct evidence that she ever met the sage, but he could hardly have come so near without her feeling his living presence.

By the older generation the author of the "Divinity School Address" was suspected of heresies too numerous to particularize. They were not content merely to deprecate his pronouncements. Once, according to an unverified legend, when he was announced to speak in Amherst only one room in the town was at his disposal, and a union prayer-meeting was appointed in the same building and at the same hour as the lecture, in order to keep godly people away. (Let us hope that some who came to pray blundered into the prophet's chamber.) His first invitation to speak in Amherst did not come from the College authorities, but from the two undergraduate literary societies. Emerson generously accepted the small glory and smaller recompense of speaking to the young men of Amherst, as he had accepted a similar call from Williams the year before, and on August 8, 1855, he delivered the address before the Social Union which was then a regular feature of the Commencement program. His subject was "A Plea for the Scholar," a topic on which he had often spoken before college audiences. Yet his *Journals* show that he reconsidered and recast his message for the new occasion, and though the tenor of his thought was the same, its outward expression was freshly drawn from his meditation.

For Amherst. Could you show the riches of the poor? Could you shame the vain? Could you make them think common daylight was worth something?

The distinction of thought is an aristocratic distinction. Instead of dealing with raw materials, it deals with methods. And it only obtains real progression. Until we have intellectual property in a thing, we have no right property. As to first coming and finding, there were comers and finders before you, already in occupation when you came. There was the bird, and the beaver, and the buffalo, and the fox. But there were meliorations these could not reach, obstructions they could not surmount.

There follow three pages, a selection only from the copious materials assembled for the moment.

The editor of *The Hampshire and Franklin Express* could find no more fitting word for Emerson's discourse than "characteristic": "He was too comprehensive and metaphysical to be at all times easily understood." But *The New York Tribune,* which was partial to advanced thinkers, gave the performance a glowing endorsement:

It flashed out bold and striking thoughts, the fire of a rich and deep brain, clear and cold and brilliant as the aurora borealis, without either heart or bitterness. He painted glowingly the immortality of the mind —the everlasting virtue of a bright dream "wedded to immortal verse," and contrasted it with the evanescence of the merely practical labors of dull manhood. He complained of the prostitution of literature and learning to trade and commerce, and appealed to the scholars to be truer to the nobility of their knowledge, and more faithful to the majesty of thought and genius.

What impression Emerson made on the Amherst faculty has

not been recorded. No doubt "the stern old war-gods shook their heads" as they had often done before. His journal-entry of a few days later allows us to infer that a courteous but unmistakable clash of opinion did occur:

August 11. At Amherst the learned professors in the parlor were pleased that the plurality of worlds was disproved, as that restored its lost dignity to the race of men, and made the old Christian immortality valid again, and probable. I said, this was a poor mechanical elevation, and all true elevation must consist in a new and finer possession, by dint of finer organization, in the same things in which buffalo and fox had already a brutish, and Indian and Paddy a semi-brute possession.

As Uriel spoke with flashing eye was he observed by eyes the color of the sherry in the glass that the guest leaves? The parlor where Emerson met the learned professors has not been identified. It may conceivably have been at the home of his cousin Mrs. Lucius Boltwood. But he spoke on the Wednesday of Commencement week, the day when Edward Dickinson invariably entertained the guests of the College at tea. In 1855 Emily was by no means a recluse, and there was nothing but her constitutional shyness to prevent her from hearing Emerson's address. It is not unlikely that she bowed to the great man in her father's parlor. But proof, unfortunately, is lacking.

When Emerson next came to Amherst he was entertained by the Austin Dickinsons, and on this occasion, if not in 1855, Emily may have heard the living voice of the sage whom she of all people in Amherst was best fitted to understand. In the autumn of 1857, a time of nation-wide financial distress, a half dozen young men in Amherst "determined upon varying the monotony of the hard times by something that should remind us that we have minds and tastes too as well as pockets." They accordingly formed an association and were soon able to announce that they had secured three lecturers "as good as the best." About one hundred and fifty people paid the admission fee of twenty cents to hear Wendell Phillips, but apparently the tickets for Emerson's lecture did not go off so well. *The Express* for December 11 announced that the price had been reduced to eight for a dollar, and added the admonition: "It is bad economy to starve the mind or the heart, and there are few people who can afford not to hear Emerson, when they can hear him for 12½ cents."

The speaker appeared as advertised in the Meeting House (now College Hall) on the evening of December 16. His subject was "The Beautiful in Rural Life." The editor of *The Express*, having done his best to draw a crowd in advance, felt free to be facetious in his next issue:

Ralph Waldo Emerson's lecture greatly disappointed all who listened. It was in the English language instead of the Emersonese in which he usually clothes his thoughts, and the thoughts themselves were such as any plain, common-sense person could understand and appreciate.

Not all in the audience, however, were moved to scoff. Mrs. Austin Dickinson, then a bride of little more than a year's standing, was greatly impressed by the distinguished visitor. Meeting him, she thought, was like meeting Abraham stepping out of the pages of the Old Testament. Years later she recalled the exaltation of the speaker's words and the excitement she felt to be walking home on his "transcendental arm." She tells us of his gentle deference, of his praising the poems of Julia Ward Howe and Coventry Patmore, and of his half amused vexation when she ventured to question him about "Brahma," then lately published in the first number of *The Atlantic Monthly*. In conversation the sage was not at all frightening: "he turned his gentle, philosophic face toward me, waiting upon my commonplaces with such expectant, quiet gravity, that I became painfully conscious that I was I, and he was he, the great Emerson." In her young hostess's elation and consciousness that she was she, Sue forgot to record the one thing that posterity would like to know, namely whether Emily Dickinson attended the lecture and sat before the fire with Emerson afterward. Though Emily rarely

appeared in public, she had not entirely renounced the world.
In the autumn of that year she had been named one of the judges
of "rye and Indian" bread at the annual Cattle Show. Could she
have watched Emerson come and go, only a house away, and
contented herself with what her family could report of him?

> Unmoved, she notes the chariot's pausing
>   At her low gate;
> Unmoved, an emperor is kneeling
>   Upon her mat.

After he had gone she wrote: "It must have been as if he had
come from where dreams are born!" which sounds as though she
had not shared her sister-in-law's privileges. But we cannot be
positive. In speaking of country walks Emerson had said: "Good
observers have the manners of trees and animals, and if they add
words, 'tis only when words are better than silence. But a vain
talker profanes the river and forest, and is nothing like so good
company as a dog." Five years later Emily paraphrased Emerson's saying when she told Higginson that she avoided men and
women because "they talk of hallowed things, aloud, and embarrass my dog." So we are left in tantalizing uncertainty.

In the autumn of 1865 Emerson delivered a course of six lectures in Amherst, and incidentally came to tea at the Austin
Dickinson house, but Emily was then in Boston. When he spoke
again before the Social Union in 1872, and at the invitation of
President Seelye in 1879, she had entered upon her life of complete seclusion. The Emerson that touched her most nearly was
the philosopher and singer of the transcendental dawn, the
Emerson of *Nature,* the *Essays,* and the *Poems.*

Echoes of Emersonian ideas, if one chooses to call them that,
may be detected in Emily Dickinson's poems as easily as in
Whitman's, but it is not profitable to single them out. The implication that Emerson created a point of view which other writers adopted is simply untrue. The resemblances that may be
noted in Emerson, Parker, Thoreau, Emily Dickinson and sev-

eral other New England authors were due to the fact that all were responsive to the spirit of the time. Their work was in various ways a fulfillment of the finer energies of a Puritanism that was discarding the husks of dogma. If we now think of Emerson as the center and soul of the transcendental movement, it is not because he invented Transcendentalism, but because in his writings the new philosophy reached a consummate fruition and received its widest applications.

All the writers who were the spokesmen of the generation when the frost was coming out of the Puritan soil gave voice to a single master thought, the conviction of self-sufficiency. Individualism become absolute was the final step in the long revolt from authority. A systematic thinker like Parker might deduce "the adequacy of man for all his functions" from a first principle of the Infinite Perfection of God, and hold to it in spite of the impossibility, which he honestly admitted, of confirming it inductively from the concrete facts of external observation. Emerson displayed a finer sense of metaphysical tactics in assuming the divine sufficiency of man as an axiom of his ethics. It was part and parcel of his ecstatic acceptance of life, an intuition beyond the reach of logic.

Emily Dickinson also required no proof, and could admit no disproof, of the soul's sovereignty. "To be alive is power." Existence in itself is omnipotence enough. But to be alive and competent to will is a state equivalent to the divine. If this is finitude, what further gift has the infinite to bestow? The brain is wider than the sky, deeper than the sea:

> The brain is just the weight of God,
> For, lift them, pound for pound,
> And they will differ, if they do,
> As syllable from sound.

A soul aware of its kingly status may well stand in awe of itself; it is "Finite Infinity," its own friend or spy, itself the most enthralling romance, itself the greatest of adventures. It knows no

Hound of Heaven but that Single Hound, its own identity. This apotheosis of individualism carries with it confidence in the soul's invulnerability:

> Reverse cannot befall,
> That fine Prosperity
> Whose sources are interior.

And the further corollary of self-reliance—the conviction of the soul's infinite resources:

> We never know how high we are
> Till we are called to rise;
> And then, if we are true to plan,
> Our statures touch the skies. . . .

In their applications of the transcendental ethic Emerson differed from Emily Dickinson in that his scope embraced human institutions and the world of affairs as well as the individual soul. Primarily he was a social critic, comparing the low estate of politics, religion, education, trade, and the other mutual relationships of men with what these things might be if they were directed toward the fullest development of individuals and inspired by a sense of the godlike powers of man. Emily, on the contrary, had no world but her house and garden. She was above economics. Society in the large held no place for her, and with one ironic gesture she dismissed it from her ken:

> 'Tis sweet to know that stocks will stand
> When we with daisies lie,
> That commerce will continue,
> And trades as briskly fly.
> It makes the parting tranquil
> And keeps the soul serene,
> That gentlemen so sprightly
> Conduct the pleasing scene!

Her sole function was to test the transcendental ethic in its application to the inner life, which was after all the key to the position. Why talk of a society of complete and self-sufficient individuals until it could be shown that a single person could maintain himself in the face of whatever disasters might befall? The problem for her was to discover what the unsupported soul could endure of loneliness, grief, frustration, loss, and pain. It was easy to state the ideal solution:

> Fate slew him, but he did not drop;
> She felled—he did not fall—
> Impaled him on her fiercest stakes—
> He neutralized them all. . . .

Was it really possible to gather the spears to her own breast, to feel them entering her side, and to neutralize every pang? She could at least render an honest report. Within the limited field of her personal experience she could tell something of the soul's capacity to stand unaided.

The virtue of poetry so conceived would obviously be akin to that of a mathematical proposition; its beauty the severe beauty of ultimate compactness and lucidity. The geometry of the soul required no decoration. "Euclid alone has looked on beauty bare." The writer's triumph would consist in producing a poem like the equation of the squares of the sides and the square of the hypotenuse, perfectly contained in itself, adequately descriptive of fact, true beyond the power of thinking to make it more or less true. Old inexact formulations of thought must be replaced by new and finer perceptions.

Emily set herself to discriminate. The theological paradox of sin as a means of grace, of good springing from evil, of spiritual gain from earthly loss, had become a commonplace of nineteenth-century idealism, frequently restated. It supplied the basis of Emerson's essay on "Compensation" and the essence of his radical doctrine in "Uriel":

> Evil will bless, and ice will burn.

Among lesser writers J. G. Holland enforced the idea with emphatic literalness in his long poem *Bitter-Sweet* (1858), which

Emily Dickinson undoubtedly read as soon as it was published. The good Doctor there instructed her to see

> In every evil a kind instrument
> To chasten, elevate, correct, subdue;

or more lyrically:

> We learn by contrast to admire
> The beauty that enchains us;
> And know the object of desire
> By that which pains us.

Sidney Lanier, too, in "The Marshes of Glynn" was soon to ring the changes on the same favorite thought in a casual simile:

> Ye spread and span like the catholic man who hath mightily won
> God out of knowledge and good out of infinite pain
> And sight out of blindness and purity out of a stain.

In its many rehandlings the sharp truth of the paradox was blunted until it became merely a current form of expression for unfounded and vague optimism. From this dullness Emily Dickinson's hard-won discernment redeemed it, giving it new exactness and edge:

> Success is counted sweetest
> By those who ne'er succeed.
> To Comprehend a Nectar
> Requires sorest need.
> Not one of all the Purple Host
> Who took the Flag today
> Can tell the Definition,
> So clear, of Victory,
> As He, defeated, dying,
> On whose forbidden ear
> The distant strains of triumph
> Break, agonized, and clear!

Her theme was precisely the perception of value won through deprivation. It was not sight, she knew, that could be won out of blindness, but a full appreciation of the miraculousness and preciousness of sight. So to "comprehend" (not to taste) a nectar, to "tell the definition" (not to have the experience) of victory, one must suffer thirst and defeat. The observation is strictly accurate, without the blur of facile generalization. The poem is original in the best sense, in that the poet has fully possessed herself of an old thought and given it fresh vitality.

Its construction is like solid masonry. No paraphrase could condense the opening sentence, which states the theme in abstract form. This simple statement is then reinforced, deepened, and humanized with mounting emotion by two illustrations, one of two lines, one of eight, each contained in a single sentence. The startlingly diverse elements out of which the poem is composed are perfectly welded by an imagination working at white heat, so that we feel no incongruity in the abrupt transition from the image of nectar to that of the battlefield. No mechanical aids to coherence are needed. "Sweetest" in the opening line expands naturally into the concrete illustration of nectar; "sorest need," interpreted in terms of the Civil War, suggests the defeated and dying soldier of the final illustration. Once the idea has been made completely valid to the understanding, the poem ends. Every part of it is severely structural. Not a word could be spared and not a word is out of order. No writing could be more stripped and sinewy. It was poetry like this that Thoreau had in mind when he penned the superb hyperbole:

> Time cannot bend the line which God hath writ.

Emerson, too, had opened the statement of his poetic creed in "Merlin" (1845) with a denunciation of the formal prettifier and a plea for poetry that should be justified by its sincerity and power.

> No jingling serenader's art,
> Nor tinkle of piano strings,
> Can make the wild blood start
> In its mystic springs.
> The kingly bard
> Must smite the chords rudely and hard.

Enough of civility and conformity, enough of poems written from the fancy at a safe distance from personal experience, enough of meticulous finish. "For it is not metres, but a metre-making argument that makes a poem—a thought so passionate and alive that like the spirit of a plant or an animal it has an architecture of its own, and adorns nature with a new thing." Let the poet not be curious of strange knowledge but find the emblems of his thought in the everyday things about him. "The poorest experience is rich enough for all the purposes of expressing thought. . . . Day and night, house and garden, a few books, a few actions, serve us as well as would all trades and all spectacles. . . . We can come to use them yet with a terrible simplicity. It does not need that a poem should be long."

Yet Emerson, submissive as always to outward conventions, did not perfectly fulfill the specifications that he laid down, except in the handful of short poems that are the most enduring part of his work. In spite of his genius for epigram he must needs write in the accepted longer forms, struggling to join "sentences like infinitely repellent particles" in the mosaic of lectures and essays, or letting a lovely thought flower unseen in the wilderness of "Woodnotes" or "May-Day." Emily Dickinson, meanwhile, was free to follow her instinct of artistry. In her swift, breathless poems she found an instrument exactly suited to her need, a form capable of containing with the utmost economy a single idea at a time. So she avoided the temptations of an æsthetic *tour de force*, and became adept in the "gem tactics" of her verse. Conquest enough if she could record with full urgency the soul's superior instants.

Both Emerson and Emily Dickinson were worshippers of integrity. Their common object was to explore the source of man's spiritual power. The plainest locutions and the most homely images sufficed them. Neither cared overmuch for the niceties of verse, but respected the form implicit in the living thought, the rugged power of sense rather than the grace of rhyme. It is not surprising, therefore, that the accent of Emerson should at times be indistinguishable from that of Emily Dickinson, especially in the sententious quatrains that both were fond of writing. It is easy to find passages that might belong to either writer, as Professor Percy H. Boynton has expertly demonstrated. Here is another pair of quotations that may baffle the expert ear to discriminate:

> To clothe the fiery thought
> In simple words succeeds,
> For still the craft of genius is
> To mask a king in weeds.

And:

> The hedge is gemmed with diamonds,
> The air with Cupids full,
> The cobweb clues of Rosamond
> Guide lovers to the pool.

Few could say with assurance that Emily Dickinson might not have written either of these passages, though in point of fact both are by Emerson. The resemblance in style, like that in substance, is not due to imitation, but to the fact that both poets were sprung from the same soil and never lost their kinship with the earth.

The moral stability and the intellectual ferment of New England were alike reflected in Emily Dickinson's poetry, and combined with these was a trick of playing with words as with counters that could be arranged in striking and unusual patterns, a faculty that she acquired from the native humor of the time. These oddly mingled elements of her style were fused as in a volcanic crucible until they became inextricably blended like the quartz, mica, and feldspar in the granite of her hills. Many of her poems remained as rough and unshaped as boulders in a pasture, but the stuff of which they were made was not apt to crumble. On occasion it could be cut and polished to brilliance under her hand.

Books and Reading

ALL HER life Emily Dickinson was an eager reader. Books, however, were not her masters but her friends. She turned to them because they offered solace and transport for the "far ends of tired days." Her attitude was Emersonian: a poet's first business was less with the literature of old than with the impressions of life thronging about him. Nevertheless, she cherished her small library of favorites as a resource when her imagination flagged. They brought her inspiration and stimulus. No English-speaking poet since Chaucer has written more engagingly than she in praise of books.

Her best known poem on the subject, "There is no frigate like a book" (46, xcix), is one of her ultimate condensations, an eight-line epitome of what she had expressed more loosely in several earlier efforts. It goes straight to the heart of her meaning, discarding as her maturest poems always do every atom of superfluous elaboration, and yet keeping the imaginative tension at a high level. In comparison she was relaxed and expansive when she wrote what was probably her first attempt to capture in verse the enchantment of the printed page, the poem beginning:

> A precious, mouldering pleasure 'tis
> To meet an antique book
> In just the dress his century wore.

Since it contains the line, "He lived where dreams were born," that Emily used on the occasion of Emerson's visit to her brother's house, this poem may be dated about 1857. At that time she was still toying with the fancies that pleased her girlish thought. It is conceivable that the Dickinson bookshelves held old volumes capable of shaking their "vellum heads" to tantalize her, but in no case could any of them have carried her back to the days "when Plato was a certainty and Sophocles a man," nor even to the era of Dante and Beatrice. In choosing to mention these authors Emily betrayed the fact that she was writing without a genuine bookman's knowledge of early editions. She did not make the mistake again. Her maturer instinct brought her well within the bounds of what she directly knew when in "Unto my books so good to turn" (35, lxxiv) she contrasted the "wilderness without" with the holiday sense of "bells within" that every born reader experiences when he turns to his "kinsmen of the shelf." Again in half the space and without loss of effectiveness she celebrated the "bequest of wings" that a book may bestow in "He ate and drank the precious words" (13, xxi). Finally she stripped the subject of every trace of ornament or circumstance till only the significant kernel remained. A book was the soul's frugal chariot, a page of "prancing poetry" its coursers.

What books were available to Emily Dickinson, and of these which did she select as her "enthralling friends"? Only a partial answer can be given to the first of these questions, but the evidence should not be neglected because it is incomplete. After briefly surveying the extent of her reading as far as it may be surmised from chance allusions in her letters, we may return to the half dozen writers that she especially cherished.

Besides legal and religious books Edward Dickinson's library contained a fair selection of stately classics, the lonely and rigorous authors that he preferred. There were sets of such historians as Hume, Macaulay, Motley, Bancroft, and Prescott; the works of American statesmen, Hamilton, Jefferson, Webster, John Adams; the British essayists, including Carlyle, Macaulay, Sydney Smith, Wilson, and Jeffrey, each in one heavy volume;

many books on the American Revolution and ponderous tomes of travel like Kane's *Arctic Voyages* and Stephens' *Yucatan.* Belles lettres were represented by Knight's Shakespeare in eight volumes, Addison's works and Washington Irving's, Cowper, Byron, and "numberless small leather-bound editions of the early [*i.e.*, seventeenth and eighteenth century] English poets." It was the standard gentleman's library of the period.

The younger Dickinsons indulged a more adventurous taste for contemporary writers, both English and American, whose books they looked forward to and bought soon after publication. Emily in 1848 mentioned "a feast in the reading line" which consisted of Longfellow's *Evangeline,* Tennyson's *The Princess,* Thomas Moore's *The Epicurean,* Tupper's *The Twins* and *The Heart,* and a tale called *The Maiden Aunt* by S. M. (Menella Bute Smedley). The light reading on Austin's desk in 1852 included Ik Marvel's *Reveries of a Bachelor,* the two volumes of prose and poetry by the elder Richard Henry Dana, Lady Georgiana Fullerton's *Grantley Manor,* Pollok's *Course of Time,* Coleridge's *Table Talk,* Hawthorne's *Mosses from an Old Manse,* and Irving's *Life of Columbus.* At about the same time Lavinia was reading *David Copperfield,* a life of Schiller, Bulwer-Lytton's *The Caxtons,* and Hawthorne's *The House of Seven Gables.* These glimpses serve to show that the Dickinson bookshelves were well lined. The young people were incessant readers and discriminating judges of what they read.

In later life Emily became more selective in her tastes. Her list of favorite authors sent to Higginson in 1862 mentioned for poets only Keats and the Brownings, for prose Ruskin, Sir Thomas Browne, and *Revelations.* "When I lost the use of my eyes [1864–65]," she wrote in 1870, "it was a comfort to think there were so few real books that I could easily find some one to read me all of them." She doubted further whether any book but Shakespeare were needed. During her mother's long illness she had small opportunity to explore new fields. "Existence has overpowered books." But before she narrowed her predilections to the few writers who spoke to her directly, she had tested many.

Her knowledge of foreign literatures, however, was certainly not large. There is no indication that she took to heart anything from the Greek and Roman classics. She speaks of Socrates and Plato only as any educated person might refer to names that have become household words. Dante also she knew as a great name, but if she ever read the *Divine Comedy* there is nothing to show for it, except that she pronounced the name of Beatrice in the Italian fashion. The *Arabian Nights* supplied her with a synonym for imaginativeness, and she once cited Don Quixote's challenge of the windmills, probably recalling her childhood reading. The only French author that we can be sure she read (and that in translation) was George Sand, whom she linked in admiration with Mrs. Browning (1861): "Women, now, queens, now!" It is more difficult to be positive concerning her familiarity with German writers. Her letters afford no evidence, but in her girlhood the influence of Jean Paul Richter was still paramount and her niece speaks of copies of his books that were eagerly read and marked by all the younger Dickinsons. Moreover, Sister Sue's library contained volumes of Goethe, Schiller, Lessing, Heine, and others, and one of Emily's close friends was Miss Maria Whitney, a scholar trained in Germany and at one time professor of German in Smith College. In all probability, therefore, Emily possessed a wider conversational acquaintance with German literature than her letters indicate. Lastly, she heard something from Higginson of the great Russian novelists whose works were appearing in English during her later years; in 1875 she wrote that she had read nothing of Turgenev's, "but thank you for telling me—and will seek him immediately." If she found what she was seeking, she gave no sign.

But we must be chary of drawing conclusions from the very fragmentary evidence of her letters. Much that she undoubtedly read passed without comment. If there was one author that she knew thoroughly it was Shakespeare. She had gone through the plays systematically with her friends of the Shakespeare club, and she returned to them continually. While Shakespeare remained she could not lack a book. A sheet of notepaper that had lain for a time between his pages was endeared to her by its resting place. To a friend who was going to Stratford she wrote in the last year of her life, "Touch Shakespeare for me." Yet in her published letters and poems together there are allusions to or quotations from only eleven of the thirty-seven plays. *Othello*, *Macbeth*, and *Antony and Cleopatra* are the most frequently cited, *Hamlet* is mentioned but twice, and *King Lear* not at all. This may serve as an approximate measure of how imperfectly her reading is reflected in her letters.

There is no positive indication that Emily knew Chaucer or Spenser or Milton, though she could hardly have grown up in Amherst a century ago without being inducted into *Paradise Lost*. Her one quotation from Milton, "Peace hath her victories, no less [renowned] than War," had become such a common saying that she was probably not conscious of its origin. It is not unlikely that Milton's poems were so associated with parsing and piety as to repel her. When she had occasion to mention *Pilgrim's Progress*, along with "Baxter on the Will," she spoke with unmistakable derision.

Any allusion from her to the religious poets of the seventeenth century would be of particular interest because of the close parallel between her work and that of Donne, Herbert, and Vaughan. Herbert at least was still in vogue with pious readers, and there is no reason to suppose that she did not know some of his poems. But her only reference to any of the "metaphysical" group consists of a line quoted, late in life, from one of the most familiar of Vaughan's pieces, which she might easily have read in Palgrave. Moreover, she misspelled the poet's name (her editor has righted that) and added uncertainly, "I think it was Vaughn." This indication, slight as it is, would lead us to surmise that she was not well acquainted with her distant predecessors.

She had, however, found one harbor in the seventeenth century. The writer of that period whom she most cherished, according to her statement to Higginson, was Sir Thomas Browne. This is the first and last that we hear of him from her, but the hint is not to be neglected. Browne, who wrote the *Religio Medici* as a "private exercise" not intended for publication, who lived much apart from the world to speculate on the mysteries of time and death, who combined the mental attitudes of skeptic and mystic, and who loved to draw hermetic meanings out of scientific and mathematical figures, was obviously her spiritual kinsman. Miss Margery McKay, in a very able honors thesis written at Swarthmore College, has pointed out that Emily Dickinson's use of the word "circumference" in the rare sense of "that which surrounds, environment," a sense which implies a radiating out rather than a shutting in, is paralleled by Browne's use of the same word following "that allegorical description of Hermes [which] pleaseth me beyond all the metaphysical definitions of divines: *Sphaera cujus centrum ubique, circumferentia nullibi.*" A further study of Browne's influence on Emily Dickinson's vocabulary and turn of mind would undoubtedly be fruitful. Here it is sufficient to note that he was one of the few writers who genuinely affected her.

No eighteenth-century author, as far as we can judge, came very close to her. Pope's *Essay on Man* served as the text for the rhetoric studied at Mount Holyoke, and was thereafter forgotten. She was brought up on Thomson's *Seasons,* which she mentioned in a poem, and on Young's *Night Thoughts,* which she quoted in an early letter. There are passing references to Horace Walpole as a person and to "Junius" as a book, to *The Vicar of Wakefield* and to "Mr. Rasselas." She once spoke of Swift's lack of heart, coupling him with Dante and Mirabeau. Cowper and Mrs. Barbauld she knew well enough to quote. Burns and the sentimental folk-songs that he made popular became at one time almost a second language to her, so that she phrased a few passages of tender feeling in the Scottish dialect, but this affectation she soon outgrew. Except for Shakespeare and Sir Thomas Browne her deepest literary affinities were with the nineteenth century.

It is safe to assume that she knew much more of the poets of the Romantic Movement than her letters reveal. Keats she named among her favorite poets—and never quoted! Three slight references to Wordsworth and two to Byron's *Prisoner of Chillon* are all that can be gleaned from her. Nothing of Blake, whom she would certainly have enjoyed, nothing of Shelley, to whom Browning should have pointed the way, nothing of Coleridge, whom her brother read, nothing of Scott, whom everybody read. Since it is inconceivable that an adventurous reader such as Emily was should not have encountered these poets, we can only remark that her omission of all mention of them is surprising and pass on.

The Victorian poets and novelists she noticed frequently. We need to be reminded that she was not guided in her selection, as we are, by histories of literature. Charlotte and Emily Brontë, Charles Dickens, Robert and Elizabeth Barrett Browning, and George Eliot, the six to whom she recurred again and again, were her elder contemporaries whose books were appearing from year to year during her own lifetime. She chose them from the stream of living literature. Two prosemen, Carlyle and Ruskin, should perhaps be added to the list of her favorites, the first because his portrait hung in her bedroom along with photographs of Mrs. Browning and George Eliot, the second because she spoke of him in the same breath with Sir Thomas Browne. We have no further word from her concerning either. Carlyle may have confirmed her belief in the redeeming power of work, and conceivably her browsings in Ruskin may have taught her to take the very moral view of the "Martyr Painters" that she expressed in one poem (387, xxiv) and have supplied her with allusions to Guido, Titian, and Domenichino (122, cx) and Van Dyke (401, xliii). But the only piece of Ruskin's writing that we can be sure she read was his inconsiderable preface to Francesca Alexander's *The Story of Ida* (1883), a deathbed biography that Emily characterized as an "ethereal volume."

We know that in her early twenties Emily devoured a considerable number of the sweetish religio-sentimental tales concocted by British lady novelists, the conventional parlor fiction of the period. She perused with approval in 1851 a forgotten novel called *Ellen Middleton,* by Lady Georgiana Fullerton, authoress of the popular *Grantley Manor.* Two years later she recommended to Sue three little books that she considered "sweet and true" though not bewitching: they were *The Light in the Valley* by a Miss Annesley, and two productions entitled *A House on the Rock* and *Only* by the author of *A Trap to Catch a Sunbeam,* otherwise Mrs. Mackarness (Matilda Anne Planché). At the same time she was eagerly looking forward to a chance to read Mrs. Dinah M. Craik's *Olive* and *The Head of the Family.* It is understandable that against a background of such innocuous fictions the novels of the Brontë sisters would emerge with thrilling power. Thanks to Mr. Bowdoin, her father's partner, Emily was reading *Jane Eyre* within two years of its publication and it is not unlikely that she read all the other Brontë novels as soon as she could obtain them. She composed one of the quaintest of her tributes in verse in Charlotte's honor, concluding with the lines:

> Oh, what an afternoon for heaven,
> When Brontë entered there!

During the last decade of her life, however, Emily Dickinson spoke less of Charlotte and more of "gigantic Emily Brontë," though it was the poems rather than *Wuthering Heights* that interested her. She twice quoted a particular stanza from "No coward soul is mine," and it was this poem that Higginson with felicitous appropriateness read at Emily Dickinson's funeral.

At the time when she was reading Mrs. Craik, Emily was also immersed in Kingsley's *Alton Locke* and Dickens' *Bleak House*, which last some one had sent her. In spite of an early reproof from her father on the score of her infatuation for "these modern literati," Dickens appealed irresistibly to her sense of drollery and she must have read all his books. *David Copperfield* and *Dombey and Son* were her favorites, if we may judge by frequency of quotation. Certain Dickensian phrases, like "Donkeys, Davy," "Barkis is willin'," and little Paul Dombey's "Weeks away?" were embedded in her familiar language. With one of her close friends she had a clear understanding as to what gentleman was intended when "Brooks of Sheffield" was named between them. A letter to Samuel Bowles ends with an echo of some unrecovered joke: " 'Swiveller' may be sure of the 'Marchioness.' " There was no waning in her regard for "dear Dickens" to the end of her life.

Like most Victorian readers Emily Dickinson probably first heard of the obscure poet Robert Browning as the husband of the better known poetess Elizabeth Barrett. None of her allusions to either of the Brownings can be placed before the year of Mrs. Browning's death (1861), but in a poem of ecstatic admiration (394, xxxiii) Emily spoke of reading "that Foreign Lady" while still "a little girl." Since she commonly thought of her childhood as extending well into her twenties, we may infer that not long before 1855 she had encountered the poetry which, if we may take her account at its face value, transfigured life for her. Responsive as always to the electrifying flash of supreme emotion, Emily felt in reading Mrs. Browning as though she were possessed by a "very lunacy of light."

> I could not have defined the change—
> Conversion of the mind,
> Like sanctifying in the Soul,
> Is witnessed, not explained.

'Twas a divine insanity.
The sorrow to be sane
Should I again experience,
'Tis antidote to turn

To tomes of solid witchcraft.
Magicians be asleep,
But magic hath an element
Like Deity to keep!

In its superficial aspects Mrs. Browning's poetry seems very
unlike Emily Dickinson's, but intrinsically the two women had
much in common. Both were intense and intellectual, both delighted in sententiousness quickened with fresh impulses of feeling and vision, both were deeply sensitive to the analogies between matter and soul. If Mrs. Browning's reach often exceeded
her grasp, Emily was not one to turn from her verse because its
occasional deeps were mingled with long stretches of shallow-
ness. What she discerned was the sincere outpouring of a great
heart: "That Mrs. Browning fainted, we need not read *Aurora
Leigh* to know." Moreover, as has frequently been pointed out,
her admiration for the poet was colored by her adoration of the
woman whose cloistered life had so dramatically bloomed in an
ideal marriage, an image of vicarious fulfillment for all closed-in
hearts. When Mrs. Browning died, Emily felt the loss as a personal bereavement. She besought Bowles, then on the eve of a
visit to Europe, to tell her any anecdotes that he might hear of
the "Anglo-Florentine." The framed portrait that hung on her
wall was a witness to her unfaltering devotion.

Her earliest references to Robert Browning are likewise personal tributes of respect and sympathy, as when she urged Mary
Bowles to name one of her sons after the poet: "He is the bravest
man alive, but *his* boy has no mama." If outsiders like herself
could "suffocate with easy woe," she wondered how the "bride-
groom" could bear his affliction. Then she was astonished to
learn that he had "made another poem." Possibly she was not

too pleased with him. Several scattered references to Browning's books in her correspondence with Higginson do not manifest quite the enthusiasm that we should expect. Thus she wrote in 1862: "I never heard anybody speak of *Pippa Passes* before. You see my posture is benighted," and we are left to wonder how Emily could have remained in ignorance of a volume given to the world twenty years earlier. *Men and Women* she knew— "That is a broad book"; but as late as 1875 she confessed that she had not seen *Bells and Pomegranates,* published in 1847, "but have Mrs. Browning's endorsement." This does not sound like the record of a devotee, and the hint of lukewarmness is confirmed when we find her writing apropos of Tennyson's *Harold,* which had disappointed her, "Tennyson declines like Browning, once so rare." She never mentioned *The Ring and the Book,* but many of Browning's shorter poems she continued to value. There are chance quotations in her later letters from "Evelyn Hope," "Any Wife to Any Husband," "The Last Ride Together," and "Love Among the Ruins," more quotations than from any other Victorian poet, even from Tennyson in whom like all her generation she was steeped. Yet she did not accept Browning's poetry in its entirety with the whole-souled acclamation that she accorded to his wife's. First and last Mrs. Browning was her poet.

She must have read other volumes of poems that every one was reading. Tupper's *Proverbial Philosophy,* for example, was much discussed in Amherst. We know that she found in Alexander Smith's poems at the height of their mushroom reputation "a good deal of exquisite frenzy, and some wonderful figures as ever I met in my life." It would be fair to assume, too, that Sue's copy of Coventry Patmore's *The Angel in the House* found its way across the lawn. Further than this we cannot guess.

There can be no question, however, that the preferred novelist of her later years was George Eliot. Her attitude is epitomized in the exclamation, "What do I think of *Middlemarch?* What do

I think of glory?" *Adam Bede,* sent her by Sue, "is the lane to the Indies Columbus was looking for." A volume of Eliot's poems, probably *The Legend of Jubal* (1874), was one of the last books given her by her father, and she could not bear to open it. But she knew the novelist's almost religious statement of her humanitarian creed in "O may I join the Choir Invisible"; a poem that Helen Hunt Jackson, when she last visited the Dickinson house, pronounced "superb." Always fastidious in her selection of books to give her friends, Emily chose *Daniel Deronda,* sight unseen, for Higginson. When he was going to England, she begged him to report every circumstance concerning George Eliot if he should happen to meet her. The look of the newspaper paragraph announcing the novelist's death was stamped on her memory like the sight of a face in the casket: one more of the mighty ones gone to that eternity where Emily possessed a special freehold. "Now, *my* George Eliot," she wrote. "The gift of belief which her greatness denied her, I trust she receives in the childhood of the kingdom of heaven."

Emily's interest extended to the biography of her favorite authors and to a variety of miscellaneous exploration in books. In the last year of her life she was "watching like a vulture" for Walter Cross's *Life and Letters of George Eliot,* which she wished also to present to Higginson. After reading it she remarked, "The life of Marian Evans had much I never knew—a doom of fruit without the bloom, like the Niger fig." We could guess that she was thoroughly familiar with Mrs. Gaskell's *Life of Charlotte Brontë,* since she described one of Vinnie's pussies as "the color of Branwell Brontë's hair," and in point of fact a copy of this book given by Emily to Sue is still extant. Possibly the account of the French actress Rachel in *Villette* led her to consult the *Memoirs of Rachel,* by Mme. de B——, of which an English translation appeared in 1858. She also quoted from a biographical notice of the operatic singer Parepa Rosa. These indications merely hint at the direction of her incidental reading.

Emily Dickinson's familiarity with the leading American authors of her time may be taken for granted, except when we have her word to the contrary. Thus she had not, in 1862, read Whitman, and if she looked at *Leaves of Grass* following Higginson's suggestion, she did not find matter there for further comment. In 1875 she refused to sample the writings of Joaquin Miller, "because I could not care about him," and of Poe four years later she knew "too little to think." But aside from these she read what every one else was reading, the poems of Bryant, Longfellow, Whittier, Emerson, Lowell, and Holmes, the prose of the three last named as well as of Irving and Thoreau, and much of the fiction of Hawthorne, Harriet Beecher Stowe, Henry James, Howells, Doctor Holland, and Helen Hunt Jackson. Her occasional remarks are almost invariably approving: "Hawthorne appalls—entices"; of Lowell's "A Good Word for Winter," "One does not often meet anything so perfect"; "Mrs. Hunt's poems are stronger than any written by women since Mrs. Browning, with the exception of Mrs. Lewes [George Eliot]; but truth like ancestors' brocades can stand alone"; "Pity me . . . I have finished *Ramona*. Would that like Shakespeare it were just published!"; "Was the sea cordial? Kiss him for Thoreau." She respected Howells and James, but perhaps missed in their books the idealistic fervor characteristic of their immediate predecessors, so that her. final verdict on them was doubtful: "one hesitates."

She met new writers in the periodicals. *Harper's Magazine* in the 1850's when it was reprinting novels by Dickens, Thackeray, Bulwer-Lytton, and others, *The Atlantic Monthly* from its beginning in 1857, *Scribner's Monthly* (not to be confused with *Scribner's Magazine*) during the decade of the 1870's when it was under Holland's editorship, and its successor the *Century Magazine*, all came to one or the other of the Dickinson households and so passed under Emily's eye. She depended on her sister-in-law, who stood "nearer to the world" than she, to pur-

vey fresh reading matter for her. Her first reaction to Harriet
Prescott Spofford's "Circumstance" in the *Atlantic* for May,
1860, was the excited note: "Sue, it is the only thing I ever read
in my life that I didn't think I could have imagined myself!
. . . Send me everything she writes," but she confessed later to
Higginson that the story "followed me in the dark, so I avoided
her." Another famous tale, one of the first examples of the new
school of realistic fiction, that she asked especially to see was
Rebecca Harding Davis's "Life in the Iron Mills" (*Atlantic*,
April, 1861). She commented on Holland's *Nicholas Minturn*
in *Scribner's*, and on the first appearance there of Howells' work.
The literary notes by Frank Sanborn in *The Springfield Republican* kept her well informed of what was going on in the realm
of letters.

Her early fondness for Ik Marvel (Donald G. Mitchell) and
her later enthusiasm for everything that Thomas Wentworth
Higginson wrote demand more extended consideration than
her quite normal response to the better known writers of the
day. Neither Mitchell nor Higginson can be classed among the
giants. What did Emily see in them that so strongly attracted
her?

Her attachment to Ik Marvel was inspired solely by his most
popular book, the *Reveries of a Bachelor* (1850). She associated
it with a thrilling afternoon in March, when the sky was blue
and warm and the white clouds sailing: "It seems to me 'Ik Marvel' was born on such a day." And it is true that Mitchell's word-
pictures have about them a delicate brilliancy of atmosphere
that reminds one of the finer lithographs of the period rather
than of any earthly air. The charm that Emily found in them
was not obtainable from Mitchell's later books. *Dream Life*
(1851) she enjoyed—"I think it full of the very sweetest fancies,
and more exquisite language I defy any man to use"—but she
wished its author "had been translated like Enoch of old, after
his bachelor reverie, and chariot of fire and the horsemen thereof

were all that had been seen of him ever after." The book that Emily so distinctly preferred was subtitled "A Book of the Heart" and carried on its title page a quotation from Burton's *Anatomy*, which read:

. . . It is worth the labor—saith Plotinus—to consider well of Love, whether it be a God, or a divell, or passion of the minde, or partly God, partly divell, partly passion.

Here, I think, is the clue to the excited pleasure that Emily took in it. The girls of her generation, even among themselves, were reticent in speaking of passion and their hearts were starved. Ik Marvel inoffensively crossed the barrier. His *Reveries* was the best anatomy of the affections available, elegant in tone and seemingly penetrating in its observation. In this bible of a sentimental age, the emotional insights and intuitions that Emily's favorite women poets and novelists sporadically gave her were neatly arranged on a gamut of fancy. Like Charlotte Brontë and Mrs. Browning, Ik Marvel fostered her interest in the workings of the human heart, particularly in its unsatisfied yearnings and tender regrets, and so helped prepare her to be a lyrist of love and renunciation.

Her relation to Higginson, on the contrary, was primarily intellectual, in fact as well as in gay pretense a relation of pupil and preceptor. There was no penetration of the heart in his writings, but there were lofty thoughts a-plenty, a diffused idealism that supplied aliment to a mind that loved to play with general ideas. She regarded his mild sagacities as a more precious boon than Mitchell's gentle sentiments. After twenty years she could still recall the thrill with which she greeted his first book: "It was mansions, nations, kinsmen, too, to me." In authority, purity, and range of intellect he seemed perfectly powerful. She did not hesitate to place him beside Shakespeare on her private shelf. His writings were an ever-flowing fountain of truth from which she gratefully drank. When "A Letter to a Young Contributor" came out in the *Atlantic* for April, 1862, the master appeared to be speaking directly to her, and Emily confidingly placed her hand in his. Not only did he cite with approval Keats, the Brownings, Ruskin, and Sir Thomas Browne, her whole list of favorite authors at that time except for *Revelations,* but he spoke of the magnificent mystery of words and the high dignity of the poet's calling in a way that matched her own transcendental convictions.

"Charge your style with life," he had written, and Emily responded, "Mr. Higginson,—Are you too deeply occupied to say if my verse is alive?" "Tolerate no superfluity that can be struck out," and Emily pared her poems to the core. "Such being the majesty of the art you seek to practise, you can at least take time and deliberation before dishonoring it"; Emily could quote this sentence from memory fourteen years later. She obeyed the precept only too well. "Literature is attar of roses, one distilled drop from a million blossoms." Emily wrote:

> Essential oils are wrung;
> The attar from the rose
> Is not expressed by suns alone,
> It is the gift of screws. . . .

Said Higginson: "Oftentimes a word shall speak what accumulated volumes have labored in vain to utter: there may be years of crowded passion in a word, and half a life in a sentence." Emily heightened the hyperbole: Could the lips that form a single syllable know the possible significance with which it is laden, they would "crumble with the weight" (45, xcv). "If your work does not vindicate itself, you cannot vindicate it, but you can labor steadily on to something that needs no advocate but itself." This too was Emily's belief: "If fame belonged to me, I could not escape her; if she did not, the longest day would pass me on the chase." She was willing to labor on indefinitely and claim no vindication.

Finally she paid Higginson the unique compliment of extracting the "essential oil" from one of his poems just as if it had been a first sketch of her own. He had written a verse for Decoration Day (*Scribner's Monthly*, June, 1874) in which after reflecting at some length on where he might most worthily bestow his wreath, he placed it on the grave of the Unknown Woman, "bravest of the brave," symbolizing the mothers, wives, and sweethearts of the soldier dead. Not later than the following autumn Emily wrote him a shade demurely: "It comforts an instinct if another have felt it too. I was re-reading your *Decoration*. You may have forgotten it." Then she added in four lines what Higginson had taken twenty-eight to say, leaving out the feminist sentiment in which his thought was entangled, preserving the crystal thought and that alone. How can one recognize the soul "too intrinsic for renown"?

> Laurel, veil your deathless tree,—
> Him you chasten, that is he.

This exchange is notable because Emily rarely borrowed either thought or phrase. Her avoidance of second-hand goods was fastidious in the extreme. Whenever she was aware of using either a quotation or a stock phrase she was particular to set it off with quotation marks. She defined her attitude early in her correspondence with Higginson when she detected a parallel between what she had written and something that she had encountered in print. "I marked a line in one verse, because I met it after I made it, and never consciously touch a paint mixed by another person." Few poets have succeeded as well as she in stamping everything they wrote with the hall-mark of a distinct personality.

The few verbal echoes that can be discovered in her poems are of the most inconsequential sort, either pure coincidences or unconscious assimilations. After going through much of her reading I can produce but a handful. Sir Thomas Browne in *Religio Medici* quaintly phrased his sense of God's unknowableness in saying, "we are ignorant of the back-parts or lower side of His Divinity," and Emily spoke of

> parts of His far plan
> That baffled me—the underside
> Of His divinity.

Dickens in *Dombey and Son* (Chap. XIV) used the words "a bustle in the house," anticipating in a totally different context Emily's

> The bustle in a house
> The morning after death. . . .

Reverend Charles Wadsworth could thunder against the stage: "And although Satan with his wonderful power might, if truly regenerated and reformed, become a most efficient teacher of morals, yet as for six thousand years he has proved himself still a devil, the Church, hopeless of his reform, will use other ministries." And Emily without reference to the theatre could declare:

> The Devil, had he fidelity,
> Would be the finest friend—
> Because he has ability,
> But Devils cannot mend. . . .

She may have been thinking of Desdemona's last words, "Nobody; I myself; farewell," when she wrote:

> I'm nobody! Who are you?

And she may have derived a striking metaphor in her best-known love poem:

> As if no soul the solstice crossed
> That maketh all things new,

by figurative extension of the opening lines of *Richard III:*

> Now is the winter of our discontent
> Made glorious summer by this sun of York.

But it was not Shakespeare who taught her to develop either of these lyrics.

Emily Dickinson's poetry is not derivable from her reading. The most we can say is that she found food for reflection in books as in life, and that in a very general way her interest in both heart and mind was prefigured in her choice of authors. But the secret of her style was like melody or witchcraft unconveyed, neither imitated nor capable of facile imitation. She earned it by the whole tenor of her life, and it was hers unmistakably, hers only.

PART FOUR

POETRY AS PLAYMATE

ᴄᴏ 13 ᴄᴏ

Thoughts in the Gown

EMILY DICKINSON'S poems do not belong to the literature of escape. She confronted all the facts of life that
came within her experience, seeking to record all she
could learn of ecstasy or anguish, and stating her conclusions without palliation. The lyric, or as she liked to call it
the psalm or hymn, lay ready to her hand as the traditional
vehicle for impassioned thought. She accepted it as unquestioningly as she accepted the alphabet. There were black symbols
on white paper, words arranged in rhythmic patterns. How
could these dead, mechanical things be made to throb with the
high excitement of the soul? How could the living truth be
flashed through them from mind to mind? She knew that the
miracle could be accomplished: "If I feel physically as if the
top of my head were taken off, I know *that* is poetry." But how
it was done no one could tell her. She experimented and besought Sister Sue for suggestions. She wrote to Higginson to
ask if her verse were alive, if it breathed. Her lifelong preoccupation was to increase the vital impact of her lines.

Like any other genuine artist she never arrived at a pat solution or easy formula. Always the finer breath of her intention
hovered for but an instant and was gone. The most carefully
woven mesh of words could not contain it. Thought was infinite, expression finite. Only imperfectly could the two be
joined. Yet what else was a true poem but a kind of finite-
infinity? She continued to experiment, never quite sure of her

success. The children of her brain were nimble, some more than others, as long as they remained "undressed," but when she "put them in the gown" they stiffened and seemed alike in their numbness.

She had no time to sift her poems, and the distinction that she could not make her editors have ceased to make for her. Triumphs and trivialities, partial successes, fragments, and failures have been published all of a piece. Let it be said at once that nearly everything that Emily Dickinson wrote is of interest to those who love her poems, as all of Wordsworth or of Browning is precious to their admirers. But let it not be forgotten that her entire workshop has been indiscriminately opened to inspection. The volume of her collected poems is not made up of pieces that have been selected, revised, and arranged for publication by the poet herself. In consequence, more than most poets, she has been exposed to the attack of formal critics. At the head of the list must be placed her chosen guide, Thomas Wentworth Higginson.

Very early in their correspondence we find Emily Dickinson thanking him for the "surgery" he had applied to her verses and adding that it was not so painful as she had supposed it would be. To his credit, be it remembered, he mingled unstinted praise with his admonitions, but he was positive in pronouncing her verses uncontrolled, sporadic, and wayward. Among the first poems sent him was the haunting but irregular lyric beginning "The nearest dream recedes unrealized." He seems to have suggested that she abandon the struggle to write in meter and rhyme and follow the example of Whitman. Emily replied that she had never read Whitman's book, but had been told that it was disgraceful, and in her next letter added that she "could not drop the bells whose jingling cooled my tramp." The figure beautifully associates the double movement of verse with the gliding of a sleigh and the pulse of harness-bells, and it also implies a perception that Higginson never reached, namely, that the jingle is not what makes either sleigh or verse *move*. After a time Higginson gave up the attempt to regularize Emily's writing, but he never could overcome an uneasy feeling that verse as unconventional as hers was somehow shocking and in need of apology.

When it came to editing her work for publication he could not permit some of her locutions to stand. In a playful poem on the grass Emily had written:

> The grass so little has to do,
> I wish I were a hay!

"It cannot go in so," exclaimed Higginson, with heat, as Mrs. Todd reports. "Don't you see? Everybody would say that *hay* is a collective noun requiring the definite article; nobody would, even in fun, call it *a* hay." And so, over Mrs. Todd's protest, the article was altered to suit the critic's preconception.

But still enough original Emily remained in the book to move Higginson to deprecation in advance. In his preface to *Poems* (1890) he thought it well to say: "After all, when a thought takes one's breath away, a lesson on grammar seems an impertinence." Whereupon the brilliant and meticulous Thomas Bailey Aldrich made the obvious riposte: "But an ungrammatical thought does not, as a general thing, takes [*sic*] one's breath away, except in a sense the reverse of flattering." Several other reviewers repeated the same opinion without offering, whether by intention or mischance, a coincident illustration.

Aldrich's comment may be found in an unsigned article called *"In Re* Emily Dickinson" (*Atlantic Monthly*, January, 1892), which was reprinted, much altered but still recognizable, as "Un Poète Manqué" in *Ponkapog Papers* (1903). The first paragraph, as originally written, will serve as a sufficient example of the plea that Emily Dickinson's poems be ruled out of court because of her high-handed evasions of the "laws of grammar," which in Aldrich's view apparently possessed a validity like that of the law of gravitation.

The English critic who said of Miss Emily Dickinson that she might have become a fifth-rate poet "if she had only mastered the rudiments of grammar and gone into metrical training for about fifteen years," —the rather candid English critic who said this somewhat overstated his case. He had, however, a fairly good case. If Miss Dickinson had undergone the austere curriculum indicated, she would, I am sure, have become an admirable lyric poet of the second magnitude. In the first volume of her poetical chaos is a little poem which needs only slight revision in the initial stanza in order to make it worthy of ranking with some of the odd swallow flights in Heine's lyrical *intermezzo*. I have ventured to desecrate this stanza by tossing a rhyme into it, as the other stanzas happened to rhyme, and here print the lyric, hoping the reader will not accuse me of overvaluing it:—

> I taste a liquor never brewed
> In vats upon the Rhine;
> No tankard ever held a draught
> Of alcohol like mine. . . .

Aldrich is forever safe from the supposition that he could distinguish between lemonade and faery wine. Both the nameless English critic and his American echo may be left to the mercy of Henry James's sister Alice, an invalid in body but not in mind, who confided to her journal under date of January 6, [1892]:

It is reassuring to hear the English pronouncement that Emily Dickinson is fifth-rate—they have such a capacity for missing quality; the robust evades them equally with the subtle. Her being sicklied o'er with T. W. Higginson makes one quake lest there be a latent flaw which escapes one's vision.

The great scholar Bentley, we recall, thought it necessary to make slashing revisions in *Paradise Lost* in order to bring Milton's grammar within the conventions of eighteenth century usage. Doctor Johnson, though he showed more respect for the text, held that Shakespeare never wrote six lines without a fault. In view of the ceaseless struggle between formalists and precisians, on the one hand, and the users of language for creative purposes, on the other, it may not be needless to insist that poetic power does not depend on conformity to grammar, logic, or any sort of mechanical correctness. Poetic truth may even be conveyed by a statement that is literally false. Balboa, no doubt, first gazed on the Pacific, but for Keats "stout Cortez" came first to mind and served equally well as an imaginative symbol. In a prose mood Emily Dickinson was as well aware as most of us that Vesuvius overlooks Naples, but if she preferred to write

> When Etna basks and purrs
> Naples is more afraid . . .

we need not quarrel with her choice. Perhaps the shock of a geographical dislocation will startle the reader to a degree of attention that prosaic accuracy could not provoke. These gross and palpable errors do not compromise the poetic value of the lines that contain them.

The same thing may be said of dislocations of syntax and other verbal abnormalities that notoriously occur in poetry. A poet has the right to create his own idiom at the risk of not being understood if he varies too widely from the customary norm. We should not have much respect for a poet whose range of expression did not strain the capacities of everyday language, and we can have no respect at all for a critic who supposes that normal usage can be made into a yardstick for the measurement of poetic achievement. If we examine Emily Dickinson's apparent lapses from grammatical convention, we shall soon discover that nearly all spring from one or another of the following causes: her preference for vernacular idiom, her old-fashioned training, her use of poetic mannerisms which she did not employ in prose, and her omission of verbal connective tissue in the effort to secure the utmost condensation of thought.

No one can read Emily Dickinson's early letters without noticing the New England provincialisms that fairly start from the pages:

Our little pussy has made out to live.

Such times as we would have would be a caution.

Aunt S—— says she sha'n't let me have many tunes now, for she wants I should get over in the book a good ways first.

I am almost a mind to take a hand-car and go around to hunt them up.

Her year at Mount Holyoke Seminary effectively ironed out most of these local wrinkles of language, but their occurrence in her girlish letters indicates that her native speech was not bookish English, but a salty country vernacular caught from living lips. This fact explains some of her variations from the norm of literary usage. She was not heedless of grammar when she wrote:

Had nature an Iscariot
That mushroom,—it is *him.*

and again:

Flinging the problem back at *you and I.*

But her instinct for the forms of expression preferred in actual speech was stronger than her regard for the rules of the purists. Yet another offense for grammar-conscious critics to pounce upon is contained in the lines:

Think of it, lover! *I and thee*
Permitted face to face to be. . . .

Strictly speaking, *thee* has no standing as a nominative case, but in colloquial practice it has long been sanctioned, quite apart from its conventional use by the Quakers.

Far from being slovenly in her handling of words, Emily was fastidious to a degree, though old-fashioned in some of her habits. If we consult Webster's *American Dictionary* (1847), the lexicon that she studied, we shall find that some of the locutions that might be cited as evidence of her illiteracy were in good standing a century ago. For example, she used four times in verse the past participle *lain* where we should expect *laid*, just reversing the common error. But one of the meanings given for *lie* was "to be reposited in the grave," and it was always in this special sense that Emily used the peccant participle, as in

Indolent housewife, in daisies lain.

Her habitual spellings of *vail* (for *veil*) and *extasy* had Webster's sanction, while *Himmaleh* and *Vevay* were names current in the geographies of her youth. Like Browning she employed *began* and *begun* indifferently as preterite forms, though her dictionary recognized only the former.

The more marked peculiarities of her language were sometimes due to a desire to give her verse a slightly archaic flavor. Thus she frequently wrote *be* instead of *is* or *are*, not only in the present subjunctive, which her grammar recognized as "ancient style," but in the present indicative as well.

The broadest land that grows
Be not so ample. . . .

.   .   .   .   .   .

Eclipses <i>be</i> predicted
And Science bows them in.

Historically, *be* as a present indicative form remained in concurrent use with *is-are* until early in the seventeenth century, and long after it had ceased to be standard it was retained in British southern and eastern dialects and in the vernacular speech of New England. One need go no further than the first number of Lowell's *Biglow Papers* for evidence. The educated classes, however, were trained to regard it as a vulgarism. To write *be* as a present indicative was, therefore, either below or above the level of ordinary discourse, depending on whether one thought of it in the vein of "thair aint no wheres a kitting spryer 'n I be" or of "The cowslips tall her pensioners be." In prose Emily Dickinson wrote *is* and *are* in a perfectly normal fashion. There can be little doubt that she preferred *be* in poetry because it gave her language an old-fashioned religious and literary flavor. It made her feel at one with Shakespeare and the King James Bible.

In her excessive employment of the subjunctive mood, whether the syntax would normally justify it or not, she was also mannered to a degree which suggests literary artifice. She reverted to it constantly in indirect discourse, in questions and comparisons, after conjunctions implying a condition or proviso, after adverbial conjunctions of time and place, and miscellaneously whenever there is a hint of doubt, desire, uncertainty, hesitation, or diffidence in what she is saying. Her prose style is not abnormal in this way, but the tension of her poetry seems to have thrown her into a state of chronic trepidation which only the subjunctive could express. In many instances her apparent failure to secure agreement between subject and predicate may be explained if we bear in mind her over-sensitive preference for the subjunctive mood. Out of countless illustrations the following are characteristic:

> I cannot vouch the merry dust
> *Do* not arise and play

> . . . . . .

> Who court *obtain*
> Within himself
> Sees every man a king.

> . . . . . .

> Diviner Crowd at home
> *Obliterate* the need

> . . . . . .

> And do I smile, such cordial light
> Upon the valley *glow* . . .

> . . . . . .

> Mirth is the mail of anguish,
> In which it cautious *arm*.

It would be too much to claim that all of these examples are defensible. Her penchant for the subjunctive was a personal idiosyncrasy, from which she might have been saved, to the advantage of her poetry, had she been willing to submit her work to the discipline of type.

Her liking for compactness of expression is everywhere manifest. Short words pleased her. The six nouns that occur most often in her verse are, in order of frequency: *day, life, eye, sun, man, heaven,* all but the last sharp monosyllables. *Summer* and *morning* are the only other polysyllables among the twenty-five nouns that she used fifty or more times in poetry. When words did not come short by nature, she sometimes contrived to shorten them. She would write "The daily *own* of love" rather than *possession,* "How *pomp* surpassing ermine" for *pompous, glid* for *glided, worth* for *worth while, inner* for *more inward.* Instead of the usual *ungraspable, inescapable,* or *imperturbable* she preferred uncommon coinages with the suffix *-less,* as *graspless, escapeless, perturbless.* They were shorter and stronger "Saxon." She even tried *vital-less,* an illegitimate combination. Like Shakespeare she made a habit of abbreviating past participial adjectives derived from verbs ending in *t,* as *create* for *created, exert* for *exerted, complicate* for *complicated.* It was briefer to say "*Much billow* hath the sea" rather than *many billows.* Other nouns in the singular were forced to serve as collectives:

> And say how many *dew*
>
> .　.　.　.　.　.
>
> Mouldered this many *May*
>
> .　.　.　.　.　.
>
> And countless *butterfly*.

Each reader must decide for himself whether such experiments as these awaken in him a pedantic revulsion or a poetic response.

When applied to matters of syntax, Emily Dickinson's instinct for economy was ruthless. She wrote sometimes as though her pen could keep pace with her thought only by skipping occasional articles, prepositions, conjunctions, relative pronouns, and auxiliary verbs. If one of the omitted words happened to be necessary to the meaning, let the reader supply it. She valued compactness even more than lucidity. At times her sentences are as crumpled as rock strata under geological pressure, seeming to the uninitiated a mere debris of fractured meanings. But her occasional obscurities are almost never due to vague thinking. When the toiling reader has filled in ellipses and bridged anacoluthons he finds that ground has been covered, though the going was rough. In her most anfractuous passages we discern the poet wrestling with language as Jacob wrestled with the angel. She was sometimes worsted, but by such encounters she developed the sinew of her art. Even in her defeats "the transport of the aim" remains.

The gnomic concision of Emily Dickinson's poems is a continual stimulus to mental alertness. She does not encourage a dreamy half-attention on the reader's part. This may be made evident if we place one of her mildly puzzling poems beside a passage of similar content by a writer of very different quality. In "A Song for Occupations," Whitman stated the transcendental conviction that the essence of a work of art is what exists in the mind of the audience, a conviction on which later critics have based the doctrine of "significant form":

All music is what awakes from you when you are reminded by the instruments,
It is not the violins and the cornets, it is not the oboe nor the beating drums, nor the score of the baritone singer singing his sweet romanza, nor that of the men's chorus, nor that of the women's chorus,
It is nearer and farther than they.

Whitman's method, as he explained it in one of his later prefaces, was to bring the reader within the "atmosphere" of an idea and there leave him to pursue his own flight. In the three lines quoted, the poet's control of the reader's mind is absolute in the initial statement of the thought, is intentionally relaxed in the succeeding list of particulars, and finally trails off in a faint, suggestive echo calculated to induce in the reader a state of revery. Emily Dickinson's treatment of the same theme is, on the contrary, a succession of challenges to keep abreast of the poet in her progress toward precision. The song of the oriole, she says, may appear a common thing or it may strike us as divine. The difference is not owing to the bird, which sings precisely the same whether there are listeners or not.

> The fashion of the ear
> Attireth that it hear
> In dun or fair.
>
> So whether it be rune,
> Or whether it be none,
> Is of within.
>
> The "tune is in the tree,"
> The skeptic showeth me;
> "No, sir! In thee!"

The thought of the poem could be stated flatly in prose, but no paraphrase could be made to contain the sense of struggle to express things never yet attempted in rhyme that the poem conveys by a gnarled, compact vitality, like that of a tree growing just below timber line. It is precisely this communicable energy of mind that we most value in Emily Dickinson's writings. Her obscurities are less frequent and less baffling than those of Donne, or Browning, or George Meredith, or Gerard Manley Hopkins, and no less than theirs are worthy of patient interpretation.

It is unfortunately true, however, that her later editors have been unfaithful in their reading of the text. Any one who doubts this fact may readily compare the printed form of one of her quatrains (267, cxxix):

> Her grace is all she has,
> And that, so *vast* displays . . .

with the facsimile facing page 266 of the Centenary Edition of *Poems* (1930), where the word I have italicized appears plainly as *least*; or again (405, xlviii), line 2:

> Stealthy Cocoon, why *hid* you so,

with the facsimile in the Limited Edition of *Unpublished Poems* (1935), where the word is *hide*. It was not Emily who committed the absurdity of speaking of the frost stiffening flowers *in March*, when there is not a flower above ground in Amherst; the fault is her editors', who carelessly transcribed her apt image for the white frosts of early October, "A visitor in *marl*," as "A visitor in *March*" (399, xxxix). In the following list of selected examples, with the true readings given in parenthesis, misprints and misreadings have been allowed to disfigure the text through several printings and still remain in the current *Poems* (1937):

> (126, Prelude). Some one the *sun* could tell (*sum*)
> (133, xiii). As if no *sail* the solstice passed (*soul*)
> (243, lxii). Whose apple Winter *warm* (*worn*)·
> (255, xci). Thy fellows,—are they Realms or *Themes?* (*Thrones?*)
> (260, cvi). Christ robs the *next*— (*nest*)
> (288, xxvi). *Than* can appal but one (*that*)
> (410, lxii). My *plans* and I together wrought (*plane*)
> (421, lxxvi). When *morn's* at full 'tis Thou, I say, (*moon's*)
> (431, xcii). A single *screen* of flesh (*screw*)
> (431, xcii). Upon my side the *vale*. (*veil*: spelled *vail*).

An early reviewer of *Poems* (1890) conjectured that when Emily said of the hemlock: "To satin races it is nought," she must have meant "Latin races." But any one who reads in their context the lines listed above will, I trust, acquit me of suggesting emendations in a like spirit of literalism.

To instances of faulty text must be added a number of blemishes due to editorial punctuation that has hopelessly misinterpreted Emily's meaning. She herself protested that the third and fourth lines of her poem on the snake (79, xxiv) should be read continuously, but her later editors have restored the question mark that keeps them asunder. Any reader may try for himself to make sense of the poem beginning "Revolution is the pod" (290, xxx) as Emily's later editors have punctuated it. When his patience is exhausted, let him move the periods from the ends of stanzas 1 and 2 and place them in each case at the end of line 3, making sense units of the first three lines and the last five. The four lines that comprise the middle section should be read continuously:

> Excellent is bloom,
>
> But, except its russet base,
> Every summer be [i.e. *is*]
> The entomber of itself.

Having done this, the reader may score a minor triumph over Chaos and old Night. Two things are clear. Emily Dickinson is not to be held responsible for the worst absurdities printed in her name. And a new edition of her poems based on a competent re-examination of the extant manuscripts is greatly to be desired.

May we hope also that future editors of Emily Dickinson will not print her poems in such a way as to disguise their metrical structure! The last three sections of her book, as arranged by her latest editors, constitute a prosodic "bad lands." Single lines have been broken into two or even three separate lines, false lines formed by joining fragments metrically distinct, stanzas divided in the middle, and the stanzaic basis of entire poems concealed by failure to divide. It is true that

Emily had little sense for the visible form of a poem. She sometimes divided or merged lines as her habit of writing in a bold hand on small scraps of paper dictated. She was quite capable of writing a poem "solid" like prose, merely capitalizing the first word of each line and not always remembering to do that. Since she freely capitalized important words within the line as well, it is often impossible to tell, except by ear, whether an apparent line in manuscript is a true line or not. The tune was in her head, and she was indifferent to its representation on paper. Her editors, however, should not permit themselves to share her indifference. A freakish display of poems on the printed page does not make them more "Emily-ish"—it makes them merely freakish.

No one who disregards editorial perversities and reads the poems metrically can avoid the perception that Emily Dickinson was both orthodox in her choice of meters, except in a very small number of poems, and skillful in blending the fixed beat of the meter with the free cadences of speech. Her preference was for iambic or trochaic measures and for the four-stress line. More than half of her published poems are written in the familiar ballad stanza, the "common meter" of the hymn books. Another large group is in "short meter," a four-line stanza differing from common meter only in having the first line a trimeter instead of a tetrameter. "Long meter," the iambic tetrameter quatrain rhymed either alternately or in couplets, does not occur in her writing nearly as frequently as it does in Watts and other hymnists. The reason may be that stated in the preface of her father's copy of *Church Psalmody* (Boston, 1854): "A hymn in long metre generally possesses less vivacity . . . than one in short metre, principally because the stanza in short metre expresses as much of thought and feeling in twenty-six syllables, as the stanza in long metre does in thirty-two. In many instances in this book, hymns in long metre have been changed into common or short metre, by merely disencumbering the lines of their lifeless members."

About one poem in ten may be described as written in irregular meter. This estimate does not include standard forms in which minor irregularities occur. Many of the irregular poems are very short,—tiny notations of some passing thought. But "I know some lonely houses off the road" (9, xv) and "In winter in my room" (246, lxx) are among the longest poems that she wrote, and in these and some others of medium length the intention of metrical improvisation is evident from the start. Another small group of irregular poems comprises those in which the writer began in a recognizable stanza form, but broke the mold rather than bend her thought to fit a procrustean bed. The rather unusual pentameter-dimeter stanza that Emily used in "This quiet Dust was Gentlemen and Ladies" (248, lxxiv) was apparently the pattern first selected for the following poem, but in the course of writing it the more familiar tetrameter-trimeter rhythm tended to intrude and Emily let herself follow the implicit cadence of her thought. (I have rearranged the lines to emphasize the stanza pattern. Many readers will no doubt prefer the freer arrangement derived from Emily's manuscript.) It commences with perfect regularity:

> The nearest dream recedes, unrealized.
> The heaven we chase,
> Like the June bee before the school-boy,
> Invites the race,

but with the third line of the second stanza the meter wavers:

> Then to the royal clouds lifts his slight pinnace,
> Heedless of the boy

and when the metrical beat is recovered at the end of the poem it has undergone a subtle transmutation:

> Ah! the bee flies not that brews
> That rare variety.

Many other poems might be cited as evidence that the substance of her writing was more precious to her than the outward form. If her mind halted or took an oblique angle, she faithfully traced its course. But with all her freedom, only one of her poems, "Victory comes late" (26, lii), is written in the unmetrical, unrhymed form that has since come to be known as "free verse."

Emily Dickinson's devices for varying the inevitable monotony that attaches to short lines woodenly written are only those long sanctioned in English poetry: the substitution of trochees or spondees for iambs, the introduction of extra unaccented syllables, and the use of the catalectic final foot. A full sense of the expertness of her performance can be gained by studying her variations of movement in their context and by comparing them with examples of merely mechanical writing. For the latter we may turn to the hymn by Doctor Watts traditionally sung at Amherst Commencements:

> Let children hear the mighty deeds
> Which God perform'd of old;
> Which in our younger years we saw,
> And which our fathers told.
>
> He bids us make his glories known,
> His works of power and grace;
> And we'll convey his wonders down,
> Through every rising race. . . .

It would be difficult to find in Emily Dickinson two successive stanzas written with a like droning correctness. Her practice is better represented by the opening stanzas of the poem which follows, in which, while the trimeter lines hold steadily to the metrical pattern, three of the four tetrameter lines are strikingly varied by one or another of the devices already mentioned:

> Dare you see a soul at the white heat?
> Then crouch within the door.
> Red is the fire's common tint;
> But when the vivid ore

Has sated flame's conditions,
Its quivering substance plays
Without a color but the light
Of unanointed blaze. . . .

In the complete poem (17, xxxiii) one may note also the frequent avoidance of end-stopped lines and the overrunning of the first and third stanzas. If the poet's thorough mastery of her medium is not sufficiently evident in her management of the simple meters that she usually preferred, an analysis of the more uncommon or complicated metrical effects in such poems as "Going to him! Happy letter!" (139, xxiii), "Safe in their alabaster chambers" (158, iv), "This quiet Dust was Gentlemen and Ladies" (248, lxxiv), "The popular heart is a cannon first" (278, iv), and "We—Bee and I—live in the quaffing" (307, liii) will convince any one that Emily Dickinson was no tyro in her art.

No feature of her verse technique has attracted more attention than her rhymes. Her practice, if not so utterly lawless as it appears to a casual eye, ran directly counter to the nicety in rhyming that was the ideal of most poets of her generation. To an old-school critic like Aldrich a failure to make rhymes chime was an evidence of slovenly workmanship; in his opinion Emily Dickinson was a poetic slattern whose intolerable verses could not even be read until a superior art had tossed a rhyme into them. More recently, her off-color rhymes have been celebrated as an anticipation of the studied inexactness affected by such poets as Humbert Wolfe, John Crowe Ransom, and Archibald MacLeish. An English writer has even argued that her inexactness was a subtly effective method of communicating her sense of fracture and discord in the world of her poetic vision. It would be unwise to accept either favorable or unfavorable view until we have considered just what Emily Dickinson did and did not do with rhyme-words and have made some attempt to trace the origin and intention of her supposed eccentricities.

Her sense of what constituted an admissible rhyme was much broader than that in vogue in her day, but she did not write at hazard, rhyming or not rhyming as might be most convenient. The instances where she completed a stanza without a rhyme of some sort if rhyme was to be expected are so rare that they may safely be dismissed as loose ends. The rhymes that she employed may be classified under five types, for all of which precedents may be quoted, though no poet before her had made such constant use of approximate rhymes as she did.

1. *Identical rhyme.* The same vowel sound preceded and followed by identical consonants occurs among her rhymes, though infrequently. Sometimes the rhyme-words, though identical in sound, are different in sense, as French usage demands: *gold-marigold, seal-conceal,* but the same word is also repeated to rhyme with itself. Had she been a sophisticated poet, she could probably not have used this type of rhyme without being conscious of its French provenience.

2. *Exact rhyme.* Most of Emily Dickinson's rhymes are such as any poet would normally use, and many entire poems are exactly rhymed throughout. Double or feminine rhymes, however, are very rare.

3. *Imperfect rhyme.* Two words may serve as rhymes if they end on the same vowel sound followed by different consonants. This kind of approximation is relatively common in folk-poetry and in hymns. From either source Emily may have acquired a tolerance for the rhymes that follow, which in her practice are hardly more frequent than in the then current hymn-books: *us-dust, thing-in, gained-spade, fields-steal, pass-countenance, fortified-described, stripped-picked.*

4. *Vowel rhyme.* A word ending in a vowel sound may be rhymed with a word ending in any other vowel sound. English poetry in general permits the laxity of rhyming final *-y* with either *be* or *die,* and certain "eye-rhymes" in *-ow* and *-ough* are not uncommon. Emily Dickinson, however, extended this

type of license far beyond the sparing use of it made by other poets. Some of her approximations are: *be-die, cloy-necessity, boy-by, caw-die, me-say, blew-sky, low-sky, snow-awe, sea-slow, plausibility-true, woe-Italy, bough-by, joy-crucify.*

Furthermore, the letter *r* was so lightly pronounced that words ending in final *-r* are not distinguished from words ending in a vowel and so follow the same rule, as: *idea-here, fear-awe, pioneer-now, stare-America, door-orchestra, saw-scimitar, drawer-rosemary.*

5. *Suspended rhyme.* Two words may serve as rhymes if they end in different vowel sounds followed by the same consonant. This is the most common form of approximate rhyme. It is entrenched in English usage in the desperate convention that rhymes *blossom-bosom, woman-human-common, heaven-even-given,* and in "eye-rhymes" like *love-move.* All poets resort to suspended rhyme on occasion, and certain modern poets have made a cult of its experimental use. As compared with poets of her time who were inclined to apologize for the license, Emily Dickinson used rhymes like these without reluctance: *gate-mat, gig-dog, near-hair, care-hour, star-door, espied-God, reach-touch, estate-cannot, grace-loneliness, crawl-cool, shawl-hill.*

As in the case of vowel rhyme, she disregarded the sound of *r: come-term, dark-spoke, stars-eyes, pearl-fool, arm-exclaim, death-earth, observe-love.* The sound of *l* is also elided, both where it is commonly silent as in *speak-talk-folk,* and where it is fully pronounced: *leaf-self, field-cloud, denied-smiled, emerald-thread, gold-inlaid, spelled-dead, cold-latitude, film-dim.* The elision of *r* and *l* may be paralleled in such hymn-book rhymes as: *wrath-north, thoughts-faults, psalm-arm.*

Within the license of suspended rhyme Emily Dickinson adopted a further license in accepting certain consonants or combinations of consonants as roughly equivalent to certain others. Though one may say that her ear was not exacting, she was not wholly without justification in supposing that a faint rhyme-echo might be secured from some pairs of words in which neither the vowel nor the final consonant perfectly chimed. Again sporadic precedents may be culled from hymns, as: *earth-chaff*, *grace-flesh*. But Emily Dickinson's verse contains so many examples that her practice can be reduced to rule, and it will be seen that her madness was not without method. She accepted the practical equivalence of:

(*a*) Nasals—M, N, NG: *time-ran, gown-hung, home-tune, came-worshipping, greens-things, refined-ashamed, warm-lain.*

(*b*) Sibilants—S, Z, SH, CH; and sibilants in combination with D, T, K, or P: *face-eyes, does-fresh, push-mice, avarice-speech, looks-eclipse, least-house, west-paradise, missed-stitch, enfolds-suffice.*

(*c*) Dentals—D, T, with ND, NT; T with CT; D with VD: *freight-adamant, mind-lead, friend-word, command-colonnade, recollect-not, act-substitute, built-erect, road-saved, repaired-removed.*

(*d*) Miscellaneous—T with P; K with NK; Z with soft G: *slope-foot; drink-look, banks-stocks; blaze-forge, freeze-privilege.*

It would be too much to claim that all these approximate rhymes are justifiable or inevitably right in their context. The poet took risks in using them and sometimes stumbled. But both sub-literary and ultra-sophisticated verse-writers have amply demonstrated that the convention of strict rhyme is an artificial one with no inherent sanction. Emily Dickinson was only following a tendency long grounded in English practice, though discountenanced by precisians. It remains to be seen how far she was aware of her boldness and what she intended to accomplish by it.

If she had been what Aldrich called her, "an eccentric, dreamy, half-educated recluse in an out-of-the-way New England village," we might suppose that she had adopted and exaggerated the slipshod rhyming of the hymn-books in unconscious innocence. But with Higginson's letters at her elbow she could not have escaped knowing that her rhymes were unorthodox. As a matter of fact she did not, under his tutelage, take any more pains to find exact rhymes than before. Instead her fondness for approximate rhymes appeared, if anything, to increase with the years. It is safe to conclude, therefore, that she knew exactly what she was doing and did it with full intention.

Incitements to experiment with rhyme were not wanting as far back as the middle of the nineteenth century. Elizabeth Barrett Browning, of whose posthumous volume Emily Dickinson wrote in ardent admiration:

> Her 'Last Poems' poets ended,

was one of the experimenters. In explanation of her departure from normal practice Mrs. Browning declared: "A great deal of attention—far more than it would have taken to rhyme with complete accuracy—have I given to the subject of rhymes and have determined in cold blood to hazard some experiments." Emily may not have read this sentence, but she must have seen and pondered the poems that occasioned it, and the example of the English poetess whom she idolized may have encouraged her to venture some experiments on her own account.

She used rhymes that did not perfectly match and she was also acutely aware of broken patterns and jarring discords within the range of her experience. Can we go so far as to affirm, as an English critic has suggested, that Emily intended the conscious disjunction of her rhymes to express her perception of a world where seams would not fit and sequences ravelled out of reach. The idea is attractive since it supplies a connection between two otherwise unrelated sets of facts, but it should be examined with extreme caution lest we mistake the desire for bringing order out of chaos for the desire to arrive at truth. Critics, as we know, are capable of constructing ingenious theories of intention which authors disclaim. This particular theory fails to take note of the fact that Emily Dickinson, besides commenting on the shortcomings of life, also expressed her sense of the ecstasy of living, of religious confidence, and even of mystic hope. If she had felt any such significance in her off-rhymes as the theory implies, we should expect to find her using them chiefly to voice her moods of doubt and dismay and returning to full rhyme in her positive and ecstatic moments. But no such correlation between rhyme and mood is observable. One of the most ecstatic poems she ever wrote opens with the faulty rhyme to which Aldrich objected. Her magnificent affirmation of love borne out to the edge of doom, "Of all the souls that stand create" (137, xix), is impeccably rhymed throughout, but " 'Twas a long parting, but the time" (135, xv), which treats the same theme of reunion in eternity, employs nothing but suspended rhyme. We are forced to conclude, therefore, that Emily Dickinson accepted inexact rhymes because their hinted tinkling served to round her stanzas as well as fully chiming syllables. There is no evidence of any such subtlety of intention on her part as the modern critic would like to discover.

An examination of Emily Dickinson's use of language and of those features of her verse technique that have excited critical objections does not indicate that her poems were faultless. They were often startlingly rough and unpolished. But it does indicate that her poetic aims were not compromised at the start by a trivial concern about externals. What she had to say would be said if necessary despite grammar, meter, or rhyme, and if it lived at all it should live by sheer inner vitality. Her willingness to pack her poems with meaning led to oddities of diction and syntax. She was moved to push against the bonds of rhyme lest they cause her to bend her thoughts. But in no respect was she a conscious innovator, seeking novelty for novelty's sake. Her instinctive preference was for simple forms hallowed by use. In poetry as in life her characteristic triumphs consisted in fulfilling patterns, not in breaking them.

Minims of Nature

A CENTURY ago Byron, Moore, and Campbell were the approved poets. We have already seen a college tutor recommending the first-named to the girls of Amherst and advising them to leave Lowell, Motherwell, and Emerson alone. Only by the few was Wordsworth recognized as the discoverer of new veins of true poetic ore. His philosophic poems were commonly regarded as obscure, his nature poems as "low." It is difficult to realize now that there was ever a time when the least facts of nature were considered as beneath a poet's notice, yet Higginson recalls in his *Contemporaries* that Emerson's lines "To a Humble-Bee," written in 1837 and published two years later in a religious periodical, were at first ridiculed by some critics as "a foolish affectation of the familiar." Slowly the public mind was educated to an appreciation of what the poets were doing, but in Emily Dickinson's girlhood the writing of nature poetry was an adventure into what was still largely a dark continent.

It is not possible to say how well Emily was acquainted with Wordsworth's poems. She seldom quoted them. The favorite poet of external nature in Amherst circles was James Thomson, author of *The Seasons*, whom she once mentioned along with Bryant. The example of Bryant, Whittier, Emerson, and Lowell, not to speak of Tennyson, all of whom she read, would have been sufficient to awaken her interest in the new poetic treatment of field and wood and garden. The world of nature in its more familiar aspects lay ready to her hand. She availed herself of it as soon as she began to write poems at all and so continued to the end. About one-fifth of her published work may be classified as nature poetry.

Her experience of uncultivated nature was gained entirely in her early years and was confined to the region immediately around Amherst, but within these limits it was intense and vividly remembered. Her schoolmate Mrs. Ford recollected many country rambles that she had shared with Emily Dickinson, and spoke especially of their excursions to Mount Norwottock, where they found the climbing fern, pink and white trilliums, and, later, yellow lady's slippers. "She knew the wood-lore of the region round about," Mrs. Ford testified, "and though her life even then was very domestic she could name the haunts and habits of every wild or garden growth within her reach."

A few passages from her letters have a bearing upon her early intimacy with outdoor things. The first suggests that she was more addicted than her family altogether approved of to scrambling through the woods:

When much in the woods, as a little girl, I was told that the snake would bite me, that I might pick a poisonous flower, or goblins kidnap me; but I went along and met no one but angels, who were far shyer of me than I could be of them, so I haven't that confidence in fraud which many exercise.

In her forty-sixth year she still recalled her rapture in the first discovery of a wildflower that was new to her:

I had long heard of an orchis before I found one, when a child, but the first clutch of the stem is as vivid now as the bog that bore it, so truthful is transport.

And finally we may note the association of the passing seasons with a strain of pensiveness that often reappears in her poems:

When flowers annually died and I was a child, I used to read

Dr. Hitchcock's *Flowers of North America*. This comforted their absence, assuring me they lived.

In later life her outlook was limited to her garden and the ample grounds around her home. These included the grove of oaks behind the house, of which she spoke in 1870 as "my own forest where I play every day." The flower garden remained to the end her particular province, its every blossom individually dear to her, though she confessed a special predilection for bulbs. In a community devoted to flower culture she was noted for a success that could not have been achieved without an intimate understanding of plants and their ways. This knowledge, as we shall see, was reflected in her writings.

An analysis by subject of Emily Dickinson's nature poems shows that fifteen are on nature in general, thirty-three on the changes of the seasons or on particular months, twenty-five on aspects of day and night, twenty-nine on the sky, heavenly bodies, and phenomena of climate, seventeen on features of the landscape, and fifty-eight on living creatures, animals, birds, reptiles, insects, or plants. Her decided preference was for dramatic and colorful subjects. The coming of spring inspired ten poems, of which no less than four are devoted entirely to praise of the gusty month of March; and the poignant transition from summer to autumn called forth an equal number. Dawn and sunset, with the latter predominating, account for all but three of her poems on day and night. Neither moon nor stars greatly occupied her attention, but there were seven poems on thunderstorms and four on the wind. The larger number of landscape poems are on mountains, though here it is observable that Emily found the names of mountains that she had read about more exciting than the modest hills that she could see from her window. Alps, Apennines, "Himmaleh," Cordillera, Etna, Vesuvius, Teneriffe, "Chimbarazu" are familiar names in her verses, to the exclusion of the Berkshires, the Holyoke Range, and Mount Tom. She wrote few poems on bodies of water. Her rivers and brooks, except for a few geographical names like Don and Dnieper, are symbolic, never actual, and her two poems on the ocean were purely exercises in imagination. "I am glad you cherish the sea," she wrote to Mrs. Todd in 1885. "We correspond, though I never met him." Running water, the "leopard-colored rills" of Emerson, apparently did not fascinate her as it does most poets, and her only poem on any watery aspect of the landscape that can be described as personally felt is one that sets forth the placid mystery of wells. Of all living things creatures with wings most attracted her, birds, the bat, insects, and flowers that like Keats's sweetpeas seemed ever "on tiptoe for a flight." Wings, in fact, are one of the most pervasive images in her poems.

We may best consider her knowledge of the local flora and fauna in terms, not of entire poems, but of references to animals and plants scattered through the whole body of her poetry. This investigation will not permit us to draw any conclusions about the extent of her nature-lore, since she was not under any obligation to tell all she knew in verse, but it will enable us to see how much of her familiarity with natural objects supplied her with poetic material, and to make some comparisons in this respect with other American poets.

The population of the barnyard Emily Dickinson was inclined to take for granted. Though she knew her family horses and the other horses of the neighborhood by name, and frequently mentioned them in her letters, she did not write poems about them. Her three poetic references to horses and her two to cattle are of the most casual kind. Sheep and pigs she does not mention at all, and chickens, ducks, geese, and turkeys provided her with but three conventional allusions to chanticleer. She viewed askance the cats fostered by her sister and deigned to name the detested animal only three times. The dog fares but little better; Carlo ("my dog") appears twice, once with a compliment to his intelligence; the mud of spring wakens a thought of dog and peddler; and "a dog's belated feet like intermittent plush were heard" in the depths of a cloudy night. The hound, three times mentioned, proved useful as a symbol. Of small furry creatures the squirrel was most frequently named, nine times in all to six for the mouse, but the rat and the bat were the only ones that she took pains to characterize. Of twenty animals alluded to in her poems, fully one half were creatures that she had read about rather than seen. It does not appear, therefore, that she found much to engage her attention in the animals about her, either tame or wild. The same may be said of most nature poets. Lowell, for instance, though he speaks of the chipmunk and the water-rat, does not even once mention the squirrels of Elmwood.

Birds, on the contrary, have always been the poets' darlings. Lowell names forty-two species (including six that are English) in his poems, Emerson and Whitman each about forty, Bryant and Whittier nearly thirty. Emily Dickinson's references to birds are extremely frequent but seldom specific. She speaks often of bird songs in general but more rarely of the note of the bobolink or the blackbird in particular. Moreover, of the twenty-five birds on her list, eight at least, like the flamingo, the nightingale, and the vulture, were not birds of her acquaintance. Her undiscriminated sparrow is usually a Biblical character, not the song-sparow of the New England meadows, and her lark, owl, peacock, and swan are likewise literary. There remain twelve birds that she really knew: bluebird, blue jay, blackbird, bobolink, crow, hummingbird, oriole, phœbe, robin, whippoorwill, wren, and woodpecker—not a very extensive list, surely, and as remarkable for what it omits as for what it includes. Though her best bird poems have to do with the blue jay and the hummingbird, Emily's favorite was the ubiquitous robin, mentioned twenty times, more than twice as often as his nearest rival, the bobolink. She loved birds and on occasion observed them closely, but she evidently did not care to ornithologize. A bird was just a bird to her, when it was not, as was too frequently the case, a robin.

Though one of her poems begins, "Sweet is the swamp with its secrets," there is little indication that Emily Dickinson studied the arcana of bogs that so delighted Thoreau, and certainly her use of swamp life does not challenge the pre-eminence of Lanier as a poet of marshes. Her references to toad, tortoise, and turtle are not intimate. Frogs she knew by their croaking; they were, she once said, her dogs. But she does not distinguish between bullfrog and hyla, and I doubt if she ever heard "the long sigh of the Frog upon a Summer's day" that one of her poems speaks of. The quaint red salamander, as apparitional as Indian pipe beside a woodland path, she never mentioned. She referred to the snake—not any particular species—more often than to all other denizens of the swamp put together, and it occasioned two entire poems, including one of her best. To the insects that haunt marshy places, dragonflies, waterbeetles, and others, she was apparently indifferent.

The small creatures that her poems favor are those of the meadow and garden, the bee, the butterfly, the cricket, and the spider. Butterflies appear thirty-one times, exclusive of a caterpillar, two chrysalises, and several cocoons (which she did not reserve for moths), crickets seven times, houseflies six; the beetle, the gnat, the midge, and the moth are also included, but only conventionally. A number of common insects that she might readily have noticed, the grasshopper, the ant, the wasp, the firefly, the cicada, and the katydid, she never used in poetry. As in the case of birds, a few old friends best served her needs. Of all nature's people bees were by all odds her favorites. She names them fifty-two times, not counting nine specific references to bumblebees. The bee might have been her emblem even more fittingly than Napoleon's. She cared nothing, however, for apiculture or the social life of bees, and never spoke of swarming, of drone or queen, of honeycomb or wax. Special knowledge of this kind was not the aliment of her poetry.

Since bees were more frequently utilized in her poems than any other natural objects, it may be of interest here to note the range of her attitudes toward them. What, in other words, did she find to express in terms of bees? The list that follows is hardly systematic, but it may serve to illustrate the variety of her sensory impressions and the still wider range of her imaginative flights:

Sensory

(color)   Bees are black with gold surcingles,
Buccaneers of buzz . . .

His helmet is of gold;
His breast, a single onyx
With chrysoprase inlaid.

(motion)   . . . Stoops to an easy clover—
Dips—evades—teases—deploys;
    Then to the royal clouds
    Lifts his light pinnace . . .

(sound)   Baronial bees march, one by one,
In murmuring platoon!

Like trains of cars on tracks of plush
I hear the level bee . . .

(touch)   His feet are shod with gauze . . .

(taste)   . . . As brew from our obtuser mints
The julep of the Bee!

(kinesthesis)   I said, but just to be a bee
Upon a raft of air . . .

Imaginative

(gaiety)   We—Bee and I—
Live in the quaffing . . .

(fancy)   When landlords turn the drunken bee
Out of the foxglove's door . . .

Imaginative—Continued

(humor)	The pedigree of honey Does not concern the bee . . .
(hyperbole)	The bees became as butterflies, The butterflies as moons Lit up the low inferior grass . . .
(sentiment)	Did the harebell loose her girdle To the lover bee . . .
(symbol)	The heaven we chase Like the June bee Before the school-boy Invites the race . . .
(mystery)	The murmur of a bee A witchcraft yieldeth me. It goads me, like the goblin bee That will not state its sting.
(solemnity)	. . . Where Bloom and Bees Fulfilled their Oriental Circuit, Then ceased like these.
(benediction)	In the name of the bee And of the butterfly And of the breeze, amen!

A well-equipped American nature poet may normally be expected to name some twenty-five varieties of trees. Bryant, Whittier, and Whitman speak of about thirty each, Lowell and Emerson of twenty. Emily Dickinson in comparison with any one of these poets hardly notices trees at all. She has but one poem on the pine and one on the hemlock. She mentions in all only seven different kinds (including the palm), and the most frequently mentioned—maple and hemlock—only three times each. This in comparison with twenty-three references to the oak in Emerson's small body of poems and still more to the oracular white pine, which last was so beloved by Whittier that he found occasion to speak of it sixty-five times in his poems. Even such common trees as the birch, the oak, and the chestnut are not on Emily Dickinson's list.

In naming the flowers, however, she was on her own ground, and here for once traces of expert knowledge are evident. She includes one or two flowers like adder's tongue and batschia (rare in Amherst) that only a fair botanist would recognize, and she refers to the popular trailing arbutus by its scientific name (*Epigea*). Her list of forty-one species, about equally divided between wild and cultivated varieties, is only slightly shorter than Bryant's and about equals Whittier's. It has not the flavor of woodlands and pastures that Emerson's preferences in flowers and flowering shrubs reveal, but on the other hand Emily Dickinson is remarkable among poets for her relative neglect of the "literary" rose, lily, and violet and her frequent mention of less poetized blooms. The rose leads with seventeen references (including one to the wild rose), but the others in order of frequency are the daisy (fifteen), clover (ten), daffodil (eight), buttercup and lily (five), anemone, dandelion, gentian, and violet (three). Whittier refers to the sentimental violet four times as often as to the plain daisy. In Emerson the rose appears thirty times to five for clover. Lanier relies almost entirely on conventional flowers. Heather and asphodel are the only flowers Emily used in her poems that she had not seen growing. She wrote delightfully of such humble growths as the grass and the mushroom. She knew, of course, many more kinds of flowers, both wild and cultivated, than she had opportunity to mention. Neither the hollyhocks that lined the Dickinson barn nor the trilliums and lady's-slippers that she found in the woods gained a place in her verse. Curiously there is only one reference to ferns ("fern-odors"), though she was fond of enclosing a frond of fern in her letters.

Except in the case of flowers, Emily Dickinson made no attempt to study nature. She was not a professed naturalist. She shared, and in two poems expressed, the not uncommon dislike of scientific analysis and classification of natural objects. It was not her intention to ticket the yellow butterfly. Nature and nature's people she accepted as companions without any desire to pry into their secrets. What attracted her attention by its dramatic quality or its individuality she wrote about, often with keen observation. One might look far for a more delicate sketch of a bird's motions than that contained in the five stanzas of "A bird came down the walk" (78, xxiii). On the other hand, she made mistakes quite apart from her fanciful distortions of fact. "Nature rarer uses yellow than another hue" is a remark that cannot be confirmed in a countryside full of buttercups in early summer and of goldenrod in early fall, not to speak of the prevailing yellow of autumn leaves.

No single formula can be given for Emily Dickinson's treatment of nature. She did not consciously set out to promulgate a doctrine or even to be a nature poet; rather she found the external world so variously and intricately related to the inner world from which she drew her poetry that she could not avoid including it. She experimented in several modes, none of which completely satisfied her. She did not entirely escape the contagion of the popular sentimental approach to nature which verged on the mawkish. In perhaps half a dozen poems she associated flowers and birds with angels and fairies or adopted the factitious romantic image of nature as a "gentlest mother" whose mild admonition restrains rampant squirrel and too impetuous bird, and whose infinite affection and infiniter care are lavished on the minutest of her children, especially about bedtime. She was capable of writing about the robin in terms that parallel Wordsworth's libel on the skylark as a prototype of the British conservative. And, as we might expect in this connection, she embodied in a single poem the gushing humanitarian sympathy that belongs with the sentimental view of nature:

If I can stop one heart from breaking,

.   .   .   .

> Or help one fainting robin
> Unto his nest again,
> I shall not live in vain.

In our ignorance of the dates of Emily Dickinson's poems we cannot be certain that this strain of sentimentalism was a girlish attitude, later outgrown. It may have remained intermittent throughout her life, for as late as 1879 we find her writing to Mary Bowles, "Nature is our eldest mother, she will do no harm," very much as Wordsworth in his twenties was convinced that "Nature never did betray the heart that loved her." But we can say with assurance that Emily Dickinson's lapses into sentimentalism were rare and that the attitude was as uncharacteristic of her as it was unworthy.

The undistinguished verses written before Emily was twenty, and printed in the second memoir by her niece, show her using birds and flowers and sunsets as threads whereon to string words like bright beads. She revels in gold, crimson, opal, ermine, purple, and cochineal, but there is little substance within all this gorgeousness. Some of her early phrases, however, she was to treasure until she could place them in a fitting context. For example, she first wrote of a "navy sunset":

> Who looks for him at morning,
> I pray him too—explore
> The Lark's pure territory,
> Or the Lapwing's shore,

a melodious but empty combination of words, which haunted her mind until it became a stanza in a poem on her favorite subject of perception won through loss:

> Who never climbed the weary league—
> Can such a foot explore
> The purple territories
> On Pizzaro's shore?

The change from her earlier to her later manner generally consisted less in development of thought than in clarification of artistry, a stripping off of loose, extraneous material until only the essential remained.

Fortunately we are able to compare her final triumphant poem on the hummingbird with an early version, and to note what happened as she condensed the original twenty lines to eight. In its first form, which we may guess took shape in the early sixties at about the same time as her poems on the oriole (72, xiii) and the mushroom (80, xxv), the lines ran as follows:

> Within my garden rides a bird
> Upon a single wheel,
> Whose spokes a dizzy music make
> As 'twere a traveling mill.
>
> .   .   .   .
>
> Till every spice is tasted,
> And then his fairy gig
> Reels in remoter atmospheres,
> And I rejoin my dog.
>
> And he and I perplex us
> If positive 'twere we—
> Or bore the garden in the brain
> This curiosity?
>
> But he, the best logician,
> Refers my duller eye
> To just vibrating blossoms—
> An exquisite reply!

This is all very well for what there is of hummingbird in it: a fine image of the rapid wings like the spokes of a whirling wheel, another of the bird's sudden departure, and a vivid sense of the adjustment to emptiness that ensues. But how much is there that distracts us from the single impression—the motion and the sound of the wings given consecutively (a "traveling mill" to blur the clear image of the "single wheel"), then the movement of the whole bird from rose to remoter atmospheres, and finally a spectator and her dog, new characters introduced, through whom the final psychological notation is registered. Surely one might come nearer to the essential object by stripping off the matrix of external circumstance and preserving simply a description of the bird as it existed in "the garden of the brain." So, it is said, Japanese artists study bird or fish or flower until they have absorbed it into themselves, and when they paint, paint not an object before them but a mental image. Perhaps twenty years later, when Emily Dickinson rewrote her hummingbird poem, she had mastered the secret:

> A route of evanescence
> With a revolving wheel;
> A resonance of emerald,
> A rush of cochineal;
> And every blossom on the bush
> Adjusts its tumbled head,—
> The mail from Tunis, probably,
> An easy morning's ride.

Here is the whole *sensation* of hummingbird: first, a dazzle of sudden sense impressions, movement, motion of wings, color, and whir (in the reiterated *r*'s), all at once; then (the bird's departure taken for granted) the emptiness emphasized by the clear picture of nodding blossoms; and finally the startled mind of the (assumed) spectator regaining its poise with a whimsical comment. Nothing could be spared and no more is needed. Emily Dickinson was never to write a better nature poem than this, but the stepping-stones that led up to her finest achievement are, many of them, monuments of an artistry only slightly less perfect.

More than any of her contemporaries Emily Dickinson preserved toward nature the attitude of the artist rather than of the philosopher. It was a model whose ever-changing subtleties of expression her pencil could approximate but never fully render.

A Route of
Evanescence
With a revolving
Wheel.
A Resonance of
Emerald,
A Rush of
Cochineal,

And every
Blossom on the
Bush
Adjusts it's
tumbled Head.
The Mail from
Tunis, probably,
An easy Morning's
Ride.

A POEM SENT TO HIGGINSON IN 1880

She was content to leave the great secret unguessed. "Nature is a haunted house, but art a house that tries to be haunted," she wrote to Higginson, and in a poem beginning, "Nature is what we see," she stated the same conviction:

> Nature is what we know
> But have no art to say,
> So impotent our wisdom is
> To Her simplicity.

She did not, so far as I know, ever conceive of the poet as capable of adding anything to nature or of improving upon nature's handiwork, though she was ready enough to alter a natural fact when it suited her purposes to do so. Nor did she blame or praise the natural order. She thought of it as an impersonal, inexorable, mysterious force, to be reverenced, accepted, studied, enjoyed, and in all humility copied. But never for a moment was her own separateness to be merged with it.

She called herself pagan in comparison with the devout souls among her acquaintance, but the truth is that her paganism, like Bryant's in "Thanatopsis," was an unconscious Puritanism. The Puritan conception of nature as a visible manifestation of God, which Jonathan Edwards and Bryant in many of his early poems overtly expressed, was so ingrained in her that she took it for granted without comment. Nevertheless she could distinguish God in a sunset and believe that even His eccentricities, as illustrated by the bat, were beneficent. In the orchard, the church that she attended after she had abandoned all others, "God preaches—a noted clergyman."

> The red upon the hill
> Taketh away my will;
> If anybody sneer,
> Take care, for God is here,
> That's all.

The beauty and harmony of nature offered a revelation of the hereafter; the rapture of dawn, noon, and sunset hinted at the

glories of paradise and inspired her with awe before the mystery.
Creation was the sign of its inscrutable and imperturbable
Creator.

> Heaven has different signs to me;
> Sometimes I think that noon
> Is but a symbol of the place,
> And when again at dawn
>
> A mighty look runs round the world
> And settles in the hills,
> An awe if it should be like that
> Upon the ignorance steals.

Her only news was "bulletins all day from Immortality," but
she generally preferred to leave the interpretation of her message to be guessed. Though the religious significance of nature
is implicit in her point of view, it is very lightly stressed in her
poems.

In her habitual presentation of sense experience as an entity
that needed no excuse for existence, she differed from most poets
of her time. Bryant in "To a Waterfowl," Holmes in "The
Chambered Nautilus," Longfellow in "Seaweed," Tennyson in
"Flower in the Crannied Wall," followed the favorite nineteenth-century fashion of viewing a natural object as a moral
symbol. The more transcendental writers, in the wake of Wordsworth and Emerson, went still further in conceiving nature as
continuously emblematic of the spirit that rolls through all
things, when they did not actually identify and exalt nature as
that spirit itself. In Emerson's view, if we may be permitted
to reduce a somewhat shifting and suggestive body of thought
to a too simple and rigid formula, nature and man were both
partial reflections of the Divine Essence or Over-Soul, the One
within the Many; hence man, the sentient but also more dis-
torted mirror, could discern in nature not merely a pattern
resembling that of his own being, but one by which he might
correct the image of God imperfectly perceived through con-

sciousness. In the light of this rhapsodic unity in duality physics and ethics merged into one system, the natural order paralleled the spiritual order and confirmed it, and nature became a flowing revelation, here and now, of man's highest leadings. An impulse from the vernal wood could teach more than the sages can. A closer walk with God could be attained by a stroll through the pines. Mystic temperaments, who would once have dreamed of religious communion with the Infinite, sought to immerse themselves in the landscape. "Margaret," as Emerson recorded of Miss Fuller, "would beat with the beating heart of Nature."

Emily Dickinson, who fully shared the self-sufficiency of the Transcendentalists, was hardly touched by their mystical doctrine of nature. The beautiful pageant of the external world thrilled her senses, but not to the point of intruding upon her identity. She could point out an occasional analogy between nature and man without implying a complete correspondence of the natural and the human. Thus she memorably characterized a November day when the feel of snow was in the air:

> A narrow wind complains all day
> How someone treated him;
> Nature, like us, is sometimes caught
> Without her diadem.

Her love of nature had in fact its reserves; she had conceived a shrewd suspicion that nature is in essence profoundly alien to man, fascinatingly unknowable, possibly hostile. This she stated tartly and once for all in "What mystery pervades a well!" (115, xcvi):

> But Nature is a stranger yet;
>   The ones that cite her most
> Have never passed her haunted house
>   Nor simplified her ghost.
>
> To pity those that know her not
>   Is helped by the regret
> That those who know her, know her less
>   The nearer her they get.

Only Lowell among her elder contemporaries was capable of combining a genuine enthusiasm for the out-door world with a like humorous common sense.

Her distrust of nature was perhaps based on the perception of nature's indifference to man's bleaker moments. The landscape that seemed to smile its accord with the lighter moods of humanity mocked at grief with unthinking drums. The sentience that she felt even in the "merry dust" was devoid of sympathy. Neither blackbird nor blossom, as she twice remarked, showed the least deference to passing Calvary, and

> *Auto-da-fé* and judgment
> Are nothing to the bee.

The natural order, therefore, like the supernatural, had no power to rescue her when life seemed to go to pieces beneath her feet. Alike in their huge impersonality, God and nature refused to intervene in her personal crisis. She realized early that a human problem must be solved by human means.

Yet though nature had no sympathy with the soul's distress, its unshakable serenity afforded a kind of discipline almost equivalent to the religious. When the reservoirs of faith run dry, men may refresh themselves with the spiritual sanity that, like dew, lies on the little things of earth, on grass and stone, tree and flower. In fullness of physical contact with nature there is a healing power, as Wordsworth and other beleaguered poets after him have discovered. The senses, the old enemies of the soul, may in adversity become its ministers. To sensuous experience, the tiny fragments of reality that do not have to be believed into being, those who wish to live freshly in an age of exhausted formulas must turn, as Emily Dickinson fixed her mind on the tone and tempo of a bee in clover, the whir of a hummingbird's wings, the bat's bisected umbrella, the snake's litheness in the grass. One feels that she watched these things with the intensity of attention that a soldier under fire is said to feel in the smallest inconsequential things about him, or an invalid in the crawling of a fly on the window-pane. Like Hamlet when he clutched his tablets and wrote that one may smile and be a villain, she craved the touch of something familiar and tangible and the relief of writing down her observations. The world of nature, then, was a distraction from piercing memories. It helped her to keep a precarious poise on the sword-edge of experience.

15

The Leaf at Love Turned Back

N HIS *Atlantic* essay on "Americanism in Literature" (1870)
Thomas Wentworth Higginson took occasion to deplore
the inadequate treatment of profound human emotion in the
work of contemporary poets and novelists, both in England
and America, but particularly in this country. To what end, he
asked, had Emerson set free the poetic intuition of America, and
Hawthorne its imagination? They had not plumbed the depths.
"Both looked into the realm of passion, Emerson with distrust,
Hawthorne with eager interest; but neither thrilled with its
spell, and the American poet of passion is yet to come." Higginson was the one man of letters then in a position to know that
the American poet of passion had arrived. Lying in his desk,
unpublished, was at least one lyric that glowed with the fire he
was seeking. Had his discernment been less decorously gloved
it would have burned his fingers.

Emily Dickinson was the only American poet of her century
who treated the great lyric theme of love with entire candor
and sincerity. But it is not enough to say of her, as we may say
of Catullus or Burns, that she wrote love poems of extraordinary
intensity. The individuality of her contribution lies in the fact
that these poems are not merely reiterated expressions of passionate longing and regret, but successive moments in the intricate
progress of a soul through the deepest of human experiences.
They record with minute veracity the subtle changes in a
woman's nature as she becomes conscious of her heart's unalter-

able commitment, passes through self-sustained illusion and painful disillusionment to an agony of frustration, and emerges at last impregnably fortified on a new plane of being. Not many poets have traced the stages of a like psychic journey to the very edge of doom and back. But somewhat the same pattern of spiritual growth through deprivation we may recognize in the grave symbolic pageant of Dante's *Vita Nuova*. Emily Dickinson was probably not aware of the parallel between her course and the great Florentine's, and where the road branched she elected a different turning. She was not tempted for long to look for solace on the heights of mystical sublimation; the way that she followed kept closely to the human level.

The story of her heart is developed in a series of lyrics written with the concision that brief verse demands. Within each tiny poem exists a shaping principle like the inner law that compels a snowflake to assume symmetrical form. Yet in the mass these myriad poems are something more than the fall of so many separate flakes, something more even than a snowdrift sculptured by an exigent wind. They have the organic coherence that belongs to the record of an inward drama. Their cumulative effect, if they were properly arranged, would be many times that of their sum when each is read singly.

Unfortunately the accidents of posthumous publication have seriously obscured an intrinsic design which the writer of the poems was never at pains to express by ordering her work and which her editors have missed entirely. In the three selections from the Dickinson manuscripts published during the 1890's the material was loosely divided into the four groups entitled Life, Nature, Love, and Time and Eternity that still constitute the first four sections of the poems as currently printed. Later editors have merely added on three volumes of further selections, within each of which some attempt has been made to group like poems together. But the essential task of organizing the whole body of Emily Dickinson's work has never been faced. Until this is done so that it can be seen how poem leads on to poem, the larger form and significance of her achievement will not be generally recognized. Higginson's failure to perceive the distinction of her writing shows what will inevitably happen as long as her lyrics are regarded as separate units, not as parts of an articulate whole.

As the poems now stand in print, the majority of those that reflect Emily Dickinson's experience of love are contained in Part III (Love), Part VI (Further Poems), section 6, and Part VII (Additional Poems), section 3, but the classification is not exact. A few poems included in these groups do not refer to the principal crisis of her life, and many others which do refer to it have been placed elsewhere in the volume. When her authentic love poems are brought together and carefully studied, it is possible to discern some indications of how these separate star-points of light may be combined and related to each other in nebular clusters. To bring out such connections, even in the most tentative way, is a service that criticism must perform before Emily Dickinson's full stature as a poet can be appreciated.

She does not leave us for a moment in doubt as to where to look for the sun of her poetic universe:

> Wait! Look! her little book,
> The leaf at love turned back.

The. fact ever present to her consciousness was that what she most asked of life had been denied her. Around that denial a large number of her poems revolve. To disengage herself from a subject that so piercingly concerned her was the achievement of an instinctive artist, and Emily Dickinson attained it not without difficulty. She had to learn by experiment that an outcry verging on the hysterical is not equivalent to a poem. It took many attempts for her to transcend the pang of negated affection, and in some of her poems we may agree with Howells that "touch often becomes clutch." Not until she realized that a death-blow to her heart had become a life-blow to her mind was she able to look upon her grief as though it were the agony of another person, a supposed person even. Only then did the mature poet in her come into being.

It may be useful, before we attempt to reconstruct her experience in full, to define her development from aggrieved woman to disembodied intelligence in the simplest possible terms. By reference to three distinct points we can in a sense plot the curve of her progress. She was all woman when she wrote (176, xliii):

> At least to pray is left, is left.
> O Jesus! in the air
> I know not which thy chamber is,—
> I'm knocking everywhere. . . .

The poem is a cry of despair, immediate and poignant. It is a record of a mind overwhelmed by an emotion from which it cannot detach itself, as the consciousness of a heartbroken child has no room for anything but its sense of grief. Emily had still to learn how to be impersonally aware of what she was personally undergoing. In another and, I assume, a later poem (296, xxxviii) a sense of perspective begins to appear:

> Of course I prayed—
> And did God care?
> He cared as much
> As on the air
> A bird had stamped her foot
> And cried, "Give me!" . . .

The poetic expression rises as the emotion is brought under control. The poem still contains indignation, but its mood is predominantly historical. The writer is able to look back at her despair, and has had time to collect herself and to estimate results. In her maturer judgment her former desperation comes to seem like that of a petulant bird; God might mark the sparrow's fall, but not the sparrow's childishness. Finally, after the harrowing experience has long mellowed in memory and lost its harshness, it becomes the occasion of completely impersonal reflection in "Prayer is the little implement" (39, lxxx). Behind the laconic precision of language is a glint of ironic understatement and a mischievous delight in the unexpected juxtaposition of great things and small, as though prayer were a kind of pea-shooter:

> [Men] fling their speech
>
> By means of it in God's ear;
> If then He hear,
> This sums the apparatus
> Comprised in prayer.

None of these poems can be dated by external evidence, but in terms of Emily Dickinson's favorite educational metaphor we might say that the first was written while she was still a pupil in the school of suffering, the second shortly after her graduation, and the third at her twentieth reunion. It is possible to give other poems an approximate position on the curve thus established, and to check the resulting arrangement by occasional references to actual events. Even without knowing the exact chronology of the poems we may reconstruct a kind of sequence of states of mind.

The first poem on prayer quoted in the last paragraph clearly rises out of an emotional crisis, though the nature of the crisis is not specified. It is a plausible assumption, however, that it refers to the main crisis of her life. A number of Emily Dickinson's love poems, on the other hand, contain no hint of pain or loss, and are so far from sharing the agonized mood of "At least to pray is left, is left" that it is natural to suppose that many of them were written before she had undergone the shipwreck of her hopes. Without being too positive about it, therefore, we may say that they reflect a state of mind characteristic of the time, between 1854 and 1861, when Emily was exulting in her heart's commitment. The number and variety of these poems would seem to indicate also that her love affair developed slowly and did not instantly pass into a phase of tragic frustration. Their tone is that of a woman in the early stages of an attachment, deliciously aware that she is falling in love, and speaking sometimes with playful assurance and again with maidenly modesty. Some of them display a Keatsian luxuriance of fancy unusual in Emily Dickinson, as though she were on the point of bursting into bloom. Their mood is echoed in a letter to Mrs. Holland dated in late summer, 1856: ". . . if God had been here this summer, and seen the things that *I* have seen—I guess that He would think His Paradise superfluous. Don't tell him, for the world, though. . . . Dear Mrs. Holland, I love, to-night—love you and Doctor Holland, and 'time and sense'—and fading things, and things that do *not* fade." We might call the group, using one of her preferred symbols, images of Eden.

The testimonials of her devotion vary in poetic competence from the youthful jingle of "Summer for thee grant I may be" (147, xl) to the fully mature "One and One are One" (356, cxl). Among the most characteristic are those that express her longing for a sight of her "bright absentee" in the relaxed and expansive mood of "I come to buy a smile today" (347, cxxv), "I tend my flowers for thee" (347, cxxvi), and "What would I give to see his face?" (353, cxxxv). But she was also able to achieve the powerful lyric condensation of "Wild nights! Wild nights!" (141, xxv), which comes as close to innocently erotic imagery as she was ever to go. The direct projection of her feelings blends imperceptibly with dreams of what might come to pass. In "The night was wide" (141, xxvi) she draws a fond picture of two married lovers cozy beside the parlor stove:

> To feel if blinds be fast,
> And closer to the fire
> Her little rocking-chair to draw,
> And shiver for the poor,

[274]

> The housewife's gentle task.
> "How pleasanter," said she
> Unto the sofa opposite,
> "The sleet than May—no thee!"

We must, of course, imagine a manly form stretched upon the sofa and expand the little housewife's cryptic remark to read: "How much pleasanter is a night of sleet and storm with you at home than the loveliest night of May without you." Elsewhere the imagined fulfilment of her imperative wish leads to even more insistent distortions of reality. When she says of her lover that she makes "his crescent fill or lack," that his letters tell her how infinite she is "to—no one that you know," she is assuming a relationship of requited affection that is contradicted in other poems where she faces the truth that he is hers only "in vision and in veto." Even her tropes of pure fancy do not suggest the bliss of surrender: her lover is "Immortal Alps" and she one of the myriad daisies at his feet; she is the coy harebell and he the bee; she is the little arctic flower strayed to the tropics. And in a moment of clear sight she could write:

> Love, thou art deep,
> I cannot cross thee,
> *But were there two*
> *Instead of one,*
> Rower and yacht some sov'reign summer,
> Who knows but we'd reach the sun?

In the first stages of her attachment, then, Emily Dickinson played with the perilous joy of picturing to herself what companionship with a man whom she unreservedly admired would mean. She was perhaps not aware until too late of how completely this pleasant fancy would come to possess her, or of what it would cost her to realize the disparity between dream and fact. There are signs that the more insubstantial her hopes became the more tightly she clung to them.

> Let me not mar that perfect dream
> By an auroral stain. . . .

Disaster was soon upon her. A second cluster of poems deals with the departure and, as Emily believed, the final loss of her beloved friend. "There came a day at summer's full" (133, xiii) and several more recount the lovers' last interview with a considerable element of dramatic elaboration, as I have tried to show in a previous chapter. Here we are not so much concerned with the writer's biography as with her emotional and imaginative responses to the first shock of frustration.

The parting that seemed to cut her life in two left her bewildered, though not too bewildered to record what she was undergoing:

> I clutched at sands—I groped at shapes—
> I touched the tops of films.

This is an accurate description of the poems that exhibit her first efforts to achieve an adjustment. The relatively long poem "Because that you are going" (Taggard: *The Life and Mind of Emily Dickinson*, p. 123) was evidently written in immediate connection with the lover's departure. It is a confused piece, far from clear; one might describe it as an attempt, not altogether successful, to take account of stock, as though Emily were struggling to write off her losses and to renew her life after a staggering blow. "Because you are going and never coming back," she writes, "and I may lose track of you, let this present instant, however grievous it seem to us now, be suspended forever above mortal change. At least it is something that we have found each other, a discovery that not God himself can now annihilate." There follow protestations that her life meant nothing to her until it became "the Realm of you," and that immortality is so bound up with thoughts of her lover that all the remaining glories of heaven are as dim to her as to an unbeliever. But "If 'God is love' . . . If 'all is possible' with him,"

> He will refund us finally
> Our confiscated Gods.

Closely related to the foregoing poem, and probably written not long afterward, is a brooding survey of her situation, beginning "I cannot live with you" (131, xii). Since it is sometimes misread as though it were addressed to a lover already dead, I paraphrase the essential meaning here, stanza by stanza.

1–3.   I cannot live with you, for that would be life, and life for us two must be postponed to another existence. . . .

4, 5.   Nor could I die with you, since one of us must wait to perform the last offices for the other, unthinkable though it may be that either you or I could bear not to share the other's agony.

6, 7.   Nor could I rise with you, for your face would eclipse the Lord's and the glory of heaven show flat and strange beside your glory.

8–11.   How then will we be judged? You served heaven (or tried to), while I never had a thought save of you. Were you lost I would ask nothing better than to keep you company. Were you saved and I not, our separation would be the bitterest hell I could know.

12.   But as it is, there is nothing for it but for us to keep apart,
You there, I here,
With just the door ajar
That oceans are,
And prayer,
And that pale sustenance,
Despair!

In both these poems Emily Dickinson is indeed clutching at sands in the desperate effort to find some basis for prolonging her devotion. Meanwhile the thought ever present to her consciousness was the thought of his absence. In "The sunrise runs for both" (354, cxxxvi) she speaks of her lover and herself as "weeks wide away," one lying upon midnight's bosom and one "upon her hem," as would be true if he were in California and she in New England. "I envy seas whereon he rides" (153, lv), "I would die to know" (430, xc), and "You see I cannot see your lifetime" (359, cxliv) all poignantly express her longing for sight or word of him, and her jealousy of the common

things and trifling circumstances of his daily life which enjoy
the priceless boon of a companionship which

> The earrings of Pizarro
> Could not obtain for me.

The most noticeable quality of the poems composed under the
immediate stress of her loss is their unevenness. Many of them
are longer than her poems were wont to be. Many are irregular
in metrical form. They look like improvisations, outpourings
of feeling that has not been poetically assimilated. Only by
dramatizing a single episode such as the scene of the lovers' last
farewell could Emily get any part of her experience under
artistic control. The subject as a whole was as yet too huge for
her skill. Little by little, however, she mastered every aspect of
her lot.

As falling in love had meant the joining of many streams of
being into one main current, so frustration led to branchings
out like those of a river at its delta. On a map these alternative
channels may be seen all at once, but to explore them in detail
we must follow each in turn. Somewhat arbitrarily then we may
divide the poems that register the aftercourses of calamity into
three groups, which in time were probably not successive but
concurrent. With one side of her nature Emily protested her
everlasting constancy and further claimed a union in spirit that
transcended the bounds of reality even while another side of her
was engaged in scrutinizing the inexorable fact of renunciation.

The group made up of protests of constancy may overlap somewhat the earlier group that I have called images of Eden. A few
of them, like "Forever at his side to walk" (352, cxxxiii), breathe
the same air of rapt dedication. Among these is a poem that
contains one of the most astonishing "metaphysical" images that
Emily Dickinson ever conceived, an image equivalent in its

unexpectedness and ingenious elaboration to Donne's famous comparison of two lovers to a pair of compasses:

> My life had stood a loaded gun
> In corners, till a day
> The owner passed—identified,
> And carried me away.
>
> And now we roam the sov'reign woods,
> And now we hunt the doe. . . .

For five stanzas the extraordinary image holds good. To picture the flash of the rifle and the impact of the bullet without losing touch with the human side of the metaphor is an amazing piece of virtuosity, but Emily took it in her stride:

> It is as a Vesuvian face
> Had let its pleasure through.
>
> . . . . . .
>
> None stir a second time
> On whom I lay a yellow eye
> Or an emphatic thumb.

After these triumphs, however, the poem falters to an obscure and inappropriate close, which does not confirm the central idea but runs off on an odd tangent of speculation. The gun, of course, is speaking:

> Though I than he may longer live,
> He longer must than I,
> For I have but the art to kill—
> Without the power to die.

Apparently this means that the physical existence of the gun may outlast the life of the owner, but the owner must live longer because he has the power to die to immortality, whereas the gun's "art to kill" applies only to temporal existence. But whatever the meaning, the stanza is a collapse, not a conclusion.

Most of Emily's protests of constancy are not tranquil poems.

Their mounting intensity is that of a woman whose dearest wish is threatened, and who throws fervor after fervor into the balance to incline the scales of destiny her way. One or two poems, for example "Doubt me, my dim companion!" (128, v) and "Split the lark and you'll find the music" (147, xli), imply that her faithfulness has been questioned by her lover, though if I am right in insisting that this love affair was entirely one-sided, no such situation could actually have occurred and these poems must be taken as imaginative dramatizations. If it was not mere force of circumstances that challenged the permanence of her devotion, it may have been some intimate friend or member of her family trying to console her by assurances that she would get over her heartbreak in time. Later Emily was to find perfect expression for what she instinctively felt:

> Time is a test of trouble,
> But not a remedy.
> If such it prove, it prove too
> There was no malady.

At the moment of crisis, however, she did not philosophize but wrote her unshakable commitment in flaming assertion. "Alter? When the hills do." To empty her heart of her chosen one would be "Simply extinction's date. . . . The Heavens stripped, Eternity's wide pocket picked." If she could not be a wife in fact, she could at least claim to be a wife in spirit, and on this consolatory crumb she banqueted in several poems. Yet she could not even in imagination conceive of robbing another woman's table. Her lover was hers only "by the grave's repeal," which loosed all bonds. In one of her most fervent poems, "Title divine is mine" (154, lvii), with every temptation to compensate for her loss by dwelling upon an ideal union, she shows a remarkable preference for fact, even though it involves the pain and wistful longing so poignantly expressed at the close.

> "My Husband," women say,
> Stroking the melody. . . . Is this the way?

On this earth her true estate was that of "Empress of Calvary" and she was grimly honest about it.

For an imagination steeped in Puritan convictions the prospect of eternity offered the only escape from intolerable actuality. It is no surprise, therefore, that Emily's protests of constancy on earth should rise to a climax in a further group of poems which picture the almost unimaginable bliss of union with her beloved in immortal life. An early intimation of the thought of marriage beyond the grave appears in "If you were coming in the fall" (128, vi), a poem written perhaps not long before the final parting while Emily was still on tenterhooks of expectancy. "If you were coming in the fall. . . . If I could see you in a year. . . . If only centuries delayed." . . . Then:

> If certain, when this life was out,
> That yours and mine should be,
> I'd toss it yonder like a rind,
> And taste eternity.

To "file this mortal off" and "wade in liberty" with her lost— this desperate solution appears once more in a poem of crisis, "What if I say I shall not Wait?" (145, xxxiv):

> They cannot take us any more,—
> Dungeons may call, and guns implore;
> Unmeaning now, to me,
> As laughter was an hour ago,
> Or laces, or a travelling show,
> Or who died yesterday!

Her gradual reconcilement to the idea of waiting, with a shining hope at the end of the dark vista, finds later and more quiet expression in "The grave my little cottage is" (203, cv) and "I sing to use the waiting" (206, cxiv), where she effectively employs the household imagery natural to her years of seclusion. About midway between anguished thoughts of suicide and patient looking forward to a cottage in eternity just big enough for two we may place the curious poem beginning "If I may have it when it's dead" (211, cxxvi), in which Emily uses the neuter pronoun to refer to her lover's disembodied spirit in somewhat the same way as Emerson preferred to speak of God as IT. Halfway through the poem, however, her attempt to be impersonal breaks down, and the last lines are a direct and intimate appeal in the second person singular:

> Think of it, lover! I and thee
> Permitted face to face to be;
> After a life, a death we'll say,—
> For death was that, and this is thee.

Abstractly considered, her lover's death was a prelude to everlasting reunion, but it was also a human event involving pain and stress. His imagined agonies stirred her womanly tenderness. In three poems Emily wrote of the death of a man so dearly beloved that it is difficult to suppose she was not thinking of the one preferred above all others. "Promise this, when you be dying" (422, lxxviii) embodies her wish to be with him during the last moments so sacred to the Puritan imagination. After his death, apparently, she described her cautious inquiries in "If he were living—dare I ask?" (364, clvi) and upon learning that he was buried, condensed all his consequence to her in the one exclamation: "My life holds just the trench." Again, in "To know just how he suffered would be dear" (164, xix), she returned fondly to the thought of the deathbed ministrations she would so gladly have performed for him, had fate permitted. The last lines:

> Till love that was, and love too blest to be,
> Meet—and the junction be Eternity,

connect this poem, and by implication the other two, with the marriage in heaven group.

The thought of her own death, regarded as a mortal incident, did not distress her. She could manage that alone, without any one to hold her hand. Dying, as she briefly remarked, was not double. It was a solemnity too precious to be shared. Beyond the grave was a bliss that assumed in her mind a pageantry of images resembling those of *Pilgrim's Progress*. There is no parallel to the exalted fervor of her language, except in that high moment when Bunyan describes Faithful entering into glory, while "all the trumpets sounded." For Emily, too, there were mountains, seas, deserts to cross, but

> Sahara is too little price
> To pay for thy Right hand!

We may be sure that she did not mean God's right hand. Her eyes thirsted for the sight of a face in paradise that "would put out Jesus'." Her only scruple was lest "Death be scant for opportunity" to display the boundlessness of her long-pent love.

> The River reaches to my feet,
> And yet my heart be dry!
> Oh Lover, Life could not convince,
> Might Death enable thee!

With sunrise and flags she passes from her long midnight "Unto the East and Victory."

> Eternity, I'm coming, Sir,—
> Master, I've seen that face before.

The fleshless lovers' first interview "before the judgment-seat of God" is anticipated in several poems which perfectly illustrate Emily Dickinson's capacity to rationalize deprivation until it becomes almost an equivalent for fulfilment. It is

> Joy to have merited the pain
> To merit the release;
> Joy to have perished every step
> To compass thee at last.

Even renunciation becomes dear since linked with the idea of her lover and in some dim atavistic way conceived of as a propitiation that must be paid for him. Stand a New Englander on his head and he will soon arrive at an antipodean philosophy.

Emily's mind achieved a similar adjustment to an unnatural posture long sustained. This "consolation upside down," as she called it, is fully exhibited in one of the longest of her love poems, "Fitter to see him I may be" (276, *Prelude*). Since the wording is somewhat obscure, I have ventured to paraphrase the thought.

1, 2.   The long waiting may make me so much more worthy to see my lover that I shall be half sorry he chose me in my imperfect state.

3.   I shall have time to anticipate his gaze—his delighted surprise in greeting me, his searching scrutiny to see if I am indeed the one he left behind, so much less fair then that he will need assurances that I am really the same person.

4, 5.   I must not become so different that he will fail to recognize me and ask me for news of myself when I rejoin him; that, however, can never happen, for love will make me perfect in his sight.

6.   If he perceive the "other truth" (i.e. the sincere devotion that I felt for him on earth) upon "an excellenter youth" (i.e. combined with my new celestial loveliness), then indeed it will be sweet to me that out of loss and grief has come this gain: that I have achieved the beauty that can best reward him, "the beauty of Belief at rest."

The length and devious involutions of this poem mark it as a rough sketch. Emily was still a long way from perfect expression. She comes closer to it in "'Twas a long parting" (135, xv), which runs clear for two stanzas and then clogs into a veritable log-jam of cryptic phrases. But the artist in her was finally to triumph, discarding in effort after effort what was too personal and poignant until only the pure quintessence of impassioned thought remained. In one of her finest, and we may guess one of her later poems (137, xix), since it survived in a single pencilled draft, she reached the ultimate condensation of all that she wished to say of her sense of spiritual union with her dearest friend. The apocalyptic imagery of the poem gives it magnificent perspective. Human desire is dwarfed to the status of a wave moving on the surface of a vast deep. Among the stark,

clear shapes of the verities emerging from earthly blur, the truth
of the heart's affection has its place and must at long last share
the triumph of all intrinsic things, but the lover so often extravagantly craved, the face that would "put out Jesus'," is now but
an atom in the great scheme of things.

> Of all the souls that stand create
> I have elected one.
> When sense from spirit files away,
> And subterfuge is done;
>
> When that which is and that which was
> Apart, intrinsic, stand,
> And this brief tragedy of flesh
> Is shifted like a sand;
>
> When figures show their royal front
> And mists are carved away,—
> Behold the atom I preferred
> To all the lists of clay!

There would be no more to say if we were dealing with an
Emily Brontë or a Christina Rossetti. But Emily Dickinson
would not be Emily Dickinson if she did not somehow manage
to convert even her heartbreak into mischief. Like a Greek
tragedian in miniature she must supply an elvish afterpiece to
her trilogy of woe. The same crisis that moved her to write
poem after poem almost too deep for tears inspired also the
whimsical conception of a buggy-ride to the Day of Judgment:

> Tie the strings to my life, my Lord,
>   Then I am ready to go!
> Just a look at the horses—
>   Rapid! That will do!
>
>   . . . .
>
> Good-by to the life I used to live,
>   And the world I used to know;
> And kiss the hills for me, just once;
>   Now I am ready to go!

Besides picturing moments of exaltation when her heart overleaped boundaries of time and space and stormed eternity, Emily faithfully recorded her moments of depression—and there must have been many—when, as she quaintly put it, Nature sent a fact to "scuttle her balloon." Renunciation, she wrote, is a "piercing virtue," and she continued in breathless definition:

> Renunciation is the choosing
> Against itself,
> Itself to justify
> Unto itself;
> When larger function
> Make that appear
> Smaller, that sated vision
> Here.

But only intermittently could she sustain the idea of herself as a heroine who had chosen the better part. A light had gone out of her life. Her "daily night" had begun. In desperate need of distraction she turned to her poetry:

> I told my Soul to sing.

> She said her strings were snapt,
> Her bow to atoms blown;
> And so, to mend them, gave me work
> Until another morn.

In analyzing the frustration and despair that threatened to break her spirit forever she found a saving occupation. The most flinty soil could be made to yield a crop, and from her stony acre she gathered a little sheaf of poems that describe her prostration: "After great pain a formal feeling comes" (365, clviii), "There is a languor of the life" (366, clix), "There is a pain so utter" (366, clx), "At leisure is the soul" (371, clxvii), and others. The mechanical performance of life's little duties helped to fill the appalling emptiness, and writing about it in "I tie my hat, I crease my shawl" (368, clxiii) doubtless helped still more.

To her surprise she learned that it was possible to grow accustomed to deprivation, even to find it dear. She had the companionship of her loneliness. So though she considered herself "dated with the Dead," her soul stood up and walked.

> Either the darkness alters—
> Or something in the sight
> Adjusts itself to midnight—
> And life steps almost straight.

As she "plated the residue of woe with monotony" and became able to survey her experience in retrospect, she saw that it brought compensations. Her one draught of life had cost her "precisely an existence" in one sense, but in another she had tasted a "dram of Heaven." Her legacy was double; it included love as well as pain. She could be proud of her broken heart. New perceptions animated the numbness of her misery. She could fill out from her own knowledge the words that gentle Mr. Whittier had declared the saddest of tongue or pen:

> This might have been the hand
> That sowed the flowers he preferred,
> Or smoothed a homely pain.

Her fresh insight confirmed what Tennyson had written of love and loss:

> To lose thee, sweeter than to gain
> All other hearts I knew.

Time in its lowly way was teaching her the certainty of immortality. Emily was a New Englander in every fiber of her being, less concerned with outer than with "inner weather." She could not be mistaken about it: she had passed through the valley of the shadow and reached the hill of vision. Out of loss had come an enrichment of her nature, a proved vitality of consciousness, a power to savor and discriminate, a multiplied intensity of inward life. The discovery lifted her above caring whether she were happy or not. She was better than happy—she was occupied, possessed, absorbed, "inebriate of air." Ideas, convictions, sensations, memories, the manifold implications of her new life, pressed upon her with startling vividness. Here was news too momentous for the supper table, but in the seclusion of her room Emily wrote again and again the definition of her victory: it was possible "to learn the transport by the pain."

Love to be viable in poetry must be of a rarer birth than consummated passion; it must be "begotten by despair upon impossibility," and subtly transmuted into an intellectual thing. Emily Dickinson had by her own efforts recaptured the position held by Donne, Marvell, and other Platonizing poets of the seventeenth century. Her long struggle to face down frustration gave her a curious doubleness of vision, as though her two eyes did not make one in sight but, bird-like, were focused in opposite directions, one upon the world of sense and one upon the world of changeless things. In her mind the two sets of images were sometimes whimsically blended, sometimes violently contrasted. This doubleness gives her maturest poetry its peculiar fascination.

We may suspect oblique references to her own experience in a considerable number of poems that are so impersonal and detached that they elude identification with it. Was she asserting anything personal to herself when she wrote:

> That Love is all there is,
> Is all we know of Love;

or was her final conclusion embodied in the contradictory poem that denies love's all-inclusiveness?

> We outgrow love like other things
> And put it in the drawer. . . .

Each stated an aspect of the eternal paradox. She knew only too well that gods proved half-gods not long after their arrival. To match the paradoxes of life she invented and applied a paradox of imagery by means of which she could squeeze infinity into finite garments. If Jehovah's watch was wrong, she could tease

Him about it in spite of the inconvenience He had caused her.
Once in all simplicity she had prayed for a heaven large enough
to suffice her modest needs. And what happened?

> A smile suffused Jehovah's face;
> The cherubim withdrew;
> Grave saints stole out to look at me,
> And showed their dimples, too.
>
> I left the place with all my might,—
> My prayer away I threw;
> The quiet ages picked it up,
> And Judgment twinkled, too,
>
> That one so honest be extant
> As take the tale for true
> That "Whatsoever you shall ask,
> Itself be given you."

Could not the victim take the cosmic swindle in good part and
even share the cosmic joke?

In her first access of her trouble Emily Dickinson had thought
Calvary not too large a symbol for her woe. Of that domain
of agony she was the chosen queen. But the tremendous figure
that she invoked gradually changed its meaning. Could it be
that those tortured limbs were convulsed with celestial laughter?
If the drama of the cross ended in salvation, would not Jesus
be inwardly smiling? She could not think it otherwise:

> Gay were Gethsemane
> Knew we of Thee.

Midnight might be long, but the stars, it seemed, twinkled at
her, and while twinkling back at them she could forget her
tears.

16

The Landscape of the Soul

B Y WRITING about bees and hummingbirds and sunsets Emily Dickinson learned to analyze her external perceptions and to keep them distinct from her feelings. Only rarely, as we have seen, did she allow any interfusion between the world of sense and outward things and the inner world of sentiment. Only once, in a crisis of despair, was she led to an outpouring of sheer emotionalism and to a confusion of desire and fact. Little by little she gained the power to measure her grief with analytic eyes and to record her progress along the old road through pain with the same impersonal precision that she applied to a bird hopping down the walk. Thus, by steps that were probably less consecutive and assured than they appear when we attempt to retrace them, she arrived at what was to be her special province in poetry, the region of dramatic tension between the mind and experience. The most intense event of her life occurred when a hope long cherished was brought into sudden conflict with realities that she could not ignore. Could not poems achieve the same intensity if molded in the image of her inward drama? She explored the possibilities of the field and found them inexhaustible.

Hence, on the basis of an exceptionally narrow experience she was able to rear a poetic structure that surprises us by its amplitude. If we disregard the very small group of poems dealing objectively with men and women and public affairs, her only external subject was nature as seen from her garden. Her passional knowledge was confined to an unfulfilled love which in point of fact she barely touched with her fingertips. In the whole body of her lyrics there is little admixture of narrative. She seldom adverts to any story but her own, and that she merely hints at. Yet she does not impress us as a poet of limited range. Among English poets Blake is her only rival in the faculty of making a little count for much, but the superstructure of visionary mythology that Blake conjured into being is so huge and obscure that only the most elaborate scholarship can discern its connection with reality. Emily Dickinson, on the contrary, never lets us forget the world of here and now. It was vital to her method to bring fact into paradoxical conjunction with thought, not so much to merge or reconcile the two as to establish their dramatic interplay. No great variety of actual experience was necessary for her purpose. The perceptions that a small New England town afforded would serve as well as any. The minutest intuitions could be made to ramify in all directions like the scriptural grain of mustard seed.

The variety of her attitudes is so notable that it has induced many readers, Higginson among the first, to characterize her as elusive and unpredictable, a doubtful compliment, since really elusive minds are generally shut up in institutions. Emily Dickinson's poems are not the vague mumblings of a pythoness. Her constant effort was to be clear and exact in every phrase. But neither are they the product of a systematic or philosophical intelligence. Of this she was herself well aware and for a time at least it bothered her. She turned to Higginson for guidance because, as she said, she had no monarch in her life and could not rule herself: "when I try to organize, my little force explodes and leaves me bare and charred." But Higginson could not give her the kind of control that she was seeking. Without any philosophical commitments, therefore, she continued to set down, as in a poetic journal, her detached observations of the nature of things and the misgivings of a soul moving about in worlds unrealized. Before long the pattern she was weaving assumed a doubleness that closely conformed to the paradox of life itself. She became acutely aware of an inner world of dream and desire and an outer world of fact and experience. The two crossed and contradicted each other continually. Emily would not favor either at the expense of the other; she summoned them both as "concave and convex witness," and enjoyed drawing out their conflicting testimonies. Consequently, like Emerson's Brahma, she was able to be both doubter and devotee in a fashion that puzzles more single-minded readers.

For the sake of clarification we may divide her intellectual lyrics into two groups, one dealing with the analysis of the mind, the other with the analysis of experience. The terms "mind" and "experience," which Emily commonly used are not strictly scientific, and we must expect the two groups to shade into each other and overlap. A popular distinction, however, has always been made between man's conviction of his destiny and the reality of his destination. She accepted it as Milton for poetic purposes accepted the astronomy of the spheres.

If we consider the group of poems in which Emily is concerned primarily with the inner life of the mind, the line of her thinking may be described as parabolic in the geometrical sense, in that it follows a curve that returns upon itself. Starting from direct objective notations of the data of consciousness, it rises to a second level where abstract ideas are personified and dramatized, filled with vital breath, and placed in exciting relation with each other. But never are these abstract entities permitted to slip the tie that connects them with the ground. Just as they seem about to float away on airy missions of their own, Emily mischievously twitches the subtle thread that brings them back into shattering juxtaposition with the solid earth. The third stage in her poetic method is, therefore, critical of the mind's untrammelled activity, and involves a return to fresh notations of reality.

The simplest of her intellectual poems are those that merely record a mental phenomenon. She was curious to see how the brain worked, eager to find words for every thought she ever had, as though thoughts were a kind of inner fauna and she a new Adam naming the animals. Such notes on the mind could have been written only by a poet who was ceaselessly interested in the natural history of the intellect. For instance, it teased her, after she had studied her ideas until each wore a familiar aspect, to encounter one that she ought to be able to recognize but could not identify:

> A thought went up my mind to-day
> That I have had before,
> But did not finish,—some way back,
> I could not fix the year.
>
> .   .   .   .
>
> But somewhere in my soul, I know
> I've met the thing before;
> It just reminded me—'twas all—
> And came my way no more.

Again she recorded without comment the shock of finding a gap in the sequence of her reflections where she had not expected a break to occur:

> I felt a cleavage in my mind
>   As if my brain had split;
> I tried to match it, seam by seam,
>   But could not make them fit. . . .

These two poems, and others like them, amount to little more than field notes, the immediate jotting down of psychological observations. They are exactly like her notations of the physical world. She does not express a feeling or obtrude a preference; she watches and records.

But careful observation was only a starting point. Once an observation has been raised into the realm of thought it may take on there a fresh vitality. Time, for example, may be divorced from association with material clocks and considered as an abstract idea that exists only in the mind. Once established as a subjective concept, it may then be given a new imaginative objectivity by identifying it with other concrete things, as in *"tempus edax rerum,"* or in Shakespeare's vivid freshening of the old phrase, *"cormorant* devouring time."

The steps in Emily Dickinson's progress from the mere noting of mental phenomena to the complete dramatization of her thoughts as integers of the mind may be illustrated in a series of poems that show her weighing the data of consciousness, making distinctions and generalizations, and finally personifying the resultant isolated abstractions. In seeking to draw a line of demarcation between similar states of feeling she commenced the process of individualizing each as a separate psychological entity:

> The difference between despair
> And fear, is like the one
> Between the instant of a wreck,
> And when the wreck has been. . . .

Simile serves the purposes of definition, but to give each concept a more vivid distinctness Emily was obliged to pass from simile to metaphor and equip her thought with a machinery, if not a personality, of its own. Metaphor, accordingly, became her habitual language, as in the following poem where a generalized observation has been mechanized:

> The brain within its groove
> Runs evenly and true;
> But let a splinter swerve,
> 'Twere easier for you
> To put the water back
> When floods have slit the hills. . . .

But the greatest of metaphors is the human one. Emily employed

it continually, endowing abstractions with personal character-
istics so that they seemed to act and live like independent beings:

> The heart asks pleasure first,
> And then, excuse from pain;
>
> .   .   .   .   .   .
>
> And then, if it should be
> The will of its Inquisitor,
> The liberty to die.

On this second level of her intellectual poetry Emily Dickinson delighted in playfully reanimating the bloodless creations
of the brain. She was doing with particular zest and brilliance
what all poets do. Eternity, for her, was no bodiless abstraction
but a close personal acquaintance:

> He joins me in my ramble,
> Divides abode with me,
> No friend have I that so persists
> As this Eternity.

Time is a quaint stream down which we are forced to glide
without an oar; the Future cannot speak—he has no office save
"to execute Fate's telegram to him"; the Past is a curious and
possibly dangerous creature in feminine guise whom it is best
to avoid, for

> Her rusty ammunition
> Might yet reply!

Remorse is memory awake—not a very vivid figure to begin with,
but before she has finished Emily makes it a visitation from a
spectral Ku Klux Klan:

> A presence of departed acts
> At window and at door.
>
> Its past set down before the soul,
> And lighted with a match,
> Perusal to facilitate
> Of its condensed dispatch.

Hope is a thing with feathers that perches in the soul and sings to keep it warm; contrariwise, it is a subtle glutton that feeds upon the fair, and yet whatsoever is consumed the same amounts remain. Anger as soon as fed is dead, 'tis starving makes it fat. Fame is a fickle food upon a shifting plate, a banquet table

> Whose crumbs the crows inspect,
> And with ironic caw
> Flap past it to the Farmer's corn.

One need not illustrate further. It is hard to read a page of Emily Dickinson without meeting examples of the immaterial stated with startling elaboration in terms of the material. The identification of seemingly unlike things was her constant habit, and the amazing virility of her metaphors constitutes a chief element of power in her poems.

The poetic mind may enjoy the setting up of conceptual puppets and endowing them with the attributes of life, but there is a day of reckoning to come. If we let ourselves believe in the actuality of these pretty creations, we are apt to dull our awareness of fact, and when an unexpected reality breaks in upon us we are in for a painful awakening. Emily Dickinson was keenly perceptive of the subtle transformation involved in the replacing of a fact by the idea formed of it. She described the process in a remarkable poem, beginning:

> Perception of an Object costs
> Precise the Object's loss.
> Perception in itself a gain
> Replying to its price. . . .

And she went on to remark how the mind takes the concept that it substitutes for fact and "sets it fair"; then finding itself misled, "upbraids a Perfectness that situates so far," or in plainer terms, resents the illusion of perfection that it has inflicted upon itself. She had once been the victim of this process and was not to be caught twice the same way.

Hence she was not content merely to induce a suspension of belief favorable to the imaginative dramatization of abstract ideas, but insisted on testing what her mind had wrought by active disbelief. Few poets have cared so much for mental honesty. She was wary of anything that resembled wishful thinking, and was suspicious of whatever induced a feeling of satisfaction, even of the most tranquil expectations. She could not trust a pleasure until she had discerned behind its smile a trace of austerity. The mind's complacence was a danger signal: "Good, without alarm, is a too serene possession." The part of caution was to check the exuberant mind by constant reference back to experience. The two, she found, invariably failed to correspond:

> Experience is the angled road
> Preferred against the mind
> By paradox, the mind itself
> Presuming it to lead
> Quite opposite. . . .

Following the rough path of experience might oblige her to adopt a precarious gait, as of one stepping uncertainly from plank to plank, but it was better than trying to walk on air. The mind was so given to seeing mirages. Only the mute testimony of fact could be trusted:

> The rainbow never tells me
> That gust or storm are by;
> Yet she is more convincing
> Than philosophy. . . .

So at the conclusion of her analysis of the mind Emily found herself facing the hard facts of experience, the ineluctable reality. But she had discovered by the way that wherever desires ran counter to fact there arose a tension that might successfully be captured in poetry. Such conflicts were implicit in every aspect of existence, and hence, for her, drama's vitalest expression was the common day. If nothing more than three walls and a passion were needed to make a play, she required only a single taste of life and a lead pencil to make a whole series of lyrics. But her parabolic method could be best applied where the divergence between fact and dream was widest. In such situations there was ample opportunity to sample the texture of the fact, to dally playfully with the substance of dream, and finally to point the contrast between the two.

The subject of death and immortality was well adapted to treatment on all three levels of her method, and it is not surprising that she recurred to it more frequently than to any other. She, of course, noted various aspects of death in the village and wrote little elegies for departed friends. These we may leave aside. Our present concern is with the poems that deal with death and the hereafter, first, as a phenomenon of consciousness, second, as an abstract conception that tempts the mind both to dramatizations and to rash conjectures, and third, as an illusion to be subjected to sharp critical examination.

Strictly speaking, the only adequate poem on the unknowable would consist of a blank sheet of paper, but speculation has always balked at that austere solution. In several poems Emily Dickinson attempted by a kind of imaginative triangulation to measure the subjective realization of death, projecting consciousness into the negation of consciousness with extraordinary success. "I heard a fly buzz when I died" (212, cxxviii) anticipates the sensation of dying, and the poem that follows describes the feeling of being present at her own funeral:

> I felt a funeral in my brain,
>   And mourners, to and fro,
> Kept treading, treading, till it seemed
>   That sense was breaking through.
>
> .   .   .   .
>
> And then I heard them lift a box,
>   And creak across my soul
> With those same boots of lead, again.
>   Then space began to toll

> As all the heavens were a bell,
>   And Being but an ear,
> And I and silence some strange race
>   Wrecked, solitary, here.

Death, abstractly considered, might become also a concept in the mind to be personified and put to figurative uses and associated with the human longing for a future existence. Emily unleashed her fancy in the poem beginning:

> Because I could not stop for Death,
> He kindly stopped for me;
> The carriage held but just ourselves
> And Immortality. . . .

which pictures with the usual vivid detail the start of a stage-coach journey to eternity. She also created a little hinted drama of mortality (170, xxxi):

> Death is a dialogue between
> The spirit and the dust,

wherein Death urges the claims of dissolution while the Spirit defends its trust in its eternal inviolability; when skeptical Death "argues from the ground,"

> The Spirit turns away,
> Just laying off, for evidence,
> An overcoat of clay.

The thought of death in both these poems leads to the idea of immortality, to which Emily Dickinson was by no means insensible or indifferent. She tried it on in all its forms, as she tried on every mental garment that came within her reach. While she wore the costume of faith, she could write:

> I never spoke with God,
> Nor visited in heaven;
> Yet certain am I of the spot
> As if the chart were given.

But she possessed an uncanny faculty of slipping out of all cos-

tumes. The heaven that the poets disclose might be a dream
too beautiful to live up to; she would not make it hers until
she had scrutinized it from every angle.

In contrast to her poems of affirmation, therefore, we find a
number conceived in a purely skeptical mood. Beside her mystical certainty of heaven may be placed:

> Heaven is so far of the mind
> That were the mind dissolved,
> The site of it by architect
> Could not again be proved. . . .

She was willing to grant that heaven is excellent—"when earth
cannot be had":

> How hospitable, then, the face
> Of our old neighbor, God!

But when she tested the lovely dream by reference to her own
experience she was more than half convinced that she would not
feel at home in "the handsome skies." Moreover, she could not
avoid the perception that most of humanity seemed to feel much
as she did:

> The Maker's cordial visage,
> However good to see,
> Is shunned, we must admit it,
> Like an adversity.

And, in full accordance with the preference for one world at a
time often attributed to Thoreau, she expressed her distaste for
"medicine posthumous" and emphatically signed off from any
implied obligation to an eternity not available here and now:

> Is Heaven an exchequer?
> They speak of what we owe;
> But that negotiation
> I'm not a party to.

When the mind had finished its ingenious play, Emily put
its toys back on the shelf. Experience did not confirm any of the
proposed answers to the final mystery. She had sampled all the
"myrrhs and mochas" that the mind could suggest, and had

found none to satisfy her. "All but Death can be adjusted," she wrote. Honesty required that she record it.

She did not stop, however, with an analysis of the mind's activities and a testing of its pleasing fictions by contrast to the truth of experience. As opposed to the illusions of desire or the structures of philosophy the solid certainty of fact offered distinct advantages. But what was this fact that it should be exalted to a position of supreme trust? Concurrently with her probing of consciousness she carried out an analysis of experience, examining and criticizing the texture of the goods it offered with the same appraising eye that she applied to the tapestries of paradise. The mind that proved so fallible when it brought her visions of hope might still serve a useful purpose if it could be made to reveal the shortcomings of reality.

Emily Dickinson was not, like Herman Melville or the second James Thomson, overwhelmed with a sense of the world's blind malice, nor had she the opportunity to acquire as extensive a collection of life's little ironies as Thomas Hardy possessed. But no sheltering hedges could protect her from pain and disillusionment and loss. She knew enough of God's ways to men to be keenly aware of what she called "the underside of His divinity." She had learned early that a human soul in search of either certainty or happiness found itself dealing with a "thrifty Deity." His universe seemed a hit-or-miss affair, "a gambol of His authority." It was full of defects that she felt obliged to report to the management. Why were the fairest promises so seldom fulfilled and golden opportunities so often hidden? Why was victory postponed until it had lost its relish and bliss hung within sight but out of reach? Why was knowledge of what we long to know obscured in shadow, but misery enlightened with a flood of daylight? Why was honey never steadfast, peace never assured? Her imagination supplied appropriate images to embody the satires of circumstance: the shipwreck—four saved, forty gone down together into the boiling sand; the gallows—

a wretch hanging there the sole object of a mother's love, her "livid boon"; two swimmers wrestling for the spar that can uphold but one; grand old Moses permitted to see the Promised Land, but barred by God from entering it, "as boy should deal with lesser boy to show supremacy." Listen as she might, the murmur of earth's "Perished Patterns" drowned out the alleged harmony of the spheres. Experience, it seemed, had only quandaries to offer. What were its certainties worth when tested by inner criteria?

Emily scanned the fact of pain. Its nature fascinated her. Here was an undeniable certainty. She could write:

> I like a look of agony
> Because I know it's true.

Was it also irreducible and ultimate? She pushed her analysis further. "Pain has an element of blank" (12, xix); it absorbs both past and future within itself and tolerates no consciousness of a time when it was not. "Pain expands the time" (336, cv), and equally "Pain contracts the time." What then becomes of time in any objective sense? It appeared to have no fixed external value, but to be fluctuant and relative. "Two lengths has every day" (232, xxxii): its "absolute extent" and a totally different area lent it "by hope or heaven." This was matter for reflection. Perhaps experience was not such granite after all. Time varied at the touch of pain or joy.

The terms of the problem might also be reversed. What becomes of pain when viewed in relation to time? Emily could not deny that time had softened the remembered woes of childhood:

> Bisected now by bleaker griefs,
> We envy the despair
> That threatened childhood's citadel.

Project these bleaker griefs again into time and the fact of present agony lost something of its rigidity. At the touch of time the harshest experience changed its value. Like the solid terrain seen through the eyes of the geologist it became fluid. Emily recorded a new insight: "We see comparatively" (291, xxxii). The mountains of yesterday dwindled to the molehills of today. Viewed in this morning's fresher light,

> A furrow our Cordillera,
> Our Apennines a knoll.

Once possessed of the notion that the value of any particular experience is determined by its context, Emily found confirmations wherever she turned. In fully a score of poems she dwelt on the idea in one or another of its aspects. Even the simplest impressions of the senses were not constant, but relative. The ear colors what it hears. The eye lends beauty to a face imperfectly beheld. The apple that hangs out of reach always seems better than the one we hold in the hand. We do not recognize hardships until we have grown used to comforts. A starving man attaches undue significance to food, a beggar to riches. Conversely, a craving disappears as soon as the possibility of satisfying it is attained; "the palate of the hate departs" when the chance for vengeance arrives. We minimize pleasures while we have them, but magnify them as soon as they are lost. Things look differently when seen in prospect and in retrospect. Life is not precious save as mortality makes it so. Death, above all else, "reorganizes estimate." The facts that loom large in time dwindle in the light of eternity. The more Emily tried to grasp the ultimate nature of experience, the more she was impressed by its protean shifts.

And yet the flux of things moved within bounds. Through all experience ran a principle of counterpoise, a vibration between extremes. This law of balance could be grimly stated:

> For each ecstatic instant
> We must an anguish pay
> In keen and quivering ratio
> To the ecstasy. . . .

The apprehension of an approximate equality of pain and pleasure brought little comfort. Positive and negative factors merely cancelled out, leaving a zero satisfactory to mathematics but savorless to a searcher for ultimate meanings. Emily, however, like Emerson before her, was Compensation's child. To her deeper scrutiny it appeared that opposites did not destroy each other but brought each other into being. Without black there could be no white, without cold no heat, without peril no security, without anguish no ecstasy. Only when viewed through pain did delight become pictorial. All that could be known at all was known by antithesis. Without the eternal interplay of contradiction there could be no experience. Whatever was negative, therefore, became a contribution to the positive:

> Water is taught by thirst;
> Land, by the oceans passed;
> Transport by throe.
>
> . . . .
>
> Defeat whets victory, they say;
> The reefs in old Gethsemane
> Endear the shore beyond.
> 'Tis beggars banquets best define;
> 'Tis thirsting vitalizes wine,—
> Faith faints to understand.

Conceive of life in terms of education—the metaphor was as inevitable for Emily Dickinson as for Henry Adams—and not a moment of it need be wasted or regretted. Day and night, loss and gain, were equally parts of the cosmic curriculum. Even to know the worst would be sweet, since that knowledge brought a fuller realization of the best. Out of pain and calamity came revelation, the precious attar that sunshine alone could not produce. "Essential oils are wrung." Only suffering can "bend the eye best beauty's way." The gentian must wait the frost to evoke its Tyrian hue, the lily pass "through the dark sod as education" tc attain its bloom. The defects of God's universe that Emily so sharply noted were from this standpoint potential beneficences. The darker the great enigmas the brighter might the little candle of man's intelligence shine. And so "it is true that the unknown is the largest need of the intellect, though for it, no one thinks to thank God." Emily could not feel at home "in a life that stopped guessing." Possibility was a fairer house than prose. Nothing could happen that did not advance the soul in its quest for knowledge.

Thus if the fair promises of the mind turned out to be delusive dreams, the harsh lessons of experience resolved themselves into spiritual gains. Emily recognized the doubleness in her reading of life, and being a poet rather than a philosopher, revelled in it. Besides things that fly and things that stay, "there are [things] that resting rise." Life's contradictions were dynamic, its baffling paradoxes the seeds of growth. It was not her business to "expound the skies" or chart the seas. Enough for a passenger of Infinity to feel and record "the divine intoxication of the first league out from land."

In examining the complex pattern of Emily Dickinson's thought we must guard ourselves from attributing to her an undue consistency or an undue solemnity. Her states of mind were not progressive, but approximately simultaneous. She did not move in a systematic fashion from one intellectual position to another, nor set herself to defend a single point of view. Her delight was to test all conceivable points of view in turn. At any moment she was ready to acknowledge in herself the claims of rationalist and mystic, Pyrrhonist and Transcendentalist. A mood of faith that possessed her in the morning might become matter of delicate mockery in the afternoon, a piercing grief could be sublimated overnight into a rapture of spiritual purgation. She enjoyed every extension of the multiplicity of metaphor. Hence a reader who looks to her for a single attitude invariably finds her inconsistent.

A study of her mind, moreover, is almost sure to risk misrepresentation by its formality. It may point out certain directions that her thoughts took, but it fails to catch the darts and ripples that distinguish their movement. She could write of solemn things without becoming permanently solemn. The swift intuitions of her intelligence were a continual surprise, an adventure, a joy sufficient in itself. She glanced from one to another with the lightness of a metaphysical ballerina. In poetry she found the freedom of mastery. Translated to that realm pain and heartache, like sunset and autumn, became incitements to artistic activity and occasions for artistic triumph. Like her own "Martyr Poets" she discovered "in Art the Art of Peace." There she could obtain sure transport when the everlasting arms proved not to be a "sufficient phaeton." Poetry was her playmate, not her taskmaster, and she came to it with a sparkle in her eye and mischief on her lips.

Yet if her poems rose above circumstance, they also rose from it, not merely in reflecting her surroundings and her personal history, but likewise in their unconscious anticipation of the dilemma that her generation and its successors were bound to face. Emily Dickinson was born into a world of expanding opportunities, when the air was electric with awakened energies. Before she died, stagnation had begun. In her youth every American vaguely expected to rise in the world. The national dream was embodied in the progress of the pioneer boy from log cabin to the White House, of the barefooted immigrant from the steerage to a palace on Fifth Avenue. But in the decades after the Civil War the industrialization of the country neared the point of completion, the frontier closed. A widening gulf separated expectancy and the possibility of its material fulfillment. Frustration, dissatisfaction, criticism, and revolt replaced the old optimism. "America the Land of Promise?" exclaimed Lowell, "The Land of Broken Promise!" Confidence in the power of the individual to master his destiny was meeting its first major test.

Emily Dickinson rather earlier than her contemporaries was obliged to deal with the problem of a narrowly constricted life. Cut off from any form of external activity, she was forced to fight a private battle to preserve her self-respect and personal integrity. Her individual struggle was a replica in miniature of the greater conflict that was breaking out around her; the acute accidents of her experience paralleled and intensified for her the spiritual predicament of the age. Her isolation, her helplessness as a gentlewoman, forced her immediately to face the thwarting of her hopes without shuffling or evasion. So, more than Emerson or Whitman, whose optimism was sustained by winds from the West, Emily Dickinson realized in her loneliness the full implications of the individualist's defeat by circumstance. She knew what it cost in anguish, and she had worked out at first hand the tactics of wresting triumph from seeming disaster.

Her adjustment to a static life involved no compromise with her New England heritage. She never lowered the flag of individual dignity and responsibility. Behind her and speaking through her were seven generations of a self-sufficient stock, able to take care of themselves, delighting in strenuous liberty, and willing to risk all they had on an uncertain future. Her people had braved a wilderness to find a home to their liking; they had challenged the power of England to win the right to shape their ends. Within living memory her grandfather had pledged his entire property to support a tottering educational project in the full conviction that the enlightenment of the world could be achieved if he and his neighbors could succeed in kindling the beam. New Englanders had seen their faith translated into visible substance too many times to permit them to think of the future as circumscribed. To the strong of heart the world was boundless and life was not to be meanly enclosed in formula or plan. If one door was shut, another could be opened. This habit of mind was ingrained in Amherst's child as positively as it ever was in the sons of the American frontier.

Mark Twain may be credited with inventing the master-symbol of nineteenth-century America in the image of a small boy floating down the Mississippi on a raft, uncertain of his destination, but confident of meeting any emergency with pluck and ingenuity. Emily Dickinson without leaving her sheltered garden had drifted on a vaster stream than Huckleberry Finn ever knew, and her watchword was like his: "Trust in the Unexpected." Valor in the dark she acknowledged as her Maker's code. Sophocles long ago, facing the perplexities of the human lot, had found no better solution.

BIBLIOGRAPHICAL P(

Bibliographical Postscript

S INCE I have avoided footnotes in the text, I list here, with one important exception, the sources of information upon which this book is based. The exception consists of holograph letters or groups of letters by Emily Dickinson now in private collections or in the possession of the descendants of her correspondents. All told I have examined more than two hundred such manuscripts, about half of which have not been printed. Since the owners of these letters have with one accord requested me not to divulge their names, I can only make this general acknowledgment of the valuable assistance that they have given me.

It should be clearly stated that I have not asked or received aid from any surviving member of the Dickinson family. Whether this independence is considered an advantage or a disadvantage to a biographer of Emily Dickinson will depend on one's point of view. I am inclined to value it.

With the exception of "A Valentine," "The Snake," and "Success," all of Emily Dickinson's poems were published after her death. Between 1890 and 1935–36 six installments have appeared in book form, as follows:

Poems by Emily Dickinson. Edited by two of her Friends, Mabel Loomis Todd and T. W. Higginson. Boston, 1890.

Poems by Emily Dickinson: Second Series. Edited by . . . T. W. Higginson and Mabel Loomis Todd. Boston, 1891.

Poems by Emily Dickinson: Third Series. Edited by Mabel Loomis Todd. Boston, 1896.

The Single Hound: Poems of a Lifetime. . . . With an introduction by her niece Martha Dickinson Bianchi. Boston, 1914.

Further Poems of Emily Dickinson. . . . Edited by her niece Martha Dickinson Bianchi and Alfred Leete Hampson. Boston, 1929.

Unpublished Poems of Emily Dickinson. Edited by her niece Martha Dickinson Bianchi and Alfred Leete Hampson. Boston, [1935], 1936.

The first four titles named form the basis of *Selected Poems of Emily Dickinson*, edited by Conrad Aiken, London, 1924.

The Complete Poems of Emily Dickinson, with an introduction by her niece Martha Dickinson Bianchi, Boston, 1924, reprints the same four volumes, with one additional poem.

The Poems of Emily Dickinson, edited by Martha Dickinson Bianchi and Alfred Leete Hampson, Centenary Edition, Boston, 1930, adds the text of *Further Poems*, with one omission and one additional poem.

The Poems of Emily Dickinson, edited by Martha Dickinson Bianchi and Alfred Leete Hampson, Boston, 1937, adds the text of *Unpublished Poems*, now called "Additional Poems."

Four books contain selections from Emily Dickinson's correspondence, as follows:

Letters of Emily Dickinson. Edited by Mabel Loomis Todd. Boston, 1894. Two volumes, paged continuously.

At least one important group of letters preserved by Mrs. Todd's industry is supposed to have been destroyed before any other collection of the letters was attempted.

The Life and Letters of Emily Dickinson. By her niece Martha Dickinson Bianchi. Boston, 1924.

Part I contains letters or parts of letters not elsewhere available. Part II reprints in chronological order, with omissions and changes of text, and without acknowledgment, the material previously assembled by Mrs. Todd. See Morris U. Schappes: "Errors in Mrs. Bianchi's Edition of Emily Dickinson's *Letters,*" *American Literature*, IV, p. 369 (Jan. 1933). Important corrections affecting the dates of Emily Dickinson's birth and death, her full name, etc., were made in the fifth printing of this work (1929), which should be consulted in preference to earlier printings.

Letters of Emily Dickinson. Edited by Mabel Loomis Todd. New and enlarged edition. New York, 1931.

Contains additional material, both original and editorial, of the greatest importance.

Emily Dickinson Face to Face. Unpublished Letters with Notes and Reminiscences. By her niece Martha Dickinson Bianchi. Boston, 1932.

Chapter V contains early letters to Susan H. Gilbert and later notes to members of the Dickinson family which are not included in any other book.

Besides the *Letters* and the two biographical works by Emily Dickinson's niece mentioned above, three books that appeared on the occasion of Emily Dickinson's centennial contribute to an understanding of her life. The first two, however, give untrustworthy accounts of her supposed love story.

Emily Dickinson: The Human Background of her Poetry. By Josephine Pollitt. New York, 1930.

Contains many previously unknown facts and first emphasized the importance of Emily's friendship with Charles Wadsworth.

The Life and Mind of Emily Dickinson. By Genevieve Taggard. New York, 1930.

Valuable for critical comment. Contains (p. 123) the only published text of "Because that you are going," an important love poem.

Emily Dickinson, Friend and Neighbor. By MacGregor Jenkins. Boston, 1930.

A slight but charming sketch of Emily and her family as seen by a child. Mr. Jenkins was seven years old when he left Amherst.

I shall make no attempt to list critical material or magazine and newspaper articles to which I am not specifically indebted. A fairly complete index of such material is provided in *Emily Dickinson, a Bibliography,* compiled and published by the Jones Library, Amherst, 1930. Articles published since that date may readily be traced by consulting the periodical lists printed in either *American Literature* or *The New England Quarterly.*

The general sources for each chapter are listed below. I have given a page number only where the reference is limited. On occasion I have yielded to the temptation to comment briefly on some controverted or confusing points with which I did not wish to encumber the text.

CHAPTER I

Confusion in regard to the date of Emily Dickinson's birth is due to her niece, who allowed an incorrect date to stand through the first four printings of *Life and Letters*. December 10 is given by the Town

Records, and is indirectly confirmed by Emily herself (*Letters*, p. 68).

Emily Dickinson's birthplace and home from 1830 to 1840 and from 1855 to her death is usually supposed to have been built by Samuel Fowler Dickinson about 1813. But a paragraph in *The Hampshire and Franklin Express* for April 20, 1855, after congratulating Edward Dickinson on repossessing the "Old Homestead," adds: "Here was born in 1790 the Hon. Chester Ashley, U. S. Senator from Arkansas, who died in Washington in 1848." It is possible that another house stood on the same site before the brick house was built. Emily Dickinson's other home on Pleasant Street is no longer standing.

For information about Amherst and Amherst College, see the following:

Allen, Adèle. "The First President's House—A Reminiscence." *Amherst Graduates' Quarterly*, February 1937. (XXVI, 93.) "The Boltwood House—Memories of Amherst Friends and Neighbors." *Amherst Graduates' Quarterly*, August 1937. (XXVI, 297.) Contains three previously unpublished notes by Emily Dickinson.

Burgess, John W. *Reminiscences of an American Scholar* (1934), p. 60–3.

Carpenter & Morehouse. *The History of the Town of Amherst* (1896).

Dwight, Timothy. *Travels in New England and New York* (1821), II, p. 360.

First Church of Christ in Amherst, Massachusetts. *One Hundred and Fiftieth Anniversary* (1890). Contains papers by W. A. Dickinson on "Representative Men of the Parish, Church Buildings and Finances"; Rev. A. M. Colton, "Reminiscences"; Rev. E. S. Dwight, "Reminiscences." A manuscript record of members of the First Church, now in the Edward Hitchcock Memorial Room, shows that Mrs. Edward Dickinson joined by letter on "1st Sab. in July 1831"; Edward Dickinson and Susan H. Gilbert on August 11, 1850; Lavinia N. Dickinson on November 3, 1850; and William A. Dickinson on January 6, 1856—the last four by confession of faith.

Fish, C. R. *The Rise of the Common Man, 1830–1850* (1929), p. 22.

Fletcher, Robert S., and Young, Malcolm O. *Amherst College: Biographical Record of the Graduates and Non-Graduates, 1821–1921* (1927).

Fuess, Claude M. *Amherst: The Story of a New England College* (1935).

Hammond, William Gardiner. *Journal, 1844–49.* Typewritten copy of the original unpublished manuscript made under the supervision of Juliet Hammond in 1928–29; two volumes, paged continuously, in the Edward Hitchcock Memorial Room. (Quoted also in Chapters III, IV, and XI.)

Hitchcock, Edward. *Reminiscences of Amherst College* (1863).

Jackson, Helen Hunt. *Mercy Philbrick's Choice* (1876), p. 49. Further discussed in Chapter VII. Seth Nims was at one time postmaster of Amherst. Orra White, who taught in Amherst Academy, became the wife of President Hitchcock, but the Amherst Female Seminary which from 1832 to 1838 was located in the Brick Row was presided over by Miss *Hannah* White, an intimate friend of Mary Lyon.

Park, Edwards A. *Memorial Collection of Sermons* (1902), p. 45. Professor Park of Andover Theological Seminary was a member of the Amherst faculty in 1835–36 and declined the presidency in 1845. His famous "Judas Sermon" was almost certainly the one described by Emily (*Letters,* p. 99) and later recalled as the "loveliest sermon I ever heard" (*Letters,* p. 251). Miss Pollitt is, I think, mistaken in her conjecture that the latter reference may be applied to a sermon by Charles Wadsworth.

Reed, A., and Matheson, J. *A Narrative of the Visit to the American Churches by the Deputation from the Congregational Union of England and Wales* (1835), I, p. 355. Quoted by Fuess, p. 121.

See, Anna Phillips. *Amherst Past and Present* (1930).

Tyler, W. S. *History of Amherst College during its First Half Century, 1821–1871* (1873), p. 81.

Warfel, Harry R. *Noah Webster—Schoolmaster to America* (1936), p. 340.

Chapter II

For genealogical records of the Dickinson family, see Frederick Dickinson: *To the Descendants of Thomas Dickinson* (1897); L. M. Boltwood: *Genealogies of Hadley Families* (1862), also included in S. Judd: *History of Hadley* (1863); and George Montague: *The History and Genealogy of the Montague Family* (1886). A full résumé of this material is given in Chapter II of *Emily Dickinson Face to Face.* The alleged derivation of the family name (de Caen's son: de Kenson: Dickinson) has about the same standing in etymology that the griffins and unicorns of heraldry have in natural history.

The genealogist of the Montague family managed to go wrong in nearly every particular regarding Emily Dickinson and her sister. He stated (p. 506) that Emily's middle name was Norcross instead of Elizabeth, and that she was born in 1831 instead of 1830. He omitted Lavinia's middle name, which *was* Norcross, and declared that she was born on February 29, 1833, though 1833 was not a leap-year. Emily Dickinson's niece and biographer seems to have consulted this mine of misinformation on the subject of her aunt's name, which she gave in 1924 as Emily Norcross Dickinson and amended in 1929 to Emily Elizabeth Norcross Dickinson. *Both are wrong.* Town Records, catalogues of Amherst Academy and Mount Holyoke Seminary, Emily's signatures (Emily E. or E. E. Dickinson), her calling card (Miss Emily E. Dickinson), her death certificate, and even the index of the Montague genealogy (Emily E., not Emily N.), all overwhelmingly attest that her full name was Emily Elizabeth Dickinson. In her twenties she preferred to write her first name "Emilie," and in later life she discontinued the use of a middle initial.

The careers of Emily's grandfather, father, brother, and nephew have been conveniently summarized by W. I. Fletcher, "The Amherst Dickinsons and the College," *Amherst Graduates' Quarterly*, May, 1917 (VI, p. 179). Further details may be found in the histories of Amherst College, in *The Amherst College Obituary Record* (1875, 1896, 1899), and in the biographies of Emily Dickinson. With Miss Taggard's conception of Edward Dickinson as a heavy Victorian father, the counterpart of Edward Barrett as delineated in *The Barretts of Wimpole Street*, I am not in agreement.

For the Norcross family, see *Letters* (1931), Appendix II, and *Massachusetts Genealogy*, I, p. 411.

Some facts regarding the Gilbert family may be gleaned from the town histories and vital statistics of Greenfield and Deerfield, Mass. Susan Huntington Gilbert (1830–1913), daughter of Thomas and Harriet Arms Gilbert, was born in the old Frary house in Deerfield, which was leased as a tavern to her father from 1828 to 1830. (George Sheldon: *A History of Deerfield*, 1896, I, p. 619). From 1832 to 1836 Thomas Gilbert was the proprietor of the Mansion House in Amherst, a popular hostelry occupying the house built by Noah Webster at the northeast corner of the village common. Mrs. Gilbert died in 1837, and her husband in 1841. (Tombstones in West Cemetery.) Their eldest son, Thomas D. Gilbert, who had prospered as a lumber dealer in Michigan, was able to contribute liberally to the support of his younger sisters, including Susan. During her teens Susan Gilbert was boarded out with an aunt in Geneva, N. Y., and with her married sister Harriet (Mrs. William Cutler) in Amherst. During the year 1854–55 she taught school in Baltimore.

The children of William Austin and Susan H. (Gilbert) Dickinson were (1) Edward (1861–1898), known as "Ned." Though a confirmed invalid, he was able to take a special course of study at Amherst College (1880–84) and to act as assistant librarian in the College Library from 1886 until his death. (2) Martha Gilbert (1866–   ), known as "Mattie." She married in 1903 Captain Alexander Bianchi. Author of various novels and books of verse, and editor or co-editor of three volumes of selections from Emily Dickinson's poems. She has also written the two biographical studies of Emily Dickinson already named. (3) Thomas Gilbert (1875–1883), known as "Gib."

For Lavinia N. Dickinson, see letter signed J. K. C. (Joseph K. Chickering) in *The Springfield Republican* (I have seen only an undated clipping), and Carolyn Wells, "Lavinia Dickinson," *The Colophon*, No. III (1930).

Two letters to Clara Newman (Mrs. Sidney Turner) from Emily Dickinson, and one from Maggie Maher, the Dickinsons' Irish maid, are in the Harvard College Library.

CHAPTER III

Information concerning the schools of Amherst comes from the town history by Carpenter & Morehouse, which reproduces a photograph of the Primary School, facing p. 144. I have quoted from the recollections of Eliza S. Webster (Mrs. Henry Jones) given in Emily E. F. Ford: *Notes on the Life of Noah Webster* (1912), II, p. 145.

The main source for this chapter is Frederick Tuckerman: *Amherst Academy, A New England School of the Past* (1929), a model of painstaking investigation. I have also consulted the printed catalogues of Amherst Academy and many contemporary newspaper notices. A catalogue of Miss Hannah White's Amherst Female Seminary for 1835 lists as pupils an Emily M. Dickinson of Hadley and an Emily Dickinson of Amherst, and the latter appears again in the Amherst Academy catalogue for 1841 next to the name of Emily E. Dickinson, the subject of this biography. There were, therefore, at least three Emily Dickinsons growing up in the vicinity of Amherst in the 1830's.

Jane T. Humphrey (b. 1829) attended Amherst Academy in 1842 and was a senior in Mount Holyoke while Emily was a member of the middle class. After ten years of school-teaching she married William H. Wilkinson, and returned to her native town, Southwick.

Abiah P. Root (b. 1830), daughter of Deacon Harvey Root of West Springfield, attended the Academy probably in 1843–44. She then transferred to a school in Springfield conducted by Miss Margaret Campbell. In 1854 she married Rev. Samuel W. Strong, Yale 1843, and was still living in Westfield in the early nineties.

For Edward Hitchcock (1793–1864), who deserves a book to himself, see Frederick Tuckerman: "President Edward Hitchcock," *Amherst Graduates' Quarterly*, November, 1920 (X, p. 3), and the histories of Amherst College.

The two accounts of exhibitions at the Academy are quoted from the *Journal* of William Gardiner Hammond, already described (Chapter I). No girl named Howland is listed in the Academy catalogue for 1847, but there was an Electa Holland. The Emerson mentioned in the second quotation was Emily's friend and rather boring caller, John M. Emerson, A. C. 1849. John E. Sanford, A. C. 1851, later became president of the Amherst Board of Trustees. Hammond as a staunch member of the Psi Upsilon fraternity detested the "Alpha Delta Phi clique" and considered Leonard Humphrey in particular no better than a whited sepulcher.

Emily's letter to Abiah Root on the death of Leonard Humphrey was originally published in 1894 by Mrs. Todd, but was omitted from *Life and Letters* by Emily Dickinson's niece. This apparent suppression of an already published document naturally roused suspicion and led other biographers to place undue emphasis on this letter. Miss Pollitt and Miss Taggard were mistaken in identifying Leonard Humphrey as Emily's "earliest friend" and "dying tutor." On this point see *American Literature*, VI, p. 3.

I am indebted to the reminiscences of Miss Adèle Allen of Holyoke, who was born and brought up in the "First President's House," for much of the substance of the paragraph on Emily's garden.

The square Hallet & Davis piano that Emily used is still in the possession of her niece. See article by Richard M. Gipson in *The New York Sun*, May 16, 1936, with illustrations.

CHAPTER IV

Emily Dickinson is listed in the General Catalogue of Mount Holyoke College as a non-graduate of the *year* 1848. Since she would have completed her course if she had returned the following year, I have followed the usual convention in reckoning her as of the *class* of 1849.

The most important printed sources for the background of Emily's life at the Seminary are: *Eleventh Annual Catalogue of Mount Holyoke Female Seminary* (1848); E. Hitchcock: *The Power of Christian Benevolence illustrated in the Life and Labors of Mary Lyon* (1851); Sarah D. Stow: *History of Mount Holyoke Seminary* (1887); Beth B. Gilchrist: *The Life of Mary Lyon* (1910).

Miss Sydney R. McLean in "Emily Dickinson at Mount Holyoke," *New England Quarterly,* VII, p. 31, has written the only reliable account of the Seminary episode and was the first to make clear the fact that Emily passed through a spiritual crisis during her year in South Hadley. I am indebted to Miss McLean for knowledge of the unpublished letters from Emily Norcross, Sarah Jane Anderson, and Mary C. Whitman to Mrs. Andrew Porter of Monson, and for a copy of *A Journal for the Missionaries who have been members of the Mt. Holyoke Female Seminary* (September, 1847—August, 1848), kept by Susan L. Tolman and Rebecca W. Fiske. The originals are in the Mount Holyoke College Archives. The passages that I have quoted from the *Journal* were all written by Miss Tolman, who graduated from the Seminary in 1845 and in 1848 married Rev. Cyrus T. Mills. After eighteen years of missionary service in Ceylon and Hawaii, Mr. and Mrs. Mills became co-founders of Mills Seminary (now College) in California, an institution closely modelled after Mount Holyoke.

I have been able to supplement Miss McLean's study mainly by the glimpses of life at the Seminary quoted from the *Journal* of William Gardiner Hammond (see Chapter I) and by giving a trustworthy version of Emily's so-called "insurrection" from an unpublished paper by Clara Newman Turner: *My Personal Acquaintance with Emily Dickinson,* edited by her niece Clara Newman Pearl (type-written manuscript in the Jones Library). The legend of Emily's defiance of Miss Lyon's authority as given in *Life and Letters,* p. 25, has through much retelling become falsified in nearly every particular. Its accuracy was questioned by Miss McLean, and it may now be decisively relegated to the limbo of forgotten grotesqueries.

The brief quotations in this chapter are taken from Emily's letters to Abiah Root and to her brother Austin (*Letters*, pp. 24–35; 63–72). I have transcribed the passage detailing her daily routine directly from the original in the Mount Holyoke College Archives, keeping capitals, abbreviations, and punctuation unchanged.

Emily Dickinson's roommate, Emily Lavinia Norcross (1828–1852), was the daughter of Hiram Norcross of Monson, eldest brother of Mrs. Edward Dickinson.

CHAPTERS V AND VI

No episode in Emily Dickinson's life has been more grotesquely misrepresented than her shadowy love story. The publication of the first installment of her poems focused a disproportionate attention on this point. Thus we find a writer in *The Springfield Republican* for November 16, 1890, commenting: "What Emily Dickinson says of love has a peculiar interest, and it can hardly be forbidden that the reader should wonder what experience of her own she might have had to produce so exceptionally personal utterances as some of these voices of imagination seem to be." It is understandable that Emily's immediate kin should have been reluctant to discuss an attachment which was no more than an affair of the mind, and which could hardly be spoken of at all without suggesting implications that seemed to them discreditable.

Mrs. Todd, the first editor of the poems and letters, respected the wishes of Emily's then surviving brother and sister in guarding the poet's life from public scrutiny. She stated merely that Emily's seclusion was not due to invalidism nor to any disappointment in love. This statement, though much too summary to be adequate, possesses a certain dignity and enough truth to keep it sweet.

Lavinia Dickinson, however, seems to have felt that a confidential explanation to the neighbors was in order. She was terrified lest it should be whispered about that Emily was "in love with a married man." To several of her cronies, accordingly, she imparted an impressively secret disclosure that Emily's young lover was George Gould, a classmate and close friend of her brother's. I hesitate to assert bluntly that Lavinia was deliberately dragging a red herring, but I do not see any better way to describe her tactics. When asked why Emily did not marry Gould after her father's death, Lavinia at once became confused and gave the wrong answer. Now it is conceivable that Emily was fond of her brother's friend in an impulsive girlish way, but it is certain that Gould passed completely out of her life soon after his graduation from Amherst in 1850. There is not the slightest ground for supposing that her love poems were addressed to him; a few of them were clearly written after the lover's death, and Gould outlived Emily!

Nevertheless, the thesis that Gould was the object of Emily's lifelong devotion has been revived and elaborated by Miss Genevieve Taggard in *The Life and Mind of Emily Dickinson*. The utmost that can be claimed for Gould is that he was pleasantly acquainted with Emily in her late teens—no more than that.

An alternative and even less believable love story has been evolved by Miss Josephine Pollitt in *Emily Dickinson, the Human Background of her Poetry*. According to the revelation vouchsafed to her, Emily was secretly in love with Major Edward B. Hunt, the first husband of "H. H." Miss Pollitt's entire case is a piece of ingenious special pleading based on Emily's remark to Higginson (1870) that "Major Hunt interested her more than any man she ever saw." This is followed by a sentence, glossed over by Miss Pollitt, which specifies the nature of Emily's "interest" in Hunt: "She remembered two things he said, that her great dog 'understood gravitation,' and when he said he should come again 'in a year. If I say a shorter time it will be longer.'" The supposition that Emily became infatuated with her friend's husband is contradicted by the tradition that Hunt rather disliked Emily and thought her "uncanny." See Louise Pound, *D.A.B.*, article on Helen Hunt Jackson.

Emily Dickinson's niece and biographer, though not fully sharing the family reticence, has been so far influenced by it that she has been unable to give a clear and consistent account of the poet's emotional history. She has attempted to make the intangible tangible without benefit of documentation. Her first disclosure of a "Plutonic" (whatever that may mean) passion in Emily's life and her later, more specific references to a "Philadelphia preacher" may, I assume, be taken as adumbrations of Emily's devotion to Charles Wadsworth. But the true nature of that relationship has been badly blurred by the biographer's misguided efforts to suffuse the whole matter in a cloud of factitious glamor.

BIBLIOGRAPHICAL POSTSCRIPT

Emily Dickinson was sensitive and intense in her friendships as in everything else. Her tendency to idolize various and sundry men who came for a time within her orbit is of no particular importance to posterity. What matters is that three of these relationships, those with Newton, with Wadsworth, and with Higginson, have a bearing on her development as a poet. And with that posterity is legitimately concerned.

For a full documentation of the facts about Newton, together with a discussion of some controversial points, the reader may consult my article on "Emily Dickinson's Earliest Friend," *American Literature,* March, 1934 (VI, p. 5). Emily's letter to Hale was first printed (in part) in Thomas F. Madigan's catalogue, *The Autograph Album,* No. 1, p. 50 (December, 1933). It was purchased by a collector who has courteously allowed me to examine the original. I have slightly regularized the punctuation, but have kept the capitals as Emily wrote them. Higginson stated in "Emily Dickinson's Letters" (*Atlantic Monthly,* October, 1891) that Mrs. Child's *Letters from New York* was the book that first awakened Emily's eager enthusiasm.

Charles Wadsworth, elder son of Harry and Mary Ann (Bradley) Wadsworth, was born in Litchfield, Conn., on May 8, 1814. His father died in 1830, leaving the family in straitened circumstances. Charles earned his education by doing farm work. His freshman year at Hamilton College was interrupted by a dispute with the faculty which led him and many of his classmates to transfer to Union College, where he graduated with high honors in 1837. After a brief period of school-teaching, he attended Princeton Theological Seminary, and in 1842 commenced a fruitful ministry of forty years. He held successively four pastorates: Second Presbyterian Church of Troy, N. Y., 1842–1850; Arch Street Church of Philadelphia, 1850–1862; Calvary Church of San Francisco, 1862–1869; and a second church in Philadelphia which after several changes of name became the Clinton Street Immanuel Church, 1870–1882. In each instance he was markedly successful in transforming a feeble or disorganized body into a numerous and vigorous congregation. He died of pneumonia after a brief illness on April 1, 1882. See *Encyclopædia of the Presbyterian Church* (1884), p. 978; H. A. Wadsworth: *Two Hundred and Fifty Years of the Wadsworth Family in America* (1883), p. 160; scrapbook of newspaper clippings in the possession of the Presbyterian Historical Society of Philadelphia. I wish to thank Dr.

William S. Wadsworth of Philadelphia for courteously answering my queries in regard to his distinguished father.

Wadsworth was married on December 1, 1846, to Sarah Jane Locke (1827–1891), daughter of Oliver Peabody Locke, a well-known Boston merchant. Their three children were: Edith (1858), Charles, Jr. (1860), and William Scott (1868). See A. H. Locke: *A History and Genealogy of Captain John Locke . . . and his Descendants* (n. d.), p. 206.

Emily Dickinson's devotion to Wadsworth is sufficiently indicated by her letters to J. D. and C. H. Clark. The complete text of these letters was published for the first time in the revised edition of *Letters of Emily Dickinson* (1931), and is nowhere else available. I have added supporting evidence from Emily's unpublished letters to an intimate friend. The owner of these manuscripts has kindly allowed me to examine the originals.

James Dickson Clark (1828–1883) was born in Northampton, graduated from Williams in 1848, practised law, taught school, and engaged in business. He lived in Brooklyn, N. Y., but kept up his home in Northampton. His health was never good, and in later life he became a confirmed invalid. Emily's words (*Letters*, p. 348) would seem to indicate that when she met Clark she did not know that he was Wadsworth's friend. But Wadsworth told her about 1860 that he was visiting Clark. Therefore Emily must have met Clark before that date. The Mr. Brownell with whom he called at the Dickinsons' was his partner in conducting a private school from 1858 to 1864.

Mrs. Todd states that Emily became acquainted with Wadsworth in the spring of 1854 while she was visiting the Colemans in Philadelphia. I cannot prove in court that Emily had Wadsworth in mind when she wrote "He fumbles at your spirit" (149, xlvi), but Mrs. Todd included this description of a sermon among the love poems, and I have heard the effect of Wadsworth's preaching described in almost identical terms by one who had frequently listened to him.

Miss Pollitt, in a communication quoted in "Books and Things," *New York Herald Tribune*, December 31, 1932, states that Wadsworth's mother died on October 1, 1859. His first call, while he was wearing mourning, must have occurred within a year. An unpublished letter from Emily to the intimate friend already mentioned indicates that about March, 1860, something clandestine had recently taken place, though its nature is difficult to determine. I strongly suspect that Emily's excitement had something to do with Wadsworth's visit.

I have suggested that Wadsworth came again in the summer of 1861, but this is only a convenient hypothesis to explain Emily's "terror since September." It would also supply a sound basis for the family legend (*Life and Letters*, p. 47) that Lavinia once came running to Sue in fear lest Emily go away with "that man." The difficulties incident to accepting this story as of 1854 or 1855, before Sue's marriage, vanish if it is dated 1861. But it is quite conceivable that a letter from Wadsworth or even some rumor that he was going to "leave the land" may have accounted for Emily's distress. In that case her elaboration of a lover's parting in half a dozen poems would be pure fiction.

Wadsworth's call to San Francisco was not reported in the Philadelphia papers until January 11, 1862 (*Daily News*). On March 15 his acceptance of the call was announced. He was not finally released from the Arch Street Church until April 3. With Mrs. Wadsworth, two children, and a maid, he sailed from New York for Aspinwall on the S.S. *North Star* (May 1). The party crossed the Isthmus, re-embarked at Panama on the S.S. *Orizaba*, and reached San Francisco early in the morning of May 26. Wadsworth first preached at Calvary Church on June 1 (*San Francisco Evening Bulletin*).

I have on file four references from unpublished letters that show that Emily was in correspondence with Wadsworth about 1877–79. My account of their last interview is a conflation of Emily's two reports (*Letters*, p. 344 and 429). I am responsible for italicizing the word *you*.

A single volume of *Sermons* by Charles Wadsworth was published during his lifetime, New York and San Francisco (1869), and, of course, many separate sermons were printed in pamphlet form. After his death three more volumes appeared in Philadelphia, Vols. I and II (1882), Vol. III (1884). I have not seen the collection said to have been privately issued by J. D. Clark.

CHAPTER VII

The letters from Emily Dickinson to Bowles, Holland, and Higginson are among the most interesting of those that have been published. Her correspondence with Helen Hunt Jackson has unfortunately never been found. A single note from Mrs. Jackson is included in

Mrs. Todd's preface to *Poems: Second Series*. Emily's relations with her literary friends are extensively treated in all the biographies of her, but she is not even mentioned in the standard lives of Bowles and Holland, and Mary Thacher Higginson's *Thomas Wentworth Higginson: The Story of His Life* (1914) and *Letters and Journals of Thomas Wentworth Higginson* (1921) add little to what he has recorded in his essay on Emily Dickinson (*Carlyle's Laugh and Other Surprises*). No better notice of Helen Hunt Jackson exists than the brief but discerning sketch by Professor Louise Pound in the *Dictionary of American Biography*. For Thomas Niles, especially in relation to *A Masque of Poets,* see Aubrey H. Starke: "An Omnibus of Poets," *The Colophon*, No. 16 (1934).

Two accounts have been given of what occurred when Emily was shown *The Springfield Republican* containing "The Snake." (The poem appeared in both the daily and the weekly issues.) According to one story "the little white moth" was "almost fluttered to death, all a-tremble and ready to die of the experience and to be found on the floor next morning a mere hint of winged dust!" The other states that Emily received the paper "without glance or comment, and on the familiar phenomena of the opening door and voice from above" simply vanished. Both accounts are by the same hand. There was nothing moth-like in Emily's tone when she asserted that the poem had been stolen from her. The question mark at the end of line 3 to which she objected was removed by Mrs. Todd in *Poems: Second Series,* but was restored under other auspices in *Complete Poems* (1924) and subsequent editions. In the *Republican* version the poem appeared as three 8-line stanzas, of which I have quoted the second. "Boy" in the third line of this stanza was later changed to "child," "noon" in the fourth line to "morn." The latter is one of the few instances where Emily seems to have altered a word to secure exact rhyme. Bowles's comment on the poem is given in *Emily Dickinson Face to Face*, p. 27.

The one surviving letter from Higginson to Emily is printed in *Life and Letters*, p. 72.

Mrs. Ford's account of her conversation with Holland may be found in *Letters*, p. 131. It is not known under what circumstances Holland received the poems by Emily Dickinson that he was considering for publication.

Two volumes of the *Saxe Holm's Stories* were published, the first in 1874, the second in 1878. To the end of her life Mrs. Jackson denied the authorship of these books, but her denials were equivocal and there is no doubt that she wrote them. "Esther Wynn's Love-Letters" was originally printed in *Scribner's Monthly* for December, 1871.

Mercy Philbrick's Choice, from which I have already quoted a description of Amherst town center (Chapter I), was the first novel to appear in the "No Name Series." In view of Mrs. Jackson's connection with these anonymous books there can be little doubt that she was instrumental in placing "Success" in *A Masque of Poets*.

CHAPTER VIII

The sources of this chapter consist almost entirely of letters, both published and unpublished.

I am indebted to Professor Frank Prentice Rand of the Massachusetts State College for calling my attention to Hasket Derby's essay in *The Amherst Collegiate Magazine*, and for some biographical details in regard to Derby which he generously placed at my disposal.

Mrs. Daniel Bliss's recollections of Emily Dickinson are included in the life of her husband, *The Reminiscences of Daniel Bliss* (1920), p. 62.

For Frazar A. Stearns, see *Adjutant Stearns* (1862), a memorial volume written by his father, President William A. Stearns.

The letter to "Sweet Nellie" is one of a number of missives sent by hand to Emily's neighbor, Mrs. John Howard Sweetser, in the early eighties.

The words "Called Back" are taken from the title of a novel by Hugh Conway, one of the last books that Emily read.

In the first four printings of *Life and Letters* the date of Emily Dickinson's death is erroneously given as May 16, instead of May 15. The initials S. H. D. (Susan Huntington Dickinson) attached to the obituary notice of "Miss Emily Dickinson of Amherst" (p. 105) did not appear when this notice was originally printed in *The Springfield Republican*, nor when it was reprinted in *The Amherst Record*.

CHAPTER IX

A discussion of the complex subject of Puritanism and the Puritan tradition in our literature would be out of place here. I have made considerable use of Herbert Wallace Schneider: *The Puritan Mind* (1930), and have quoted from the final chapter of Samuel Eliot Morison: *Builders of the Bay Colony* (1930). The quotation from Santayana is taken from *The Last Puritan* (1936), p. 180.

The poem beginning "Truth is as old as God" is quoted from *Letters of Emily Dickinson*, edited by Mabel Loomis Todd (1894, 1931). It has never been included in any edition of *Poems*.

The description of Deacon Walter Colton's manner of speaking and of reading the Scripture is taken from a privately printed memorial volume, the title-page of which reads: "In Memoriam. Dea. Walter Colton. Georgia, Vermont. For the Family. By A. M. and G. Q. Colton." (n. p., n. d.)

Chapter X

My characterization of Samuel Bowles and my account of *The Springfield Republican* are based largely on George S. Merriam: *The Life and Times of Samuel Bowles* (1885). I have also examined parts of the files of the newspaper for the 1840's and 1850's.

For the background of native humor I have relied on Constance Rourke: *American Humor, A Study of the National Character* (1931) and on *Tall Tales of the Southwest*, edited by Franklin J. Meine (1930).

The complete text of Emily's valentine to George Gould, first printed in *The Indicator* (Amherst undergraduate publication) for February, 1850, is given by Genevieve Taggard: *The Life and Mind of Emily Dickinson*, p. 67.

The poem beginning "God is a distant, stately lover" first appeared in *The Christian Register* for April 2, 1891. It was reprinted in *Further Poems*, p. 198, but has not been included in any subsequent edition of *Poems*.

Chapter XI

William Gardiner Hammond's *Journal*, already frequently quoted, gives an extended summary of Professor Lord's lectures and an abstract of a sermon that he preached from the college pulpit.

Josiah Holloway Long, A. C. 1845, wrote to Professor Tyler the letter containing the words: "Miss Emily should not be absent." The original is preserved in the Edward Hitchcock Memorial Room.

The account of Emerson's visits to Amherst is condensed from an article of mine called "Uriel in Amherst," *Amherst Graduates' Quarterly*, August, 1934 (XXIII, p. 281).

For other quatrains by Emerson that possess the intangible ring of Emily Dickinson's writing, see Percy H. Boynton: *American Literature and American Life* (1936), p. 696.

CHAPTER XII

I have tried to trace every quotation and every reference to her reading contained in Emily Dickinson's published letters or in any book about her, but needless to say some still evade identification.

Information about the family library and about the reading of Austin, Susan, and Lavinia Dickinson is derived from *Life and Letters* and *Emily Dickinson Face to Face*.

I have quoted in connection with Sir Thomas Browne from Margery McKay: *"Amazing Sense"—The Application of a New Method to the Poetry of Emily Dickinson*, Swarthmore College Honors Thesis. (Typewritten copy in the Jones Library.)

Mr. Frederick J. Pohl should be credited with first identifying Robert Browning as the person after whom Emily wished Mary Bowles to name a child "Robert."

CHAPTER XIII

Besides "Emily Dickinson's Literary Début" by Mabel Loomis Todd, *Harper's Magazine*, March, 1930 (CLX, p. 463), I have examined many unpublished letters by Mrs. Todd, Higginson, and Austin and Lavinia Dickinson relating to the first publication of Emily's poems and letters. These documents have since passed into the possession of Mrs. Walter V. Bingham of New York.

The quotation from Henry James's sister is taken from *Alice James—Her Brothers—Her Journal*, edited by Anna Robeson Burr (1934).

The line which in *The Single Hound* reads:

"Flinging the problem back to you and I,"

has in later editions of the *Poems* been altered to read, "you and me."

Statistics on Emily Dickinson's use of nouns are drawn from Margery McKay: *"Amazing Sense"* (see Chapter XII).

The misreading of *vast* for *least* (267, cxxix) was first noted by Ralph Marcellino in a communication to *The New York Herald Tribune Books*.

The quotation from Elizabeth Barrett Browning on the subject of experimentation in rhyming I encountered in Virginia Woolf: *Flush —a Biography*, p. 174, and have not traced to its source.

Miss Susan Miles in "The Irregularities of Emily Dickinson," *London Mercury*, December, 1925 (XIII, p. 145) advanced a theory of relationship between Emily's rhymes and her view of life.

CHAPTER XIV

For statistics on the nature lore of various American poets other than Emily Dickinson I am indebted to Norman Foerster: *Nature in American Literature* (1923).

CHAPTERS XV AND XVI

These two chapters are based entirely on a study of Emily Dickinson's poems. The point I am interested in making is that the poems should be read in sequence rather than as unconnected lyrics. The sequence that I have followed in Chapter XV is based on an assumed succession of states of mind. It should not be taken literally as an indication of the chronological order in which the poems were written.

Index

INDEX

Brannan, William P., 176
Briggs, George N., 25, 28
Brontë, Charlotte, 88, 212, 213
Brontë, Emily, 100, 212, 213, 285
Brook Farm, 89, 189
Browne, Sir Thomas, 208, 211, 222
Browning, Elizabeth Barrett, 81, 208, 209, 212, 214–15, 247
Browning, Robert, 81, 208, 212, 215–16, 233, 237
Bryant, William Cullen, 218, 250, 254, 257, 258, 264, 265
Bull, Ole, 56
Bullard, Lucretia Dickinson (Mrs. Asa), 30
Bullard, O. A., 6
Bulwer-Lytton, Edward, 208, 218
Bunyan, John, 210, 283
Burgess, John W., 15, 33, 36, 146–7
Burns, Robert, 269
Burton, Richard, 220
Byron, Lord, 191, 212, 250

Calisthenics at Mount Holyoke, 62, 63
Calvinism, 10, 20
Campbell, Thomas, 250
Carlo (Emily's dog), 134, 253
Carlyle, Thomas, 212
Cattle show, 16, 17, 55, 198
Catullus, 269
Cazamian, Louis, on humor, 181
Century Magazine, The, 218
Chaucer, Geoffrey, 206, 210
Chickering, Joseph K., 37, 143
Child, Lydia Maria, 88–9, 191
Choate, Rufus, 61
Circus, 17, 67
Civil War, 32, 105, 140
Clark, Charles H., 99, 142
Clark, James D., 99, 100, 104, 323
Clemens, Samuel L. (Mark Twain), 173, 174, 175, 181, 184, 308
Coleman, Eliza, 56
Coleman, Lyman, 45, 47, 102, 103
Coleman, Olivia, 14
Coleridge, Samuel Taylor, 208, 212
Colton, Aaron M., 7, 9, 166
Colton, Walter, 166–7
Congregational Church in Amherst, 6–7
Cooper, James Fenimore, 29
"Cousin Sally Dilliard," 171
Cowper, William, 211
Craik, Dinah M., 213

Currier, Elizabeth Dickinson (Mrs. Augustus N.), 30

Dana, Richard Henry, Sr., 208
Dante, 80, 91, 207, 209, 211, 269
Dartmouth College, 23
Darwin, Charles, 173
Davis, Rebecca Harding, 219
Delano, Charles, 11
Derby, Hasket, 136
Dickens, Charles, 88, 208, 212, 214, 218, 223
Dickinson, Edward (Emily's father), a pillar of Amherst, 5; church going, 6; opinion of Rev. Mr. Colton, 7; joins the church, 8; drives to mill, 10; life and character, 24-27; Emily's devotion to, 28; marriage, 28; compared with his son, 31; a parental stratagem, 46; prefers Emily's bread, 55; disapproves of "modern literati," 88; possible rejection of Newton's suit, 91; idolized his daughter, 139; his library, 207–8
Dickinson, Edward (Emily's nephew), 36, 155
Dickinson, Emily
(1) *Life:* birth and birthplace, 3; child portrait, 6; describes the village choir, 7; comment on sermons, 8–9; friendship with clergymen, 9; glimpse of her schoolmates, 14; withdraws from social life, 15; appearance at the Dickinson teas, 16; watching the circus pass, 18; her mental development, 20; an unrecognized lyric poet, 21; family and ancestry, 22-3; devotion to her father, 27–8; change of relationship with her mother, 29; cousins and aunts, 30; early enthusiasm for "Sister Sue" and later disappointment in her, 34–6; Lavinia her lifelong companion, 37; her inheritance, 38; education, 39; at the Primary School, 41; at Amherst Academy, 42–3; vignettes of Emily as a schoolgirl, 43–4; studies and teachers, 44–5; visit to Boston, 46; study of sciences, 47–8; literary exercises, 48–9; dread of examinations, 50; comment on preceptresses, 50–2; friendship with Leonard Humphrey, 52; letter on his death, 52–3; Mrs. Ford's account of Emily as a schoolgirl, 53–4; housekeeping and gardening, 55; music, 56;

INDEX

INDEX

INDEX

SELECTED ANN ARBOR PAPERBACKS

works of enduring merit

For a complete list of Ann Arbor Paperback titles write:
THE UNIVERSITY OF MICHIGAN PRESS / ANN ARBOR